BRITISH SOCIAL SERVICES

THE SCOTTISH DIMENSION

BRITISH SOCIAL SERVICES

THE SCOTTISH DIMENSION

John Murphy

assisted by

Gill McMillan

Foreword by

Barbara Kahan

SCOTTISH ACADEMIC PRESS

EDINBURGH

Published by
Scottish Academic Press Ltd.,
56 Hanover Street
Edinburgh EH2 2DX

SBN 0 7073 0718 X

Typeset by Trinity Typesetting, Edinburgh
Printed in Great Britain by Redwood Press Limited, Melksham, Wiltshire

CONTENTS

General

Fundamental changes are at present in progress – the work fills a gap in the literature, and would be invaluable for students, in-service included, as well as for members of staff and researchers. It is also of major interest to students of social administration and policy.

FOREWORD

The history of welfare services in some respects stretches back through several centuries, but their modern manifestations are postwar and therefore relatively recent. Perhaps because of this, there is little awareness by many current practitioners or users, of how the services in which they work or from which they benefit acquired their present identity and dimensions. This is regrettable, because a knowledge of how things came to be what they are, is an essential element in the understanding of what is possible in the future. The questions 'when', 'why', 'how', 'where' are part of a sense of history and also part of social work's daily tools.

There is also little real understanding of the fact that in these islands we have separate social services systems in England and Wales, in Scotland and in Northern Ireland. Even when the differences are recognised, how they came about and what they are remain obscure. This book will make a valuable contribution to filling these gaps not only for Scotland but for other parts of Great Britain as well.

The author in spite of having spent much of his working life outside Scotland in the forces and the London civil service, has a deep understanding of Scottish culture and traditions and illustrates these against his informed perceptions of the wider British scene. His sympathy for the subject and his enthusiasm for recording Scotland's unique history of social services is clear throughout the book.

He is not a social worker but read classics at the University of Glasgow and then trained as a teacher. After wartime army service and some residential teaching he joined the Home Office Children's Department Inspectorate which had been given the task of monitoring and encouraging developments under the Children's Act 1948. In 1961 he returned to Scotland where he worked till 1969 in the Scottish Education Department as HM Inspector of approved schools. Then until 1975 he was the first director of social work for Stirling County, and for the new Central Region till 1978. He has since carried out work as a commissioner for mental welfare in Scotland and as chairman of the Bield Housing Association concerned with sheltered housing for elderly people in Scotland. Occasional opportunities to study child welfare, children's courts and housing for elderly people in Denmark, Sweden and Holland have added to the breadth of his experience.

The author's daughter Gill McMillan ably collaborated with him, providing the chapter 'Social Workers and the Social Work Act'. She is a history graduate and professional social worker.

The book begins by tracing the immediate postwar 'welfare revolution', and identifies a recurring theme of the impact of small groups of powerful women, whose influence on public opinion, politicians and fellow professionals was significant not only in the 1940s but also in the 1960s.

The differences in child care services between Scotland and England are examined in Chapter 2 which illustrates how early beginnings set the patterns of development for a number of years. Chapter 3, 'The Wilderness Years' explores pre-war attitudes and services for elderly people under the Poor Law.

The next three chapters deal with the separate services provided between 1948 and 1969 in the fields of health and welfare, probation and child care. Differences between Scottish and English practice are highlighted and critically assessed.

Chapter 7 describes developments concerning young offenders through the Kilbrandon Committee and leads logically into Gill McMillan's Chapter 8 which traces in some detail the processes leading to the Social Work (Scotland) Act of 1968. It also links them with similar but different developments in England which led to the Local Authorities Social Services Act 1970. The development of the social work profession itself is particularly examined, and how it was affected by, and affected the establishment of a family service.

The last chapter 'The Making of Social Work Departments' looks at the situation which arose at the grand amalgam of 1969 resulting in increased demand and expectations from the public, other services and social workers themselves, against a background of resource constraints and other difficulties. The Introduction's concise summary of Scottish administration, attitudes and traditions is particularly valuable at this juncture in history for all those studying or working in the country.

Although the author regards this book as only a beginning in the historical study of social services and their development in Scotland, it is an important start. Very little has been written on developments of the separate specialist services between 1948 and 1969 and apart from work on Children's Hearings, there is little about the post 1969 period.

Much of the information presented is new and arises from research into original sources, and conversations with some of those influential persons who were active at crucial points of change in the field or as committee members on the Curtis, Clyde, Morison and Kilbrandon Committees. There is also new information coming from the author's own first had contemporary observations in the context of the Home Office Children's Department, and the Scottish Education Department. Use has also been made of sources in the Scottish Record Office and Social Work Services Group Records.

An attractive feature of the book is the fact that though the author is a dedicated Scot he is able to be critical of the traditions and culture of Scotland in an outspoken and refreshing way. He demonstrates that Scottish services which were to some extent backward and late developers, nevertheless achieved in the late 1960s by the means outlined so clearly in the book, an earlier and more radical reorganisation of social services than in England. Another feature is the engaging and readable style, flavoured with interesting and unusual allusions and comparisons drawn from a lifetime's experience and scholarship.

The book will be of interest not only to Scots but to English, Welsh and Irish readers. The chapter on the Kilbrandon Report, which launched the Scottish juvenile justice experiment, may well have wider appeal, not least in the United States. The book provides fascinating material demonstrating not just the development of social services but the way in which public opinion, tradition, powerful individuals, legislation and professional influences all interact in achieving change. I have greatly enjoyed reading and learning from the book and warmly commend it to others.

Barbara Kahan, OBE, MA (Cantab.), (M(Univ.)

INTRODUCTION

Everything is in a state of flux; nothing is fixed.
Heracleitus 500BC

This book traces the path and causes of the emergence of a strong, radical social work service in Scotland against the general background of British personal social services and the peculiar Scottish cultural institutions and attitudes, which had also influenced the earlier infra-structure of specialist services.[1]

The Social Work (Scotland) Act of 1968 became operational in November 1969 through the formation of social work departments which combined the previously separate agencies of children, proba-tion, health and welfare departments. Its radical provisions for a new system of juvenile justice — the Children's Hearings — were imple-mented in 1971. There followed two decades of development and growth in the Seventies and Eighties, at which point the pace of change again accelerated with the arrival on the Uk scene of the Griffiths Report in 1988, the White Paper 'Caring for People' (1989) and the National Health Service and Community Care Act of 1990.

As they entered the Nineties, Scottish social work departments not only came of age, but also reached a major crossroads where the pace of impending change, if not the scale, seemed to rival the earlier upheavals surrounding their birth.

The new community care provisions, recognising significant changes and unmet needs, raised the profile of the major client groups of elderly, physically handicapped, mentally handicapped and mentally ill people, previously secondary to the main pre-occupation of the agencies — child protection and families. While some 70% of departmental budgets had been disbursed on the former, it is estimated that in 1990 they enjoyed less than 20% of the time of qualified social workers.[2] A prime problem of the 1990s is to balance the rightful place of child protection alongside better supporting measures for the handicapped and very elderly, and against a background of impossible public demands for the former and unrealistic expectations on the latter.

Such a major change of direction implied also changes of methodol-ogy and skills needed to achieve the varying objectives of assessment, placement and support in the community through a variety of agents such as family, private contractors, or voluntary and local authority provision. Emphasis, of necessity, had to be on planning, financial and

1

quality control as well as the basics of case assessment and case management, with these two latter taking on new and unfamiliar dimensions. This obviously required radical re-thinking of roles, considerable retraining and some re-staffing of departments. Many of these new activities are more appropriate to others than social workers, for whom considerable re-orientation appeared inescapable.

In the relevant and wide-ranging article of 1989, *Social Work in Scotland; Problems and Perspectives*[3] Margaret Yelloly risked the following prediction. 'In future the role of social workers in local authorities may focus more sharply on child protection, and on assessment and co-ordination of care; while career opportunities in direct counselling and therapeutic work, attracting the most able staff, may come to lie (as they do in the United States) with the private and voluntary sectors. The constriction of the role of local authority social workers to that of 'street level bureaucrat' concerned with people-processing is not, it may be said, a scenario likely to hold much appeal for Scottish social workers'.

By mid 1991 the first part of that prophecy was being realised by the general trends of community care and by the imperatives of dramatic developments in Scottish (and English) child care. The extreme case of proliferating private practice or mere management roles was not immediately imminent. It had become clear however that the established local authority semi-monopoly and the field social worker's acquired hegemony in the provision of social services were likely to be moderated by the advent of community care as a major operational form.

On the one hand there is difficulty in visualising a situation where the local authority could retreat substantially from its wide powers under the Social Work Act, or where the social worker abdicated the key roles which have substantially developed the service, and played a subordinate role to the accountant or the manager. On the other hand, personal social services cannot escape the spirit of the age already affecting other agencies such as health, housing and even education. The themes of accountability, consumer choice, private provision and cost effectiveness cannot be dismissed as transient political dogma. They have gained considerable acceptance even among consumers, where private pensions, housing and health, and for the elderly private sheltered housing or residential care, became in the Eighties a major aspiration of many. Even without the full realisation of 'Community Care' major change for social work practice in the 1990s was imminent.

The 1980s heralded the beginnings of return to some specialisms in mental health and offender services. The 1991 'cause celebre' of alleged sex abuse in Orkney, following similar such cases in England, together with media spotlighting of endemic difficulties and deficiencies on the residential side, focused public as well as professional concern on major issues and problems of child care and accentuated the already perceived need for specialism and specialist training. Child care became once again the public face of social work, as reflected by one journal's sweeping comment 'The reputation of the social work profession is at an all time low. The Orkney case has surpassed even Cleveland and Rochdale in the way that it has shaken the foundation of public confidence in child protection services'.[4] These explosions in a few authorities and sectors of social work carried a fall-out, however temporary, for all. The major departmental daily works of compassionate care for elderly and handicapped persons normally pass unsung. When child care is tarnished even such undisputed virtues avail little to ward off the general stigmatising of social work.

A further possible dimension of change and uncertainty was introduced in 1991 by the government's announced intention to examine the possibility of single tier local authorities. Changes as radical and wide-ranging as listed above must always be threatening to fieldworkers, and disturbing to the much greater number of staff, too often overlooked, who are engaged in home care, day centres, residential work and management. This was the case a quarter of a century earlier when workers of all categories were confronted with radical changes of agency, setting and role, at the amalgamation of the separate departments in 1969, and at the subsequent local government reorganisation in 1975.

The difference was, however, that in the 1960s there still existed a firm unchallenged belief in the welfare state, and in the local authority's duties to protect and ameliorate its citizens' lives. By the 1980s governmental and popular philosophies had veered from these traditional liberal values towards an irresistible tide of hard-nosed individualism and survival on market-place principles in health, education, housing and personal services as well as in industry and commerce. Antagonism to 'professional welfare', implicit in government thinking, was more than matched by open hostility in the media and the market place. In such periods the perspectives of the past can be particularly relevant to understanding the present, and may serve for illumination of possible future paths. It is particularly important also to appreciate what part, beyond mere reactive roles, workers in the field may play in the influencing of change and transition.

The landscape of personal social services in Scotland has changed out of all recognition since 1969. In place of a multiplicity of separate specialist departments serving cities, counties and large burghs — some too small, most too poorly resourced, to provide more than a rudimentary service — there were, post the 1975 reorganisation, 12 social work departments, one of which, Strathclyde, is the largest of its kind in Europe. Exceptionally, the three island authorities' populations remained very small — Western Isles 30,000, Shetland and Orkney both 20,000 approximately — the last being obliged to supplement services from mainland sources in their emergency of 1991. Expenditure on social work in Scotland rose from a mere £20m in 1969-70 to £471m in 1989-90. In real terms the rise, initially rapid, was continuous, making social work the second biggest spender to education in the 12 authorities. In 1969 many councillors viewed the new social work department with some suspicion; by 1979 the committee had generally secured status, and there was competition for its seats.

The total number of staff, field, community and residential, doubled from 15,000 in 1971 to 30,000 in 1984. In 1969 the separate departments on combination mustered 959 staff for fieldwork and management. In 1989 the comparable total was nearly 5,000.[5]

Perhaps the most impressive indicators of the Scottish metamorphosis are the statistics for qualification. In 1969, 30% of field staff had a full professional qualification. In 1989 the level of qualification for main grade social workers in the 12 departments varied between 89% and 100%, giving a national average of 97%, a figure substantially higher than that for England and Wales.[6] In stark contrast to 1969, Scotland by 1989 deployed a trained, qualified force of field social workers, and debate had moved on to the question of more intensive training for certain specialisms. There was, however, a continuing area of weakness in residential care, where the general level of qualification was well below 20%, and the specific level for child care was just above that figure.

As regards compulsory measures 'The Children's Hearings system has for two decades embodied and made operational child-centred concerns that are only now being recognised as goals round the world' was the verdict of Sanford Fox, U.S. and U.N. authority on juvenile justice, given at Glasgow University in the Kilbrandon anniversary lecture of 1991.[7]

To comprehend fully the relatively surprising and sudden launching of generic family social work departments in the backwater of Scotland 1969, we must consider in depth the Kilbrandon Report, the resulting White Paper and the Act, and review and evaluate the separate services of the period 1948-69. These in turn cannot be fully understood without some short account of the crucial influences of wartime social upheavals from 1939 to 1945, and a brief look at the basic condition of services pre-dating 1948.

This book is concerned not only with the events leading up to 1969, but with the cardinal points of change, and with the part played by social forces, official enquiries, individuals, civil servants, political climate and politicians in bringing those about. Amongst such factors not least was the role the of social workers of the time, who actively intervened in the debate and direction of change, a process whose by-product was the establishment in Scotland of a unified social work profession. The work therefore takes us from the original omnibus Poor Law service, which had lasted 400 years, through the specialist services of 1948-69, to the generic emporium of a social work service, set to extend, diversify and modify in the 1990s. We stop short of speculation as to whether it has become so unwieldly as to some day fragment, and merely note that a considerable degree of specialism must re-emerge for major client groups.

The progress from the pre-1948 Poor Law regime to the social work era of 1969 was comparatively rapid. Such major change in itself is remarkable. That it happened in 20 brief years is more remarkable. That it happened in the relatively unpromising soil and backward climate of pre-1969 Scottish social services is most remarkable. This must be the central mystery — how such a progressive provision as the Social Work Act was so readily conceived and liberally implemented in a small fringe country, whose children, welfare and probation services were, at the time, comparative laggards and followers. Add to the mixture of negative concomitants the traditional parsimonious attitudes and low standards of many pre-1975 local authorities, a dearth of trained social workers and an almost complete lack of public pressure or indeed interest. Further, in the Scotland of the time, wisdom and authority on social questions was generally seen to be contained in a phalanx of conservative, powerful professions, the law, medicine, education and the church, at best indifferent to such changes, at the worst actively opposed.

This then was the setting for the genesis of one of the most progressive and extensive systems of personal social services in Europe, two years ahead of less radical developments in England, where, for a decade or more, well-resourced agencies with central government support had been advancing ideas and practice accompanied by a flurry of white papers and reports.

Change in Social Policy

At this point it may be helpful to look at the main factors which influence change in social policy and at the specific Scottish elements arising from our history, national character and values. Much has been written on the causes of change, and the subject may be studied in such works as *Change, Choice and Conflict in Social Policy* by Hall, Land, Parker and Webb (1975), and more specifically in *Reforming the Welfare* by Phoebe Hall (1976), which relates to the Social Services Act of 1970 for England and Wales. In these works a wide variety of different agents of change are identified, which are individually assessed. For present purposes a quotation from a Scottish sociologist of the time may suffice '. . . the formulation of policy is dependent on a wide variety of sources. There are the philanthropists and the social reformers, the official reports, the private social enquirers, the advisory committees, the pressure groups, the trade unions, the voluntary societies, and the churches'.[8] All of these in turn are promoted or neglected by the media and public opinion, but ultimately depend for fruition on the political climate and the spirit of the age.

In this last connection the ethos created during the second world war by common needs and suffering, which stemmed from shared experience of service activities and war work or public protection and welfare, was one of the most potent influences for major change in the middle years of the century. Whether to stave off threats of revolution as in the first war, or to maintain morale as in the second, governments responded by formulating extensive plans of reform. Most notably, the post-war Acts for National Insurance, National Assistance, National Health and Children, the framework of the welfare state, and the infrastructure of our social work service, were largely informed by this spirit, as is well illustrated by Titmuss in his *Essays on the Welfare State*, 1958. A certain degree of this idealism, optimism and belief in social planning, also survived into the 1960s.

In the 19th century initiatives for social services were usually taken by great individual reformers, often women of religious conviction, such as Florence Nightingale, Mary Carpenter and Elizabeth Fry. In the period under consideration the thinking, if not the action, has been largely led in England by university figures such as Curtis, Wooton, Warnock and Titmuss. To these must be added Beveridge — academic, civil servant and also man of action. Scotland has not been so well endowed in this respect, though a handful of social work teachers in the universities of Edinburgh and Glasgow played a significant part in the inspiration of the Social Work Act. The Scottish establishment, whether through caution or a more restricted field of choice, has relied heavily on legal luminaries, such as Clyde, Kilbrandon, Wheatley and Birsay, to guide the debates on measures of change. This practice derived largely from the 19th century legal dominance over the Poor Law, and their influence on public affairs through the great 'Boards', which preceded local authority administration.[9]

The major official reports of the period which led to legislative change in British social services were Beveridge 1942, Curtis 1946, Ingleby 1960, Kilbrandon 1964, and Seebohm 1970. Of less legislative consequence, but with great impact on social work thinking in Britain was the Younghusband Report of 1959. There were also influential non-governmental reports by individuals or committees, which provided basic materials for future developments. These included Seebohm Rowntree's *York — Poverty, a Study of town Life 1901*, its 1935 sequel, and the Nuffield Committee's report *Old People* of 1947. In Scotland the eminent dietitian Boyd Orr, later to become first director of the Food and Agricultural Organisation, produced in 1935 his *Food, Health and Income*, a seminal work which influenced thinking on health and poverty in Britain and the wider world.

Yet the ultimate determinant of social policy is not the reforming individual, nor the pressure groups, nor reports official or unofficial, powerful as these may be, but rather the political dimension. Derek Fraser sums up the issue 'Choice between social options is essentially a political choice, and social policy receives its proper dimensions when related to the political system'.[10] In this context the civil service plays a vital determining role, which Hall, Land, parker and Webb illustrate by 'The upper reaches of the main government departments contain many of the most influential policy-makers in British political life'. They restate this diagnosis succinctly as 'The principal to deputy-secretary grades of the civil service are the source and graveyard of many ideas, initiatives and issues'.[11] Even granted this cardinal role of the senior civil servant on the road to reform, parliament is still the main gate, to which only ministers and government hold the key. Parliament is usually sensitive to social issues, and at the time of the major reforms of the 1940s and 1960s which concern us, was largely sympathetically predisposed. At the crucial points of change in social services, reforming ministers have played a leading, and at times dominant role, such as Lloyd George for pensions, Aneurin Bevan for health, Rab Butler for education in England and Judith Hart for social work in Scotland. In later chapters we shall see an almost text-book illustration of these principles in the speedy passing of the Social Work (Scotland) Act though the combination of a powerful committee, professional aspirations, a guiding civil service, a committed minister and a favourable parliamentary climate.

The Scottish Dimension

Having surveyed briefly the general factors leading to social policy change we need to look in some detail at the peculiarly Scottish aspects which have promoted, hindered or diversified developments. While the lives of most readers have probably been conditioned by these, there often seems an insufficient awareness of their importance, due in no small measure to apparent neglect in the schools, universities and professional training. A Scottish sociologist identified this in 1991 as follows — 'It is very important that Scottish students are not always given American or English examples when they are being taught the social sciences. This is not parochialism; it is about giving Scots some intellectual self-confidence, of which they do not seem to have an abundance'.[12] Unfortunately, as regards the underlying Scottish culture, institutions and social history, the educators may sometimes be as blithely ignorant as the educated.

In 1707, by the Act of Union, the Scottish state ceased to exist and was submerged in a British polity, dominated by English custom, practice and institutions. 'Scotland was a nationality which resigned statehood but preserved an extraordinary amount of the institutional and psychological baggage normally associated with independence'.[13] The important separate institutions of law, education and church were preserved by the settlement of 1707. Under a joint parliament and government administration, the different national character and traditions persisted, and with the growth of government responsibility for civil affairs, a separate 'Scotch Office' (sic) was established in 1885, followed in 1894 by a Scottish Grand Committee of Parliament. That Scottish Office, now completely in Edinburgh, apart from a service station in Whitehall, has grown to be the biggest civil service department in Britain. Relevant to our subject are three of its five main branches of that time; the Scottish Education Department, responsible for education and social work, the Scottish Home and Health Department with obvious responsibilities, and the Scottish Development Department, responsible for local government, housing and planning. In 1991 these departments were given the publicity prefix of 'Scottish office', instead of 'Scottish', and Social Work Services Group was transferred from SED to SHHD, now SOHHD.

Some observers have seen this as a highly advantageous arrangement whereby national independent systems of law and education, together with distinctive traditions in health, housing and local government, are administered from Edinburgh by a Scottish, involved and seemingly sympathetic civil service, not immediately subject to Westminster nor Whitehall, apart from overall Treasury control. Add to this the advantage of being set in a larger unitary state, which to date has been not ungenerous in its financial maintenance of this settlement, with per capita spending, both under health and social services headings, substantially higher than for England and Wales.[14]

There is a view however that 'The Scottish Office has evolved for 99 years into a peculiar weapon of Government, administratively devolved, but democratically unaccountable, a perfect device for a colonial viceroy to employ'.[15] This has considerable validity, particularly when the government in London has minimal support in Scottish parliamentary or local authority representation.

It must be added that substantial dissatisfaction with the status quo has existed in post-war years, first peaking with the devolution referendum of 1979, which achieved an insufficient majority. These feelings continued to be expressed through political parties, and at a national level through the Scottish Constitutional Convention, a joint forum of two political parties, trade unions, and the churches.

By 1991, in the face of persistent national sentiment, the Labour and the Liberal Parties had been driven to explore a form of devolved government. The Nationalist Party was already committed to complete independence, and the Conservative Party in government was being pushed reluctantly to recognise that a problem existed.

By January 1992 opinion polls indicated that half the Scottish population favoured some major constitutional change. While the government in London and Edinburgh studiously ignored or played down the problem, serious British newspaper and broadcasting commentators treated it with understanding, and the fall out was registered and analysed in Madrid and other European centres.[16] Following the April 1992 election the new administration was constrained 'to take stock' seriously of the constitutional position.

In legislation, there are United Kingdom or Great Britain common statutes covering the main fields of government activity in external affairs, defence, economic and fiscal matters. For Scotland there is separate legal provision in much of the field of civil, criminal and family matters, and also in the regulation of public affairs, such as shopping, alcohol consumption or sporting events. In this regard Scotland is very much a separate country, whose viable legal provisions are largely ignored in Westminster and Whitehall even when they might be relevant to major problems being considered there, such as Sunday shopping, licensing hours or football crowd control. These Anglo-Saxon attitudes have changed little in the 300 years since Clarendon, Charles the Second's chief minister, exclaimed, 'When the whole nation was anxious to know what passed in Germany and Poland, and all other parts of Europe, no man enquired what was doing in Scotland, nor had that Kingdom a place of mention in the Gazette'.[17] Such muted curiosity is not unknown even in the parallel fields of social services as, for example in 1968, when the Seebohm Committee managed to report while virtually having ignored the relevant and revolutionary ideas of Kilbrandon and White Paper, separated from them only by a few months and Hadrian's wall.[18]

As regards social service legislation, the main Acts in this century, up until Social Work (Scotland) 1968, have been common, such as the Children Acts of 1908, 1948 and 1963 and the National Assistance Act of 1948. Because of their operation through different court and educational systems the Children and Young Persons Acts of 1933 (England and Wales) and 1932 and 1937 for Scotland were separate. We therefore see the situation of two adjacent countries in one island, where social services, usually under the same or similar legislation, have varied considerably from time to time. They are now in most respects radically different, though centralising and anglicising tendencies have recrudesced in the 1980s, notably in education. There have existed substantial differences in education, health and personal social services for various reasons, including social attitudes and economic conditions, as well as legislation. Sometimes Scottish systems have gone ahead of English, as in the early establishment of widely available public education, sometimes the reverse; sometimes they have converged, sometimes diverged. Not infrequently in Scotland there has been complacency and lack of standards, fostered by the chauvinistic illusion of the superiority of our own systems. Part of the interest of this book lies in these comparisons, and the riddle of how such variations of similar systems could arise in a comparatively small island state.

Important clues to these differences lie in national outlook and philosophy. Scottish attitudes to life, work, success and failure, and to public services are the result of many strands of history, but may be seen as particularly conditioned by three main influences — the economics of a poor, fringe country, a dominant calvinist religious tradition, and an education system shaped by both of these. Comparative lack of affluence until the second half of this century, on the part of all save a minority, was conducive to general acceptance of simple standards of food, dress, housing, furnishing and public services. A need to strive to escape poverty was widespread, and this was reinforced by frugal and saving habits often to the point of parsimony. This tendency was not confined to the more provident in the working class, but those who had achieved power in industry, commerce, the professions and local government usually believed in the efficacy of running works, businesses or services on the simplest and cheapest lines. Until the reorganisation of 1975 local government salaries, like wages in the country, were kept comparatively low, as were staff ratios and the level of supporting services. At the time of the reforming acts of 1948, even major Scottish authorities were seriously proposing that, to justify the post, the Children's Officer should also act as clerk to the burial ground. Times had changed little from 1901, when, as his tombstone in Dollar indicates, a certain William Hunter had completed 33 years as schoolmaster, and 45 years as inspector of the poor in Fossoway — perhaps a justifiably economical arrangement for that rural parish at that time.

In the past there has been a prevalent simplistic view of Scottish society as a presbyterian democracy, which valued education, independence and human worth, while scorning rank, power and riches. Alongside this noble egalitarianism, part real, part projected by Victorian writers and sentiment, there are, however, discernible the sterner aspects of 19th century reality and fundamentalism. These inculcated not only individual responsibility, but also respect for authority, whether that was minister, doctor, teacher, laird or just 'the corporation'.[19] Free thinkers there have been in both religion and politics, many of them distinguished, but, till recent times, acceptance, conformity and respectability have been to the fore among Scottish virtues.

In contrast to some aspects of 19th century philanthropy and caring, most of the 20th century in Scotland has not been distinguished, apart from early missionary and temperance movements or the more recent welfare provision of the churches, by sympathetic public attitudes to failure in the spheres of employment, marriage, housing, personal finance or law-breaking. Just as success and respectability have been generally admired, so failures have been the subject of censure, spoken or implicit, as much by those who have just escaped such vicissitudes, as by the more comfortable classes. Nor until recently, has charity and understanding for the unfortunate, inadequate or deviant been readily discernible from the educated, religious or political quarters from which it might have been most expected. All this does not deny a people essentially helpful and hospitable at basic community level and generous to a fault in private or official charity. Generalisation is of course difficult and dangerous. There are many Scotlands, much myth and too little serious sociology.

The third and perhaps strongest leg of the stool of Scottish culture is education, shaped by the factors just discussed — economics and religion. The historian, T. C. Smout, writing in 1986, was emphatic about this, 'Perhaps then, it is in the history of the school, more than in any other aspect of recent history, that the key lies to some of the more depressing aspects of modern Scotland. If there are in this country too many people who fear what is new, believe the difficult to be impossible, draw back from responsibility, and afford established authority and tradition an exaggerated respect, we can reasonably look for an explanation in the institution that moulded them.' That conclusion is based on his assessment, 'In short, anything but the most basic curriculum taught in the most traditional way was regarded as superfluous in most schools until after the Second World War: most education was what it always had been, drilling in the Rs. If the child did not understand the lesson, the tawse was on the desk'.[20] He did not need to add the old Russian aphorism on drama 'If the gun is on the wall in the first Act, it will be used by the third'. The above analysis, shocking to those reared on the myth of our educational superiority, would have smacked less of overkill, if superlatives had been moderated, and instead of 'most education' and 'most schools' it had rested at 'much' and 'many'. Yet it carries a certain ring of truth for those with first-hand experience of the period as pupils, parents or related professionals.

The merits and demerits of Scottish education may be debated endlessly, but for present purposes the author's generalised summary must be as follows. In its heyday there was much to be proud of, not least widespread basic literacy and access to secondary and higher education. By the 20th century, however, the system had become somewhat formal, repressive and knowledge-based, rather than child-centred, at a time when the new child psychology was having its impact on many developed countries. Thus it was that a substantial percentage of children escaped the system at the earliest opportunity with little achievement and no taste for further learning. They often took with them strong feelings of inferiority, inarticulacy and resentment in the face of authority or superior persons. The fortunate minority who fitted the system, found it a ladder to the respected professions, or less frequently managerial success. In these roles they were naturally predisposed to maintain the ethos that had made them, and operate the kind of communications and controls against which they had been tested. The educational pattern was constructively changed in the 1960s, but the earlier attitudes influenced industry, professions and local government in the first seven decades of this century, an aspect of our sociology which has been insufficiently recognised in some Scottish social work education.[21]

In relation to change and standards, a further specific feature of Scottish society needs to be mentioned — the restricted extent of an educated, leisured, influential middle class, which in England in this period found a field of interest and service as magistrates, prison visitors and chairmen of children's and other welfare committees. In so doing they became involved and concerned with social services. This involvement extended beyond the local sphere, and some took leading parts as individuals or pressure group members in the reforms of child care in the 1940s, and the debates on crime, delinquency and family services of the 1960s. There is limited evidence of such a class operating in Scotland this century. Nor is this imbalance likely to be speedily rectified with a continuing high annual emigration rate which consists largely of the upwardly mobile. This included in the late 1980s a substantial proportion of all new Scottish graduates from the universities of Glasgow, Strathclyde and Edinburgh.[22]

These then, in outline, are the principal factors which have moulded Scottish thought and attitudes, and have produced the peculiar Scottish social climate and identity. Against this social background and framework of institutions the Scottish social services developed between 1948 and 1969. The separate child care, welfare and probation services of that period grew slowly, were starved of resources, and lacked stimulating leadership. At central government level there was, apart from the few latter years, limited positive direction. Indifference and meanness towards personal social services characterised many local authorities whose priorities of the period were generally education and public health. (Since 1975 the new regions have produced a fresh climate much more favourable to social work services.) There had been no powerful, vocal groups for the post-war reform of child care, and later there was no widespread interest or demand for better family services outside some limited professional or political circles.

The metamorphosis was as sudden as it was unforeseen. The surprising, rapid and complete evolution of a new social work service in the 1960s had, as we shall see, to depend on an unexpected conjunction of a handful of professionals with a few civil servants, ready and able to advance the ideas of the hour and to use the freedom and encouragement afforded by sympathetic ministers. The close, integrated pattern of the Scottish Office at that time made the process easy and rapid by comparison with English developments, which had to defer to the entrenched powers and jealousies of the separate, large, London ministries.

This book attempts, for the first time, a comprehensive survey of the slow and predictably limited development of the pre-1969 separate services, and the equally rapid and unpredicted birth of a generic service in the late 1960s. As a basis it has been necessary to outline the nature of the pre-war welfare services, and the main war-time social conditions and evolving ideals which established the welfare state.

The literature of policy and practice for the period in England and Wales is extensive and detailed: for Scotland it is contrastingly sparse and limited. It has been necessary to rely largely on central and local government department documents, reports of the major committees and other papers. At the same time the author has had easy access through acquaintance or introduction to the memories, views and papers of those involved at the central points of action either as members of the major enquiries, Curtis, Clyde, Morison and Kilbrandon, or as Scottish Office advisers and administrators, or as the key figures in the field at the crucial junctures. To all those, to the many others who have read and commented on chapters in draft, and not least to the friends and colleagues who first inspired, often criticised, but always encouraged me, I acknowledge a considerable debt. Lastly, without the typing expertise, hard work and patience of Jean Ellis, Rena Milligan and Elsie Craig the text would not have been so well prepared for the publisher.

Much of this ground is being researched, assessed and recounted for the first time, and the breadth of the subject has made it difficult to treat certain aspects as intensively as some readers might have wished. For others some of the detail which the author has seen fit to preserve, perhaps due to his own earlier involvements, may seem superfluous. Prejudices may be suspected at times, and some of his judgments which conflict with received wisdom may be strongly questioned. It will be appreciated that given the wide canvas, the dearth of existing literature, and the limited time and resources available for work, there is room for further refinement.

The responsibility and the credit for 'Social Workers and the Social Work (Scotland) Act' lies with Gill McMillan, who has produced this chapter based on her own researches, and who has also contributed comment and material utilised elsewhere.

This book is intended as a foundation text rather than a definitive work. It is believed that as a distinctively Scottish history it will provide for all readers a clear outline of the origins and recent developments of personal social services in Scotland and in England. It is hoped that for serious students it will provide a useful background for further reading and research into the many topics and questions identified here, but still insufficiently explored. It is offered as a stimulus to study of the Scottish dimension of social work services.

NOTES

1. Local authority social services include education, health, housing as well as personal social services. The latter are referred to in England simply as social services, and in Scotland as social work. Social Work was deliberately given a wider interpretation in Scotland to emphasise the varying element of personal social work in all the activities of the departments. This element, with its knowledge and ethos, was seen as the main influencing and unifying force in the new organisation. 'Specialist services' refers to the Children, Welfare, Probation and Mental Health Services between 1948 and 1969.

2. Allocation of Social Work Resources between Client Groups, Table 2, a paper presented to the Joint Consultative Group on Social Work Resources by SWSG Research Section, based on a study (1990/91) of data from six regions.

3. Professor Margaret Yelloly, Social Work in Scotland; Problems and Perspectives, Scottish Government Yearbook 1989, pp. 279, 280.

4. Community Care, 11 April 1991.

5. SWSG, Statistical Bulletin, Oct. 1989, Tables 1 and 6.

6. Ibid., Table 7.

7. Sanford, J. Fox, Children's Hearings and the International Community. The 1991 Kilbrandon Child Care Lecture, HMSO, C 2.5, 6/91.

8. John Spencer, Professor of Social Administration, Edinburgh University; Social Policy in Europe. Paper given to the Sixth European Symposium of the International Council on Social Welfare, Edinburgh 1971.

9. Clyde   —   Report on Homeless Children, HMSO 1946, Cmnd. 6911.
   Kilbrandon   —   Children and Young Persons HMSO 1964, Cmnd. 2306.
                        —   Commission on the Constitution 1972/73.
   Wheatley   —   Royal Commission on Local Government, HMSO 1969, Cmnd. 4150.
                        —   Committee on the Teaching Profession 1961-63.
   Birsay   —   Advisory Committee on Travelling People 1971-77.

| | — | Committee on Medical Services in the Highlands and Is lands 1964-67. |

Clyde   —   In 1991, 45 years after his father reported on 'Homeless Children' in Scotland, Lord Clyde was appointed to enquire into the care of children in Orkney.

10. Derek Fraser, The Evolution of the British Welfare State, Macmillan 1973, p. 223.

11. Hall, Land, Parker and Webb, Change, Choice and Conflict in Social Policy, Heinemann, 1975, pp. 58, 59, 66.

12. Steve Bruce, Professor of Sociology, Aberdeen University. Quoted in the Glasgow Herald, Weekender, of 23.3.91.

13. Tom Nairn, The Break-up of Britain, NLAB, London 1977, p. 129.

14. Hunter and Wistow, The Scottish Difference, Policy and Practice in Community Care, Scottish Government Yearbook, 1988, p. 101.

15. David McCrone, Scottish Government Yearbook, 1985, Commentary, p. 2.

16. Article in the leading Spanish newspaper El Paris, Madrid 2.2.92.

17. Clarendon as quoted by Bishop E. A. Knox in his biography Robert Leighton, Archbishop of Glasgow, J. Clarke, 1930, p. 84.

18. The Seebohm Report, apart from a statement of the position in N. Ireland and Scotland, devotes one paragraph — out of seven hundred — to Scottish developments. See also, Phoebe Hall, Reforming the Welfare, Heinemann 1976, pp. 74, 75.

19. Until 1975 nearly half the population of Scotland was governed by the 'Corporations' of the four cities, and authority in matters of education, housing or child care was commonly referred to as 'the corporation' or 'the council'.

20. T. C. Smout, Professor of Scottish History, St Andrews University, A Century of the Scottish People, Collins 1986, p. 229.

21. The year 1965 may be seen as a watershed when the Scottish Education Department produced, interalia an overdue progressive report Primary Education in Scotland, and also Circular 600 which announced reorganisation of secondary education on comprehensive lines. Some of the concomitant changes of this period were seen by practising educationists as more confusing than helpful or necessary. In 1965, however, 70% of children left with no qualification; by 1990 two thirds had some Highers, 'O' or Standard Levels, and only a third left with no such achievement (Scottish Government Yearbook, 1990, pp. 156-158).

22. E.g. Office of the Appointments Committee, University of Glasgow. No. of first degree domiciled Scots leaving Scotland immediately after graduation 1988 — 698 = 33.1%; 1989 — 642 = 31.2%; 1990 — 699 = 32.9%

CHAPTER 1

War, Peace and Reform

'The object of government in peace and in war is not the glory of rulers or races, but the happiness of the common man.' William Beveridge.

Now, and at most times under most regimes, those words would seem naively idealistic. In the 1940s, in Britain, they fairly reflected the spirit and the sentiment of the age, and, far from being empty rhetoric, they embodied the standards against which the statutes and policies for social security and social services were to be framed.

The year 1945 was a landmark of the century in European and world events. It was also a major watershed in British social planning. The necessities of war had produced widely shared social experiences through participation in the armed services, civil defence, evacuation, and the industrial shop floor. Previously unknown culture-contacts had been established. Public services, medical, social and economic, had been sampled at first hand by a wider population, and found to be in many ways outdated and inefficient. The common efforts and sacrifices of the Second World War promoted high expectations of transformed material and social conditions. The government had not forgotten how near at times riot and revolution had loomed at the end of hostilities in 1918. 'A revolutionary moment in the world's history is a time for revolutions, not for patching,' was a further Beveridge dictum.

As early in the war as 1941 there was a Minister for Reconstruction, who set up the 'Inter-Departmental Committee on Social Insurance and Allied Services', to be chaired by Sir William Beveridge (academic and government adviser on employment and insurance). By November 1942 Beveridge had compiled the report, with some assistance from his Civil Service colleagues, and signed it on his own responsibility. In 1941 also, the Minister of Health and the Secretary of State for Scotland had made their historic declaration of intent — 'It is the objective of the government, as soon as may be after the war, to ensure that by means of a comprehensive hospital service, appropriate treatment shall be available to everyone in need of it'. These radical, planned initiatives for Social Security, National Assistance and Health, were therefore ready and waiting for peace and the new peace-time government of 1945. Their proposals, the blue-print for the Welfare State, were ultimately implemented together in July 1948 as follows:

The National Insurance Acts of 1946 covered unemployment, sickness and retirement. The National Assistance Act, 1948, made provisions to secure or supplement resources to persons in need. Part Three of that Act, in replacement of Poor Law provision, gave duties and powers to local authorities for the accommodation and welfare of elderly and physically handicapped persons. From this sprang Welfare Services Departments. The National Health Service (Scotland) Act 1947, following its counterpart for England and Wales of 1946, established the National Health Service. This was done by taking over the municipal and voluntary hospitals, and introducing free medical, dental, ophthalmic and pharmaceutical services for all, to replace a patchwork of Poor Law, 'panel', and private medicine. Another part of the Act required new local authority health departments to provide community services for mothers, young children, elderly and mentally handicapped persons, the foundation of the Home Help, Day Nursery and Occupational Centre provision inherited by Social Work Departments.

In 1945 the wartime state-planning furnace, stoked by experience, ideals and new social values, stood fired and ready to forge new systems. The needs of infants, mothers, handicapped and elderly, had been identified, and certain provisions planned. There was grave public unease over children's services, which badly needed reform. Education was brought up to date by Acts of 1944 for England and Wales and 1945 for Scotland. However, a picture of the condition of children, particularly children of broken or inadequate homes, was emerging from the crucibles of evacuation, service vicissitudes, and the death throes of the Poor Law. To the administrators this presented a major problem, whose solution could not be indefinitely delayed. To a cohort of interested, informed, and influential women in England, it signalled the call for an urgent crusade to be fought in every possible arena.

In retrospect, the Children Act of 1948 is sometimes seen as the miraculous response to two dramatic events — Lady Allen's letter to *The Times* of 15 July 1944, and the death in remote Shropshire in January 1945 of foster child, Dennis O'Neill. These happenings merely, but effectively, aroused public pressures, and concentrated ministerial minds on plans already in train. The events of these few pregnant years are significant in the history of social reform, are relevant for comparison to later Scottish happenings, and so merit some outline description. Students seeking a fuller treatment of the subject will find it in R. A. Parker's well-researched *The Gestation of Reform*.[1]

The impending demise of the Poor Law in 1948, would in any case have required new provisions for children in public care. The ending of evacuation was expected to raise problems of resettling large populations from country to city. Amongst these were thought to be as many as 10,000 unaccompanied children. In the event, the Curtis Report (Para

33) gives for March 1946 a figure of 5,200 children in England and Wales, who for various reasons were unable to return to a home of their own.

In 1943 the Ministry of Health set up an informal committee to consider the implications of ending evacuation. They soon produced *The Break-up of the Poor Law and the Care of Children and Old People*.[2] It recommended that all homeless children should be the responsibility of a Children's Committee appointed jointly by Health and Education in each local authority. The implications alarmed the Home Office which, as the Ministry for the existing Children and Young Persons Acts, already had a separate 'Children's Branch' and a strong, experienced Inspectorate. Home Office, Health and Education, had competing interests here, and these might have delayed child care reform for further years by inter-departmental rivalry, but for the active extra-parliamentary interventions of able and vocal crusaders, mainly women.

After a London Conference on Child Welfare, Mary Stocks, at that time Principal of Westfield College, wrote to the Manchester Guardian in March 1944, expressing concern about 'the legion of lost children'. Lady Allen, a protagonist of nurseries, promptly followed this up with a similar letter to the Home Secretary, Herbert Morrison, and to R. A. Butler at Education. Morrison temporised, and Lady Allen, not to be frustrated, sent her famous letter to *The Times* in July. This drew attention in a graphic way to seriously low standards in public care, and to inter-departmental confusions and rivalries. She ended 'The social upheaval caused by war has not only increased this army of unhappy children, but presents the opportunity for transforming their conditions. The Education Bill and the White Paper on the Health Services have alike ignored the problem and the opportunity. A public inquiry is urgently needed to explore this largely uncivilised territory'.

Further letters to *The Times* from powerful people followed, including such improbables as Bernard Shaw.[3] Shaw called for motherly women in children's homes to replace registered nurses who 'should never be allowed to come within ten miles of a healthy child'. This was the source too (letter of 2.8.44) of his famous dictum, 'All children should be tirelessly noisy, playful, grubby-handed except at meal times, soiling and tearing such clothes as they need wear'. He claims to have heard some of this 'maternal commonsense' in Moscow from Lady Astor in 1931, who lectured a bewildered Stalin on nurseries until he noted and acted on it. *The Times* of 31 July carried a leader criticising the government and demanding an inquiry. Lady Allen continued to bombard all ministers with her letters. By early November in the Commons a motion was tabled by 158 MPs of all parties, calling for a committee to investigate the institutional care of children. By this time Morrison was moved to minute 'I may have to institute an inquiry. *The Times* correspondence is impressive. I want the Home Office to lead.'[4] On 7 December 1944 he announced in Parliament the intention to set up a Committee of Inquiry. The pace of events, now mostly outwith administrative control, accelerated sharply. Over the New Year on an isolated Shropshire farm, Dennis O'Neill was dying as a result of starvation and beating by his foster parents.

News of his death on 9 January threw a bombshell into the public arena. The foster parents were tried on 20 March at Stafford Assizes and sentenced, the foster father to six years, the foster mother to six months. These happenings in the first months of 1945 stole headline coverage in press and radio from the dramatic last scenes of the war in Europe. With action and glory abroad was contrasted inaction and shame on the home front. Television was still too embryonic for projecting sensational pictures of social work failures into thousands of living rooms.

The trial and sentence of the foster parents served temporarily to absorb public anger. The Home Office now indeed took the lead by setting up a special inquiry on the O'Neill case, under the lawyer Sir Walter Monckton, who nine years earlier had played a leading role in another national drama — the abdication of Edward VIII. Monckton moved fast and his report was presented to Parliament in May. It illustrated a complete catalogue of cardinal errors and poor practice in boarding out.

The placing officer was an untrained school attendance official. The placing authority, Newport Education Committee, boarded the child in rural Shropshire, without notification in July, and did not visit until 20 December. The placement of an urban adolescent on a remote farm was random and without an assessment, which should have revealed the foster father's record of violence. There was no medical examination, and the child's ill and frightened condition was only noted too late, on 20 December, by an untrained and inexperienced visitor, who even then did not ask to see the boy on his own. Office delays compounded the final tragedy. Towards the end of December, Newport Education Department sent a letter to Shropshire expressing some concern. Because of Christmas holidays and other delays this letter was not dealt with until 10 January — the day after the death of Dennis O'Neill.

These almost incredible lapses should be seen against the pressure on places for children made by evacuation and wartime conditions. Those conditions also had their obvious effects on staffing. After due consideration of all the factors, the Monckton Report highlighted three main requirements to avoid recurrence of such malpractices ending in tragedy. These were:
— the importance of training for work with children;
— the need to rationalise the unco-ordinated network of local authorities' administration;

— the introduction of personal concern and responsibility through a
new-type chief official, the Children's Officer.

The Curtis Committee usually gets the full credit for the one
committee and the Children's Officer recommendations, but these ideas
had been raised in 'The Break up of the Poor Law' report, and Monckton
reiterated them. This was a clear and telling report. It is now sometimes
suggested that both Monckton and Curtis should have seen that such
situations could be avoided by preventive work. This particular issue
was aired by Bob Holman in 'Community Care' of 24 January 1985 on
the 40th anniversary of the case. Holman quotes from a book by the
brother Tom O'Neill who survived in public care. In 'A Place Called
Hope', Blackwells 1981, the brother's text reads: 'When Dennis was
taken away from home in 1939 he was dirty, he was covered with sores
and a rash, but he was fairly well nourished and he was alive. When he
was taken away from Bank Farm in 1945 he was dirty — his stomach
contained no trace of food. He was dead'.[5]

This is a powerful indictment of public care, with the obvious
implications that it need never have happened if the boy had been left
at home. It is idle to speculate how much this is the brother's insight,
heightened by shared tragedy, or a conclusion inspired by subsequent
training in latter day thinking.[6] At the time Monckton and Curtis of
necessity functioned within the limitations of their respective remits
and the still prevalent rescue ethos. It required a generation of empiri-
cal innovative practice in the new-style Children's Departments, culminating in the Children and Young Persons Act 1963, before break-
through to the priority of prevention was generally achieved. The fact
that Monckton did not give out preventive prescriptions is more easily
accounted for than is his positive recommendation of a special officer for
children.

As the trial of the foster parents drew to a close in March 1945,
Morrison, Willink and Butler for Home Office, Health and Education
respectively, made the formal appointments to 'The Care of Children
Committee', to be chaired by Myra Curtis, the Principal of Newnham
College, Cambridge. The remit was 'To enquire into existing methods of
providing for children, who from loss of parents or any cause whatever,
are deprived of a normal home life with their own parents or relatives;
and to consider what further measures should be taken to ensure that
these children are brought up under conditions best calculated to
compensate them for the lack of parental care'. This was probably the
historical moment when the adjective 'deprived' had its special sociological significance officially established.[7] In Scotland there had been no
comparable scandals nor recent criminal procedures, and no irresistible
public pressures. However, the systems had to move in tandem, and an
official minute anent the happenings in England opined 'We agree that

in view of the degree of public feeling on the subject, and the Parliamentary pressure for an enquiry, it is impossible not to take some action'.[8] A similar enquiry for Scotland was therefore not unduly delayed on this occasion.

It was commissioned by the famous wartime Secretary of State, Tom Johnston, on 20 April 1945 under the title 'The Committee for Homeless Children'. To the chairmanship was appointed J. L. Clyde, K.C., then a leading Edinburgh lawyer shortly to become Lord President, the senior judge of Scotland. A challenging task, affecting the doubtful conditions of a large number of unfortunate children in an otherwise caring Britain, lay before these two Committees. The Ministers and Ministries could now relax for 18 months and await the outcome of two historic inquiries.

NOTES

1. R. A. Parker, The Gestation of Reform from Bean and MacPherson, Approaches to Welfare, Routledge and Kegan Paul 1983.
2. PRO/MH/102, 1378 Sir John Maude to Sir Alex Maxwell 9.5.44.
3. Letters to *Times* from Bernard Shaw of 21.7.44 and 2.8.44.
4. PRO/MH/102, 1378 Morrison to Maxwell 26.7.44.
5. T. O'Neill, A Place Called Hope, Blackwell 1981, p. 68.
6. Tom O'Neill having survived boarding out took training in residential child care and wrote his book, 'A Place Called Hope', Blackwell, 1981.
7. The use of 'deprived' concerning children is not of course entirely new. Mary Queen of Scots, in a charter of April 1567, assigning church resources for the maintenance of hospitals (residential accommodation) in Stirling, writes — 'Hospitalia pauperibus, mutilatis, et miseris personis, orphanis *et parentibus destitutis infantibus*' — i.e., Hospitals for poor, maimed and miserable persons, orphans *and children deprived of their parents*. From Burgh of Stirling Charters 1124-1705, printed for the Burgh of Stirling, Glasgow 1884.
8. PRO/MH/102, 1161/17 Hamilton to Maxwell 23.11.44. SRO ED. 11/180. Hamilton to Maxwell 23.11.44.

CHAPTER 2

Curtis, Clyde and Children Act 1948

On appointment in March 1945, with wartime operational urgency, the English Care of Children Committee, under Myra Curtis, launched into 18 months of powerful and searching investigations. The eminence and commitment of the chairperson was matched by a committee including three concerned Members of Parliament, and leading professional and public figures of the day.[1] It was serviced by two able and sympathetic administrative civil servants. A wide interpretation of the remit was adopted to include not only children under the aegis of the Poor Law, but also those removed from home through the courts, and additionally, those physically and mentally handicapped children in institutions. They were thus looking at care in foster homes, workhouses, hospitals, remand homes, approved schools, probation and other hostels. Four hundred and fifty-one establishments were visited in 41 counties mainly without notice. Officials and committee members were interviewed in 58 authorities. Out of a total of 125,000 children in public care, arrangements for some 30,000 were surveyed. Evidence was also taken from departments of central and local government, national and local organisations, as well as individuals. In the last category, were child care authorities of the day, such as John Bowlby, Susan Isaacs and D. W. Winnicot.

The indefatigable Majory, Lady Allen, now supplemented her letters by a remarkable propaganda pamphlet *Whose Children?* (Simpkin and Marshall, London 1945). This pamphlet, now a dated and rare document, is worth quotation as illustrative of the feelings of the time. The foreword reads 'Two roads are open to the reformer: the road of gentle persuasion, or the road of fearless exposure. Charles Dickens followed the second road, and lifted the veil of secrecy which hid from public consciousness the unwanted child of his day. Since then reformers have followed the first road, but the pace has been altogether too slow. Once again the veil that has descended must be drawn aside. This time the children have no Dickens to plead their cause; those who have suffered must themselves be their own advocates.' While recourse to the voice of the clients, particularly children, may seem normal now, it was in 1945 a quite novel approach. She proceeds to quote examples from children or parents of harsh repressive conditions, where cleanliness and religion took precedence over humanity — children left stripped in cold corridors because they had wet themselves, boys with enuresis paraded in girls' knickers, floor polishing for two hours on schooldays (beginning before six am), and four hours on Saturdays. These were the physical treatments, the verbal were sometimes worse. No doubt there is exaggeration here, and no doubt these practices were not ubiquitous. However, in the writer's experience, such daily floor polishing and crude enuresis deterrents were not unknown in residential child care in the 1950s in England and Scotland.

Inevitably the Curtis Committee was not short of horror findings. Conditions nearing the nadir of provision are reported in paragraph 140. 'An example of this motley kind of collection was found in one century-old Poor Law Institution providing accommodation for 170 adults and an infirmary for senile old people, etc. In this institution were 27 children aged six months to 15 years. Twelve infants up to 18 months were nursed by their mothers. In the same room in which these children were being cared for was a Mongol idiot aged four of gross appearance, for whom there was apparently no accommodation elsewhere.'

Paragraph 144 also gives a grim example of conditions in residential nurseries. 'There were two babies with rickets, clothed in cotton frocks, cotton vests and dilapidated napkins, no more than discoloured cotton rags. The smell in this room was dreadful. A premature baby lay in an opposite ward alone. This ward was very large and cold.'

To correct the slant of such extremes the report gives an overall view in paragraph 418. 'By far the greater number of Homes were, within their limits, reasonably well run from the point of physical care, and in other ways the child has more material advantages than could be given him in the average poor family,' and again 'Where establishments fell below a satisfactory standard, the defects were not of harshness, but rather of dirt, dreariness, drabness and over-regimentation. We found no child being cruelly used in the ordinary sense, but that was perhaps not a probable discovery on a casual visit.' Obviously the Care of Children Committee had no sightings of the training and polishing practices detailed by those with firsthand experience.

In one local authority the Committee found a Chairman of the Public Assistance Committee aged 91, supported by a vice-chairman of over 80, and had the impression that they were maintaining the standards of their own early years. Some might describe these standards as Dickensian. Certainly the Curtisian conditions, revealed by the Committee and other reliable witnesses, appear to us a world apart from present child care values. They are an interesting bench-mark against which progress may now be viewed.

The Committee's other findings were that at central government level there was no co-ordinated responsibility for Child Care. At least five ministries had some responsibilities — Health, Home Office, Education, Board of Control and Pensions. Both the Ministry of Health and the Home Office had Boarding out Rules under different Acts, and where these differed the lower requirement was usually operated.

As regards local authority responsibility the report says (para. 438) 'The existing confusion is in our opinion even more acute and danger-ous. The local authority for one purpose, e.g., Child Life Protection, may be different from the local authority for another purpose, e.g., Public Assistance. This may lead to a position in which no-one feels actively and personally responsible for the welfare of the individual child, and in which we have heard there may even be wrangles between commit-tees as to who shall bear the cost of his support, where the child is left without proper care'. On this count things had changed little in the 300 years since Charles the Second's refuge at an inn was disturbed by a birth, 'which caused the constable and overseers of the poor to come hither at an unreasonable hour of the night, to take care that the brat might not be left to the charge of the parish'.[2]

Such findings and considerations resulted in the following recom-mendations: one government department should have overall respon-sibility for children deprived of a normal home life. Curtis was pre-cluded from naming a department, but the ministers and civil servants were actively warring on this count. Each county, or county borough, the large administrative units in England, should provide a service for these children through a single ad hoc committee. The Children's Committee should appoint an executive officer of high standing and qualifications, who would be a specialist in child care. This new type officer was seen as some kind of children's friend or guardian, who would exercise a personalised care and oversight. Changes were pro-posed in adoption law. Boarding Out was recommended as preferable to institutional care, where suitable. Reception Centres were seen as an urgent new priority. Whereas Monckton in 1945 appears as the protago-nist of the idea of 'Children's Officer', the idea of Reception Centres was one strongly advocated by Lady Allen in her pamphlet.

Training was regarded as of such paramount importance that early in its operation the Committee issued an interim report (Cmd. 6760) on the training of residential workers. The final report recommendations advised that training for boarding out visitors 'should be arranged with Universities'.

The report was unanimous, apart from a minor reservation re-asserting the paramountcy of placing a child with foster parents of its own religion.

The Curtis Report is a monument to the successful political influence of informed and committed women. A parallel will be seen in Scotland when we consider the approach to the Social Work Act. It also owed much to developments in child psychology by such contemporary authorities as John Bowlby, Anna Freud and Susan Isaacs. Bowlby at that time was writing *Forty-four Juvenile Thieves* (1946) and preparing his major work *Maternal Care and Mental Health* (1951) for the World Health Organisation. It is not surprising therefore that in his evidence he stressed the dangers of separation and institutionalisation, while emphasising his central theme, the need for a substitute family. Further, the report was informed by the experiences and traumas of child separation through wartime evacuation. Apart from its achievement in legislation — the Children Act — the Curtis Report, together with the school of child psychology noted, had a profound effect on child care, public and private, for the next three decades.

Clyde Committee

By comparison the Clyde Committee on child care in Scotland was inevitably a side-show. Various factors contributed towards this. Before it started, the Secretary of State by a rescript to the Chairman, excluded from consideration the 2,000+ children in Approved Schools and Remand Homes.[3] This was done to avoid prejudice to current activities of the Scottish Council on the Treatment and Rehabilitation of Offenders. The Committee were likewise barred from considering the condition of the 900 children in 'Certified Institutions', in deference to the Departmental Committee on the Scottish Lunacy and Mental Deficiency Laws. The Directors of Education, a powerful in-group, with responsibility for some 1,500 children under 'Fit Person' Orders, were not enthusiastic. They regarded the Scottish system as largely satisfactory, and thought that reform was being requested to fit in with English requirements.[4]

Neither the Scottish public nor press was clamouring for change. In these circumstances it would have required a quite exceptional committee to achieve radical reform. In April 1945 the chosen 15 members included seven JPs, six councillors, two lawyers, three arts graduates and two doctors of considerable experience in child health and social conditions. The chairman, as noted, was an Edinburgh lawyer, J. L. Clyde, K.C., whose son in turn conducted the Orkney enquiry of 1991. The Secretary was W. Hewitson Brown, whose influence in the Scottish Office ran much beyond his official responsibilities for Probation, and who soon became the first Chief Inspector of Child Care and Probation.

Neither the social conditions of the time nor the activities of the Committee have been so well written up as for Curtis. The evidence and observations on visits are not recorded in any substance in the fairly thin, *Report of the Committee on Homeless Children*. However, much of this is now accessible in the Scottish Record Office in files under the serial ED11. Forty-two years on, we were also fortunate enough to meet and talk with two of the more active members of Clyde.[5] The Committee was kept fully informed of the transactions of Curtis, and there was an overt hope and presumption that Clyde would replicate the main Curtis findings. Understandably, in the light of traditional Scottish attitudes, this did not quite happen. The position was summed up for us by one member, Naomi Mitchison, thus — 'we heard a great deal about Curtis and what they were doing, but we felt ourselves the poor relations at a distance'.

Child Care Pre-1948

The nature and scale of the problem in Scotland were indeed quite different. As in England and Wales, the Poor Law still obtained under the label of Public Assistance, and five departments had responsibilities for the protection of over 17,000 children. Health was responsible for children under the Poor Law, Education for those under the Children and Young Persons Act and the Home Department for those in voluntary and remand homes. The Ministry of Pensions looked after a handful of children, who had lost fathers on war service. The 900 Board of Control children, all mentally handicapped, were in 'Certified Institutions' except six only under guardianship.

Excluding these last, Education's children in Approved Schools (2,140), and those in remand homes and borstals, the Clyde Committee was considering the condition of some 14,000 children in public care. More details of these distributions may be found in Appendix II of the Clyde Report (Cmnd. 6911, HMSO, 1946). To supplement the Report's general review of existing methods of provision some further elucidation is required at this point.

In the decades immediately prior to 1948 there were four main agencies of child care in Scotland, two statutory and two voluntary, the Public Assistance Committees, the Education Committees, the Voluntary Homes and the Royal Scottish Society for Prevention of Cruelty to Children.

The Poor Law (Scotland) Act of 1934 gave power to local authorities to 'make arrangements for the lodging, boarding or maintenance otherwise than in a poorhouse of children under sixteen years, who are orphans, or who have been deserted by or separated from their parents'. This was implemented as regards the 7,000 children involved, mainly by boarding out or placing in voluntary homes, with less than a tenth of them, infants, sick or short stay cases, retained in public assistance nurseries, sick wards or related Homes. In some areas, however, children were, as in England, left in public assistance institutions unsegregated, or, occasionally to avoid that, healthy children were placed in the wards of general hospitals.

The Education Authorities, apart from their duty to bring before a juvenile court those in need of care or protection, also had responsibility under the Children and Young Persons Act for children made the subject of approved school or fit person orders. The latter were mainly boarded out or placed in voluntary homes, though a few education authorities ran their own Homes.

When the act became operational in 1948, there were over 120 voluntary homes, some large and national, like Quarriers, Aberlour and those run by the Catholic Church and The Church of Scotland, some small and local.

The total provision, mainly for direct admissions, amounted to some three and a half thousand places, with local authority children accounting for about a third. These were independent establishments often reflecting the traditions and views of their 19th century founders, only moderated by fairly light checks from as many as all three Scottish Office Departments — Home, Health and Education — depending on the legal category under which the children had been admitted. And yet, some provided fair standards of care for their time.

Such were the agencies caring for children after they had been removed from their families. This removal was usually long-term, and there was little contact between agency and family except at occasional visits to the child. Between the Children Acts of 1908 and 1948, the Society for the Prevention of Cruelty to Children, in spite of the education authorities having gained power to intervene in care or protection cases, was virtually the sole agency interested and active in how children were treated in their own homes.

Originating from an 1859 amalgamation of two separate societies founded in 1854 in Glasgow and Edinburgh, after a brief period of affiliation (1895-1908) to the London NSPCC, during which it was expanding rapidly, the Society became independent. In 1899 it dealt with cases involving 7,829 children; by 1908 the figure was 21,993.[6]

The pre-1948 role of the Royal Scottish Society for the Prevention of Cruelty to Children — so named by Royal Charter of 1921 — may be illustrated by the following extract from an inspector's report of 1940.

'Time 8 p.m. 9 children aged from 6 months to 12 years alone in a very bad home. All windows vandalised. Winter. No fire. Light cut off. No food. Five roomed Corporation house bare except one bed and chest. No other furniture. Father 'at Sea'. Mother having what was called 'a good time'. All telephones in area vandalised. I got message to police and Police Motor Cycle Patrol brought candles. Eldest child ill. Phoned for doctor. He arrived before midnight and moved eldest child by ambulance as she was seriously ill. Local Authority promised to collect other eight children. Took no action. Neighbours brought food and coal and by

6 a.m. agreed to take over from Inspector if Police continued to visit. Inspector walked home, some miles'.[7]

It is clear from this by no means unique example that in such cases local authority involvement was indirect as well as reluctant, and the main burden lay with RSSPCC, readily supported by police and community. This was a pattern not unknown in some places even after the new Children Act of 1948.

Such then was the complexity of the pre-1948 arrangements for the care of some 14,000 children either placed by authorities in foster homes or in voluntary homes or public assistance homes and institutions or admitted directly by voluntary homes.

It is quite amazing that in this random mosaic of provision, with relatively little oversight, co-ordination or control, so few major miscarriages or scandals were registered or even brought to light. Perhaps it was the ignorance of a public generally habituated to low expectations in personal life and not yet activated by developed national media, which led to general acceptance, if noticed at all, of low standards or backward practices of child care.

Wartime Conditions

Unlike the position in England and Wales, wartime evacuation did not leave large numbers of unaccompanied homeless children in rural Scotland in 1945. Evacuation took place in 1939 from Glasgow, Edinburgh, Dundee, Clydebank and Rosyth. After the Clydebank blitz of 1941, Greenock, Port Glasgow and Dumbarton were added. Scottish evacuation was on a lesser scale, and the drift back was rapid. One survey showed a return of 30% by September 1939 and 75% by Christmas.[8] Yet the importance of evacuation cannot be over-emphasised for its side-effects of drawing public and official attention to the poor physical condition of many town children of the time. This revelation echoed the earlier national reactions to the poor physical state of recruits for the Boer War. A study, *Evacuation in Scotland* by Dr W. Boyd, Reader in Education at Glasgow, while more a catalogue of education—related statistics than a sociological study, nevertheless gives an interesting picture of the poor physical condition of many children and families. Speaking of evacuation Boyd says 'It has quickened in the people of this country a fresh realisation of the social evils as they affect childhood and youth, and has set parents and teachers thinking in new ways about the schooling and the upbringing of the young'.

In particular, evacuation to the country of children from the more crowded Scottish urban areas spotlighted the prevalence of poor clothing, dirt, infestation, skin infection and enuresis.[9] The discovery of enuresis on a wide scale caused amazement, anxiety and concern in the reception areas. Some of these conditions were no doubt exaggerated, not just by the circumstances of separation, but also by the receiving agents for whom much of this was new, strange and taxing. At this time there were virtually no social workers, and the arrangements were carried out by teachers, ministers, nurses, students and WVS.

Titmuss, in *Problems of Social Policy*, refers to similar findings in England, Wales and Scotland. Such physical conditions of the children should be seen against the backcloth of the era. The outbreak of war came at the end of a decade of mass unemployment, Public Assistance, 'the buroo', the means test and food vouchers — all damaging experiences for millions up to 1939. In addition to economic disadvantage and degradation, the 1930s was an era of squalor and potential disease in urban Scotland, for which the many overcrowded and unhygienic houses of our tenemental towns were a natural seed-bed. In 1911, 50% of the population of Scotland had lived in one or two-room houses. By 1951 the figure for Scotland was down to 25%, but in Glasgow it was still near 50%.[10] Malnutrition, diptheria, rickets and TB, were widespread conditions. Congenital syphilis, dispersed from the first war through the 1920s, was still more than a memory. Boyd's report that 'only' six cases of venereal disease were found among all evacuated children is significant of the times. Even in the worst conditions, however, family life was often strong and close-knit.

Clyde's Views and Findings

Some of the Clyde Committee's expressed values are of interest to us. Justifying remote rural Boarding Out, paragraph 58 of the Report reads: 'moreover there are cases where owing to the conduct of the parents, it is in the child's own interest that it should reside where contact with its parents will not be easy, and therefore infrequent'. This was a viewpoint not uncommon for the next 20 years. In paragraph 99 they say, 'We consider it inadvisable that backward or maladjusted children should be placed in Homes where there are normal children. Neither type is good for the other'. Perhaps this is understandable in the light of some of the Public Assistance Institution conditions. 'There should be Infant Homes for children up to two years' was another view of the time, which favoured nursery type establishments with their hygienic but retarding regimes.

In addition to evidence from the usual government departments, the Committee heard views from the local authorities, four counties of cities, 27 counties and 20 'large' burghs. Evidence was also taken from a wide range of voluntary organisations and individuals. Education and nursing were strongly represented, as was residential child care, mainly through the superintendents of large orphanages. There were few voices from other professional associations, apart from the Scottish Association of Welfare Officers and the Hospital Almoners Association. Unlike the Curtis scenario, psychologists of the day do not seem to have made any direct impact. This is surprising in a Scotland where psychology was a thriving discipline in the Universities, and where Education had welcomed it into local authority service in the form of Child Guidance. It is known that many of the psychologists who might have contributed, had been called up, some involved with psychological systems in the armed services. It is regrettable that the potential of contributions from those still working in child guidance, mainly women, was unfortunately overlooked.

The findings of Clyde were not so sensational as those of Curtis, either in fact or presentation, whether because the investigation was less rigorous, or whether conditions in Scotland, being nearer to the community, were less dated and repressive. There was strong criticism in general terms of admission of children to the Poorhouse. Paragraph 103 says 'This practice must cease. The atmosphere and environment of the Poorhouse are very bad for these children, and their association with the inmates is the worst possible basis for securing their welfare'.

In spite of the justification of Boarding Out at a distance (para. 58), the Committee were critical of the widespread practice on crofts. Paragraph 73 reads 'We strongly deprecate the boarding out of city children on crofts in very remote areas where they have no real contact with other children, where they have no facilities for learning a trade which is congenial to them, or where living conditions are bad'. 'Instances were found where children on crofts were overworked by their foster parents.' No doubt there was understatement here.

Careful study of the setting up, the proceedings and the recommendations of Clyde, gives a hint of complacency in central departments, which found a ready echo in the local authority members and officials involved. Our national belief in the superiority of our own systems had not been dented by the scandals and excitements in the South. It was commonly thought that Scotland possessed the panacea to the problem in a fine system of Boarding Out, and that improvements, rather than major change, was all that was required. These convictions were to overshadow the early growth of Children's Departments. Such considerations made the Clyde Report less radical and strong than Curtis.

Like Curtis the principal recommendations were that the responsibilities of separate government departments should be transferred to one single Department, and the local functions exercised by education, public health and public assistance committees in regard to homeless children, 'should be exercised by one committee in each area'. Clyde then produced its central tenet as Recommendation 3. 'A good foster parent system should be encouraged as the best solution of the problem.' The next ten recommendations develop this theme. Unlike Curtis, the recommendations, (15) and (23), on training come later, and appear weak, but it must be recognised that they did recommend a central training committee, a recommendation ignored until 1963.

Unlike Curtis there is no mention of a new style Children's Officer and necessary support staff. This central and major weakness in Scottish thinking was to prove adverse to the establishment of adequate children's departments in the early years. On the contrary, they say (para 69) 'We are strongly opposed to any system under which the whole matter is referred to an official, who merely reports to the local authority committee, and under which the latter has no personal contact with the children.' This might be construed as a community responsibility approach, in tune with Scandinavian or Scottish panel Systems. In reality it reflected the elected members' attitude, prevalent in Children's Committee times, and not quite extinct in the social work era. This was due in some part to genuine concern, in some part to low esteem of officials, and probably not a little to the concomitants of official boarding out visits — Highland hotels and Highland hospitality. It appears strange that England with traditional faith in the amateur, the lay magistrates and school governors, etc., should have opted strongly for the professional, while Scotland with historical respect for learning and qualification in medicine, ministry and education, failed to recognise at this stage the need for a new professionalism.

The main area in which Clyde took the lead from Curtis was the recommendation (22) that local authority responsibility for deprived children should extend to 18 rather than 16. There was also a firm plea for after-care and further education. All in all, however, had Scotland depended solely on Clyde for real reform, we should not have had the radical legislation produced. In the event the Children Act of 1948 was a Great Britain Act.

Such were the main recommendations of Clyde. They were not unanimous, however, and some independent thinking asserted itself at this stage. The two women doctors, Nora Wattie and May Baird, with strong sympathies for child health and Scottish Education, promoted two major reservations. In this they were actively supported by Naomi Mitchison, who believed in the efficacy of progressive education. Reservation (1) recommended that instead of one new committee, the two committees with existing strong involvement in Child Care should be used, i.e., public health for children under two, and education thereafter. They saw the experienced maternity and child welfare services as the best protection for young children. This was not without good reason in the light of the widespread conditions of disease, malnutrition and poor physical care in the tenement towns.

Reservations (2), promoted by the same three members, is even more interesting. They rejected boarding out as the principal form of provision, in favour of a progressive residential education approach. This was to consist of hostels and residential schools staffed by teachers working in co-operation with foster parents. These forms of provision during the evacuation experience had been shown to significantly cater for the educational and social needs of underprivileged children. They were also in vogue through the 1940s and 1950s as features of the new Education Acts for England (1944) and Scotland (1945), pioneering provision for children with special needs.

Results of Curtis and Clyde

Clyde reported in July 1946, Curtis in September. On the latter the *Daily Mirror* headlines of 16 October proclaimed 'Shocked MPs read with dismay last night one of the most tragic documents of recent years'. In England the question of central responsibility was thereafter settled at Cabinet level in favour of the Home Office. In Scotland the question was more easily solved inside the Scottish Office by following English precedent, and administratively nominating the Home Department, which held responsibility till superseded by the Scottish Education Department in 1960.[11]

The resulting Children Bill was drafted throughout 1947 with various innovative and notable provisions. The local authority were given the duty to receive into care any child under 17 who was orphaned, abandoned or lost, or of parents unable to care for him, and to keep him so long as his welfare required and he was under 18. To fulfil this they were required 'to exercise their powers with respect to him so as to further his best interests, and to afford him opportunity for the proper development of his character and abilities'. This central duty was revolutionary when compared to the pre-1948 Poor Law requirement, 'To set to work or put out as apprentices all children whose parents are not, in the opinion of the Council, able to keep them'.

Where it appeared to the local authority to be for the welfare of the child, there was a duty to return the child to the care of parent, guardian, relative or friend — a further major break from earlier institutional practice. Care was to be provided, preferably by boarding out, but failing which, in a local authority home or hostel, preferably after a process of observation and assessment in a reception home — a radical change from random admission to, and accommodation in large multi-purpose institutions.

The relevant local authorities were to be the counties and county boroughs in England and Wales and in Scotland the cities, counties and large burghs. These authorities were each required to set up a children's committee for their functions under this Act, the Adoption of Children Act, 1939 and marginally the Children and Young Persons Acts. They were also required, as central to the whole rationale, to appoint a children's officer of suitable qualifications who was subject to the Secretary of State's approval and must not be employed in any other capacity.

The 1948 Act so designed was a liberal and great Act. It was however essentially for the protection of children once they had been deprived of a normal home life and so contained little to facilitate preventative work with the family. Further, it left largely untouched the wide provisions of the Children and Young Persons Acts of the 1930s, and so prolonged the major dichotomy between the deprived and the delinquent child for a further two decades in Scotland, and even beyond that in England and Wales.

The Children Bill because of a crowded Parliamentary timetable was not tabled till early 1948. Thereafter it passed through Parliament with great rapidity, facilitated by residual war time idealism, a state machine practised in planning, and a new reforming socialist government. The Children Act 1948 received Royal Assent on the last day of June 1948 and was ready, only just, to become operational on 5 July along with the National Insurance, the National Assistance and the National Health Service Acts.

These three pieces of major legislation created the framework for the Social Security and National Health Systems.

The National Assistance Act also, together with the Children Act, formed the basis of welfare services for the elderly, physically handicapped persons and children. Here were the beginnings of the Welfare State. Here also was the infra-structure for the future Social Work Act in Scotland.

NOTES

1. See Curtis Report, Cmnd. 6922, HMSO 1946. The author on 15 November 1988 was able to meet one of the two survivors of the Committee Miss Sybil Clement Brown, with whom he had worked in the 1950s, while she was director of training in the Children's Department of the Home Office. She gave considerable insights into the workings of Curtis, and also in another connection some of the works of her close friend and colleague, Miss Eileen Younghusband.
2. The Boscobel Tracts Part II, edited by J. Hughes, Blackwood & Son, 1857.
3. Letter of 20.4.45 from the Secretary of State, Tom Johnston, to the Chairman, Mr J. L. Clyde.
4. SWSG Records, CYP, OE10, pp. 6-8. Oral evidence given by the Association of Directors of Education to the Kilbrandon Committee.
5. Conversations with Mrs Naomi Mitchison at Carradale, April 1987, and Dr Nora Wattie 1987/88, and with both jointly in Glasgow 21.2.89.

6. Brian Ashley, A Stone on the Mantlepiece, Centenary History, of the RSSPCC, Scottish Academic Press 1985, p. 70, facing, and p. 81.
7. Ibid., p. 149.
8. Dr William Boyd, Evacuation in Scotland, University of London Press, 1944, p. 31.
9. Ibid., pp. 57-65.
10. T. C. Smout, A Century of the Scottish People — Collins 1986, p. 35.
11. Scottish Record office, SRO — ED.11/293 — Minute to the Secretary 1.5.47, initialled C.C.C.

CHAPTER 3

The Elderly — The Wilderness Years

Having considered conditions and events in pre-1948 services for children, we must now look at services provided under Public Assistance for the elderly, which were still essentially Poor Law provision.

As such, the major criterion of need was poverty. Until the post-war approach to the National Assistance Act there was little state recognition of the needs of those too frail to live independently, but not yet requiring nursing care.

Prior to 1948 the elderly, handicapped and chronic sick were scarcely differentiated for type of services. These were provided under the aegis of Public Assistance, mainly in the form of residential accommodation in Public Assistance Institutions. Even the medical care of the needy sick, whether domestic or institutional, was largely provided under this umbrella. The only category whose needs had separate recognition was the blind under the Blind Persons Act of 1920. This gave pensions to blind persons aged 50, later reduced to 40. It also promoted services for the blind through a partnership of central government, local authorities and voluntary societies. The government set the required standards, the voluntary societies made the provision, and the local authorities supplemented voluntary resources by appropriate grants.

Our picture of the elderly is of necessity limited by the fact that in general this field is less well documented than that of Child Care, and, in particular, that most of the literature on Scottish Poor Law conditions goes no further than the 19th century.[1]

In the first four decades of the 20th century the elderly and aged sick in Britain enjoyed scant priority in public sympathy or social planning. The 19th century had seen extensive consideration of the effect of the Poor Laws, terminating with the *Report of the Royal Commission on the Poor Laws and the Relief of Distress 1909* (Cmnd. 4499). This found that of 140,000 elderly persons in Poor Law Institutions only a thousand or two in all England and Scotland were in separate small establishments. The rest were maintained in barrack-like institutions of up to 1,000 persons in cramped, ill-lit, ill-ventilated rooms by day, and high, cold, crowded, large dormitories by night — human warehouses. They were separated by sex and behaviour category, and governed by harsh regulations, determining when they should rise, go to bed, eat, work, and leave the compound, if at all.

For the not inconsiderable class of old men and women given to drink and rough habits — 'The Aged Poor of Bad Conduct', the conditions described above were thought to be appropriate, even by the progressives including Octavia Hill, George Lansbury and Beatrice Webb, who signed the minority report of the Royal Commission in 1909. For the others, some general improvements in institutional life, and separate provision for the elderly were recommended by both reports. In few places had these recommendations been substantially implemented by 1948. In many the conditions of 1909 persisted into the 1950s, and even into the 1960s, as is well documented by Townsend and others.[2]

In his introduction to *The Last Refuge* Townsend paints a bleak picture of the first half of the century.[3] 'The needs of the infirm aged and the chronic sick were grossly neglected. For almost four decades there was what amounted to a conspiracy of silence on the subject'. This is strong language, but certainly there were no enquiries, and few reports or books on the subject in this period.

By the Local Government Act of 1929 administration of the Poor Law was transferred from boards of guardians to the county and county borough councils in England and Wales. In Scotland the transfer was from parish councils to the councils of counties, cities and large burghs. The service was officially re-named Public Assistance, and the Workhouse or Poorhouse in Scotland, became the Public Assistance Institution. In Scotland however, in general parlance the accepted reference was still to 'The Pairish' or 'The Puirs House', until at least 1948. In England writers on the subject and speakers in Parliament commonly used Poor Law and Workhouse up until the 1948 Act.

From this transfer to larger and more responsible authorities considerable change and improvement as recommended might have been expected. In England and Wales the effects are generally described as largely cosmetic. Means and Smith suggest that 'the period 1929-39 saw some improvements in the treatment of elderly people in PAIs, but these were often fairly marginal'.[4] Gilbert, in *British Social Policy 1919-39*, sums up the post 1929 position as 'Poor Law Relief remained Poor Law Relief, and pauperism remained pauperism, except for a few small modifications'.[5] In late 1988 we spot checked how far these latter day opinions were valid for Scotland. Thomas Tinto of Glasgow and Archie Muir of Stirling County, both leading figures in post-war Scottish Welfare Services, with first-hand experience of Public Assistance in the 1930s, testify to the contrary. Tinto expressed the clear view to us that the 1929 rationalisation enabled Glasgow to assemble the basis for better services, and Muir was emphatic that the same applied to the large burghs of Lanarkshire.

On available evidence it is hard to say how far the institutional conditions described above obtained in Scotland. From the study of

Foresthall, described below, it appears likely that similar conditions could be found in some institutions in the cities and largest 'large burghs'. For various reasons, however, it is probable that such harsh institutional treatment of the aged poor and sick was not so widespread in early 20th century Scotland. Scottish practice, with its strong church and parish community tradition, was predominantly a basic out-door relief system, and did not depend to the same extent as the English on large residential institutions.

The Nuffield Foundation survey of 1944-46, 'Old People' OUP 1947, found that the ratio of out-door relief to institutional cases in Scotland was roughly five and one-half to one compared to one and one-half to one to 1 in England and Wales.[6] Most burgh and county poorhouses were smaller institutions of under 200 places, and closer to the community served. Further, in the North there was the feature of the Parochial Lodging House, described below, and generally, Voluntary Homes, of medium size and often of philanthropic foundation, accounted for a much higher proportion of places. Before the end of the period moreover, some local authorities had produced more appropriate residential provision for the elderly, such as Coatbridge's 16 bed 'hostels' or Glasgow's 'Cottages' at Crookston. These latter were an early approximation to sheltered housing, where residents largely cared for themselves, but had a main meal and extra care as required provided by the adjacent Crookston Home. There was similar voluntary cottage provision at Whiteinch, Glasgow and Colinton in Edinburgh.[7]

The above assessment may be regarded as a novel opinion, since the prevalent view of the Scottish Poor Law has been fairly adverse. Such criticism, however, has been mainly on the out-door relief side, and based on the earlier harsh lack of provision for able-bodied umemployed.

To check further how far the suggestions of neglect of the elderly in the first half of the century, applied to Scotland, we have been able to take two samples, one of 1909 and the other of 1949. The Royal Commission, with Victorian thoroughness, undertook a separate review of Scottish conditions and reported at length. Amongst its general findings was, for whatever reason, a lower ratio of old age pauperism in Scotland than in England — 20 per 1,000 as compared to 24. It recognised that much had been done to improve the lives of the 'respectable' aged poor, particularly in Glasgow, where classification by condition and character had been introduced in 1905. However, as a result of that classification, out of 1,050 inmates in Barnhill Poor House (Foresthall), only 249 were reckoned 'respectable'. Generally the position in the large city institutions remained as described by the Commissioners, 'at best the poorhouse offers little compensation for the loss of home. The life is always cheerless and there is little room for hope'. However, some of the Commissioners unearthed examples of good

Scottish practice showing what small Homes could provide. Outside the cities, particularly in Aberdeenshire and the Highlands, there was a system of Parochial Lodging Houses or Almshouses, some quite small, which had earlier attracted disapprobation as not meeting London criteria. One of the commissioners described his discovery of the Peterhead Parish Home as 'the most delightful institution that I have seen'. It was a large, comfortable, pleasantly furnished private house with about 30 'inmates'. Some had their own bedrooms, others were in pairs and others again in small dormitories. There were pleasant dining and sitting rooms for common use. The one or two well-behaved defective residents had separate rooms under the immediate charge of salaried servants. 'The master and the matron were able and kind'. The establishment had the rare comfort of fires even in summer when cold. The final hallmark of excellence was the weekly cost of three shillings and two pence per head, which compared very favourably with the Buchan Combination Poorhouse figure of four and sixpence. Whether this eulogy was influenced by the master's whisky or the matron's cooking, or both, we shall never know. It was obviously a progressive place, with standards well above those found by Curtis and others 40 years later. Indeed this was the kind of model residential place aimed at in the run up to the 1948 reforms. Other parts of the report confirm that while Peterhead may have been pre-eminent, it was not unique for such small Homes. The Commission also commented favourably on boarding out practice in Falkirk, whereby several old men had summer placements with local farmers, which provided a pleasant break and a healthy life and diet to prepare them to withstand the winter in an institution. The Commission rounded off their report on Scotland with recommendations that there should be classification by physical condition and character, and that Parish Homes should be promoted on the grounds of increased happiness to the resident, and reduced cost to the ratepayer.[8]

The continuation or development of these ameliorations was hindered by the onset of the First World War, soon followed by economic depression and a further War. Similarly, study of the interesting advances and lapses of the period seems to have been inhibited in recent times by underdeveloped professional services, and lack of attention in academic spheres.

For our second sample of Scottish Poor Law conditions, this time of the 1940s persisting into the 1950s, in a former city Public Assistance Institution, we may look at a thesis by Dr N. H. Nisbet, entitled *The Care of the Elderly* based on her work between 1949 and 1951 at Foresthall, Glasgow, then a 'joint user' establishment. To prepare for her appointment as Medical Officer here, Dr Nisbet had gained experience in the West Middlesex Hospital with Dr Marjory Warren, UK pioneer of geriatric medicine. At that time Foresthall still compounded all the war-time and post-war residential problems dumped on the top of a Public Assistance inheritance. In war-time it had been used to house patients from hospital beds cleared for more severe service and civilian casualties. It had also been used to nurse elderly people brought from as far as Southern England and the Channel Isles. At the end of 1950 as a 'joint user' establishment it catered for a mixed bag of 1,209 persons, 623 in hospital, 479 in Part III and 107 as 'casuals'. Dr Nisbet's 400 page thesis is concerned with hospital treatment issues, but prior to embarking on her scientific work, she devotes some ten pages to her personal observations and views on the Part III standards fossilised from the 1940s and earlier.[9]

She describes the 100-year-old grey stone buildings with narrow, often spiral, staircases as dark by day and poorly lit 'by a few weak electric bulbs' by night. There was no central heating, and the few coal fires were rigidly forbidden between March and October. The dormitories were crowded and poorly furnished. The sitting rooms were mainly 'large, bleak and barn-like'. Washing and toilet arrangements are described as poor and difficult of access, some of it outside the main building. Because the dining halls were at some distance from the wards, 'a considerable distance up and downhill had to be traversed four times a day in the open air in all weathers', with the result that Part III inmates had sometimes to be transferred to the hospital for no other reason than sheer inability to make these journeys. While the men's clothes were categorised as drab but adequate and warm, the women's were strongly criticised as 'prehistoric garments' with demoralising effects on new admissions.

The daily routine with its early rising hour of 6.30, and endless cleaning is described as 'no less penitential than the living quarters and the garments'. As general assessment Dr Nisbet offers the view: 'There is much purposeless idle misery and sloth in Part III, affecting all except those who have jobs to do'. However her commentary on conditions there concludes with the admission that 'some faint eddies of improvement' had reached it after two years of reform on the hospital side.

It is difficult for readers of today to realise such pictures of mass care. Older workers may have memories of such survivals in the 1950s as illustrated by Townsend, or indeed even later examples may be known in Britain. Approximations to these conditions may still be found in parts of Europe, as the author has seen in 1987 at a large institution for the elderly outside Paris, the Chateau of Villers-Cotterets, which four centuries earlier used to entertain Mary Queen of Scots.

Such then was the description of a large Scottish city institution in 1949/50 by a concerned, reforming young doctor with experience of more modern methods. At that stage it seems to have encapsulated into the new welfare era the worst Public Assistance patterns of 19th century law and practice, aggravated by a deluge of wartime demands, and post war pressures, restrictions and shortages. This may be an extreme picture, but it is perhaps not atypical of what obtained in differing degrees in the 'joint user' establishments inherited by the new Welfare Departments in the cities. In Chapter 4 we shall look at how these conditions were gradually improved at Foresthall and elsewhere under the National Assistance Act of 1948.

The causes of such apparent neglect of the elderly were threefold. Firstly, in the early decades real hopes were centred on the effects of the introduction of old age pensions in 1908. However, from that date until 1940 these pensions were mere pittances, and many failed even to qualify because of age, type of employment, or level of earnings. Rowntree in his second York survey of 1935 found that 'only 33 per cent of all the old age pensioners in York are living below the poverty line'.[10] It took wartime and the Old Age and Widows Pension Act of 1940 to bring standards up to a tolerable level, a measure reinforced by the Determination of Needs Act, which did away with the infamous 'Household Means Test'. This last was a draconian provision whereby, when a man had exhausted his unemployment benefit, there was an obligation on employed members of the household to keep him. In the groups concerned this led to recriminations, strife, temporary family break up and general unhappiness. The Means Test is the only other financial measure of the century to rank with the Community Charge or Poll Tax for inequity, difficulty of administration and sheer social divisiveness. The wartime changes, however, led Titmuss to say, 'The spirit in which many of these services were ordered and administered from about 1941 onwards underwent a subtle but noticeable change. To an increasing degree human needs were considered and dealt with in a humane way'.[11] Moreover it then came to be regarded as an appropriate government function to ward off stress and strain for all classes and not just the poorest.

Secondly, there was the further hope that rising living standards would enable families to shoulder their responsibilities in accordance with the Elizabethan principles re-stated in the Poor Law Act of 1930 (England and Wales). 'It shall be the duty of the father, grandfather, mother, grandmother, husband or child, of a poor, old, blind, lame or impotent person — if possessed of sufficient means, to relieve and maintain that person'. However, living standards did not rise; they fell in the 1930s. The Household Means Test not only failed to promote pooled finance; as noted above it actively militated against family functioning.

Thirdly, governments and reforms did not have time for concealed misfortunes, pre-occupied as they were through the 1920s and 1930s with the priorities of housing and maternity, child health and child protection. An even greater pre-occupation was with the intractable major problems of unemployment and benefits. Against this backcloth even that protagonist of reform, William Beveridge, was still relegating the claims of the elderly by such caveats as 'It is dangerous to be in any way lavish to old age until adequate provision has been assured for all other vital needs, such as the prevention of disease and the adequate nourishment of the young'.[12]

The Pressures for Change

It required events of the early part of the second war to lift the lid off the covert sufferings and needs of the elderly and chronic sick. In the words of Titmuss, 'The problem of the aged and the chronic sick had been serious enough in peacetime; in war it threatened to become unmanageable. Thousands who had formerly been nursed at home were clamouring for admission to hospitals, when families were split up, when houses were damaged or destroyed'.[13]

Some important concomitant factors were as follows. Few elderly were evacuated from the towns. This was due partly to choice, partly to means, but largely their low priority in official schemes, when compared to school children, babies or expectant mothers. Because of this, and their greater difficulty in taking shelter, their casualty rate from air raids was high — higher at times than the other exposed category, male adults.[14] Apart from enemy action, the war years brought an increased rate of accidents and death for two categories — children and elderly. With the former these were mainly due to drowning in emergency water supplies or to accidents on badly lit roads. The hazards to the elderly are summarised by Titmuss. 'The effect of a war environment on the loneliness and limited capacity of old age to help itself, led to an excess mortality during 1939-41 of over 2,300 elderly people from falling downstairs, out of bed, elsewhere in the home, out of doors, and in unknown circumstances'.[15]

Concern was frequently expressed too on the impact of food rationing on the elderly, having regard to their difficulties of adapting to alternative foods, queuing, and surviving on rations for one.[16] It is more likely that the single main factor was inability to afford even such a ration. Largely because of these concerns, however valid, the voluntary organisations WVS, BRCS, and OPWC, took action which led to the birth of Meals of Wheels.[17] Because of these and other factors, including loss of servants or income through the exigencies of war, demands for residential beds already high, soared to unprecedented levels alongside other urgent demands for civilian and service casualties.

Where could they go? What were the resources at this time? Just as actual bombing was to reveal the straits of the sick and elderly in the community, as air raid shelter dwellers, as persons rendered homeless, as dependents of bombed out families, so the threat of air raids in 1939 had alerted Ministries to the condition of this population in institutional care. Working on an assumed 72 casualties per ton of bombs, it was decided that a minimum extra 300,000 UK hospital beds were required, apart from the needs of normal sick and service casualties. There was of course no National Health Service and no national hospital system. Sick were cared for in three separate sets of institutions, over which there was little central control and even less exact knowledge. These were voluntary hospitals, local authority hospitals and Public Assistance 'Infirmaries' or 'sick houses', the local authority sector being by far the largest in Scotland, as in England. In Glasgow and Edinburgh, provision was headed by the prestigious voluntary 'Royal Infirmaries'. At second level the Public Health Departments of these cities provided several large and smaller general hospitals, as well as special establishments for infectious diseases and tuberculosis.[18] On the bottom grade came accommodation in such PAIs as Foresthall or Greenlea. The pattern in other Scottish cities was not dissimilar. It was a three-tier graded system. The voluntary hospitals selected their sick, preferring acute cases and passing chronic sick to the Local Authority Hospitals. They in turn got rid of 'undesirable' elderly or chronic sick to Public Assistance Institutions. A Ministry of Health Survey of Eastern England in 1938 spoke of the reproach of 'the masses of undiagnosed and untreated cases which litter our PAIs'.[19] Other surveys made in the search for beds were even more outspoken.

In the event, when war was declared, in order to find the required 300,000 beds, 140,000 patients were discharged from hospitals in one massive operation throughout Britain in two days. Many of these were elderly or chronically sick, who as a result are thought to have suffered unnecessarily or died prematurely.[20] Information on the subject is sketchy, since what was happening to these people, shunted around institutions at random, was sometimes unknown even to relatives for months, as they were unable for physical, mental or other causes to notify their position. Moreover, the capacity of medical services to mislay records was, understandably, even higher in these wartime conditions.

Thus the stream of elderly and infirm seeking residential places for reasons already mentioned was swollen by the massive numbers discharged, and with the hospitals being emptied, the flow of necessity was towards Local Authority Institutions. In the process, amongst those arriving in PAIs or public hospitals of a similar character, were for the first time substantial numbers of middle-class patients. This misfortune for some became the general benefit of many, by provoking much publicity and vigorous complaints. The secrets of the 19th century social and medical gulags were at last being released. Not since Dickens had there been such revelations. 'Conditions which previously had been known only to the sick and aged poor were, as a result, more widely discussed by doctors, welfare workers and the general public'.[21] In spite of the many urgent pre-occupations of war, British public opinion in the early 1940s was awakening with concern to the treatment of the elderly. And so there began between 1941 and 1948 the steady build-up of a campaign for improvements, spearheaded by the major voluntary organisations. By March 1943 the general issue had been brought to public notice by correspondence in the Manchester Guardian, drawing attention to the desperately low standards in the PAIs. More importantly in 1944, after initiatives from OPWC, the Nuffield Foundation set up a Committee chaired by Seebohm Rowntree to survey the conditions of the elderly, having regard to pensions, housing and residential care.[6] The Committee's report, the nearest approach to a 'Curtis' for the Elderly, did not come out till January 1947. Amongst its principal recommendations it featured small Homes, and separate provision for the senile. Reporting the Nuffield Committee's findings, press comment of the day headlined the deficiencies and scandals of institutional care, as had been done the previous year with the Curtis Report, though this time in a lower key. This report of January 1947 topped out the many representations which had continued through 1944, 1945 and 1946 from voluntary, professional, and local authority sources. The motivation of these last was not entirely pure. Some welcomed reform, some feared for their rates, if they were left responsible at the end of the war for large populations evacuated from the towns. To the continuing barrage the Ministry of Health responded with a Circular — No. 49/47 'The Care of the Aged in Public Assistance Homes and Institutions'. This cited impending legislation, called for resumption of building of small homes, and outlined necessary improvements in the premises, food, clothing and routines of PAIs. The Scottish parallel was the Department of Health Circular No. 41, which was unloaded on under-resourced local authorities, still hesitant to contemplate the major new resource implications of the recently released Clyde report (July 46).

The National Assistance Act 1948

The promised Act had a long incubation period from its origins in the Beveridge report. By late 1943 the Cabinet Committee on Reconstruction had decided that the Poor Law should be abolished, income maintenance should be a central government function, and 'indoor accommodation' for aged and needy should be a local authority duty. By early 1944 the official view was 'the proposed Bill needs to do no more than take out of the Poor Law all the functions of caring for children and old people, and transfer them perhaps to a statutory Children and Old Persons, or Social Welfare Committee'.[22] By mid 1944 senior civil servants were observing 'We should watch this question carefully lest we be met with the criticism when we introduce our Bill that we have dismissed the old far too summarily'.[23] In the event the Act, or part of the Act, was indeed summary, but the relief at its arrival smothered major criticism. By February 1945 the idea of a joint Social Welfare Committee for children and elderly had been abandoned, without insistence on a separate statutory committee for old people, as was envisaged for children. The new Labour Government, returned in 1945, set up a Social Services Committee to harmonise social policy reforms. This in turn produced a 'Break up of the Poor Law Committee', which after only eight sessions presented its report together with a draft bill to the cabinet in July 1946. This report is notable for at least four major recommendations. Firstly the large general institutions should be abandoned in favour of specialised accommodation for the varying needs of those unable to lead a normal life. Secondly, small homes or hostels, as they were commonly referred to, were prescribed for the elderly. Further, to emphasise the break-away from the Poor Law dependency status, residents should enjoy a 'hotel relationship', by keeping responsibility for their own income, and paying therefrom an appropriate charge. In 1946-47 this meant that from their 26/- pension they should pay the local authority 21/- and retain 5/- for personal use — the origin of today's process. Thirdly, the local authority should be given a clear duty to promote the welfare of physically and mentally handicapped people. Fourthly, the wide responsibility laid on relatives by the Poor Law Act of 1930 should be curtailed to a point where only spouses were responsible for the maintenance of each other, and parents for children under 16. The report was approved by the Cabinet Social Services Committee.

The pace was maintained with considerable urgency and commitment. A fortnight later a meeting was held with the local authority associations. They found the general proposals acceptable, but had amendments in respect of two administrative matters. Firstly, they resisted the idea that the Bill would prescribe an existing or new committee to undertake these duties, as was to happen with the Children Act. Unfortunately this objection was duly sustained. Secondly, they requested direct grant for running the new service as for Children. After initial resistance the matter was finally settled by the Minister, Aneurin Bevan, and the Chancellor, Hugh Dalton, through a compromise. A formula was devised for capital grants towards the provision of the new residential accommodation on much the same lines as grants towards council housing. This took the form of a 60-year subsidy towards each new home at an annual rate in 1948 of £7.10/- per single bedroom provided in England and Wales, and £11.00 for the same in Scotland.[24] These figures are of interest as indicators not only of values of the times, but also of the chronic persistent higher costs of building in Scotland, which still obtain.

The Bill, published on 31 October, was generally well received. The popular press was enthusiastic, and carried allusions to hotel conditions with 'hot and cold'. Means and Smith, however, draw our attention to the more reserved welcome from such conservative organs as *The Times* and the *Glasgow Herald*. The latter's comment read, 'The proposals in the Bill will remain no more than proposals until the present period of financial stringency is past. The new services and new buildings, which will replace the old Poor Law System and Institutions, will make heavy demands on finance, building construction and manpower, all of which are not only subject to restrictions, but are needed for projects of more immediate importance'.[25] These apparently heartless reactions were in the event to prove fairly realistic predictions. Post-war scarcities and priorities delayed major replacements, in many areas for at least two decades. The Bill was introduced in the Commons in 1946. Aneurin Bevan expressed his satisfaction that 'The Workhouse' was to go, and went so far as to suggest that 'any old person who wished to go (i.e. into the new Homes) may go there in exactly the same way as many well-to-do people have been accustomed to go into residential hotels'.[26] This enthusiasm was shared in the main by both political parties, with only the lone Conservative voice pointing out that such prospects depended heavily on the degree of economic recovery. The Bill received Royal Assent on 13 May 1948 with the appointed day being 5 July as for the parallel legislation on children and health.

Did the National Assistance Act 1948 represent the best possible deal of the time for the elderly and disabled? Writing in the mid-Sixties authorities such as Townsend and Parker have stressed the inadequacy of the Act in terms of its exclusive concentration on residential provision. According to Parker 'The concern to maintain and foster family life evident in the Children Act was completely lacking in the National Assistance Act — Institutional provision was accepted without question'.[27] In the light of tradition, and the prevalent advice and attitudes discussed below, this appears an unduly severe criticism. However, with hindsight, it is indeed now possible to point to the limitations of the Act. Firstly provisions for the welfare of elderly and handicapped were covered in one modest part of the wide Act. Part I abolished the existing Poor Law; Part II described the new National Assistance Board and defined its powers of income support. Part IV, almost half of the Act, was

'General and Supplementary'. The Welfare provisions of Part III amounted to less than a quarter of the main Act, and consisted of eight sections on residential care, one on the promotion of welfare of the handicapped, and four others on voluntary organisations, compulsory removals and burial or cremation.[28] In particular there was no power for direct provision of meals services or recreation, which was visualised as happening through voluntary organisations. Indeed, for support of the elderly and handicapped in the community, there were more powers in the National Health Service Acts of 1946, and (Scotland) 1947. These Acts with their provisions for home nursing, home help, prevention, care and after-care of illness, clearly looked forward, unlike the National Assistance Act, to prevention and care in the community. Medicine was becoming community orientated, Welfare was still largely institutional in outlook.

Unlike the Children Act the National Assistance Act had no requirements for a new chief officer, nor for training of workers, nor for advisory councils. The over-concentration on residential care must be seen in the light of centuries of tradition. In particular we have Bevan's 'Hotel facility' view already quoted, and the influential thoughts of the Nuffield Foundation Committee in 1947. These read strangely now, 'If sufficient Homes can be provided, and if the home-like atmosphere found in some of them is introduced to all Homes, many old people will prefer no doubt to enter them, rather than to continue living in unsatisfactory conditions in private houses. This will lessen the need for extensive plans for home help, visiting and home meals service for old people, who would be better off in a Home or Institution'.[29] The right role for domiciliary services was thought to be in helping able-bodied old people in cases of temporary illness or during convalescence. Great weight had been given to this by senior officials in the Ministry of Health, who also viewed any necessary community services as being the province of the great voluntary agencies, such as WVS and BRCS who had developed in this field in wartime conditions.

It is clear that the philosophy of community care as the main support of the elderly and others was still a long way off. It should be remembered that there had been no great advance in the psychology and needs of elderly as there had been for children. Moreover in 1948 geriatrics was still an undeveloped medical discipline, as we shall discuss further in Chapter 4. The legislative inadequacies are aptly summed up by Julia Parker in her *Local Health and Welfare Services* of 1965 by the phrase 'The Act was a feeble instrument for such a grand design'.[30] Yet in 1948 to people emerging from a wilderness, it represented the tablets of stone which marked the end of the dark age of the Poor Law, and heralded a mighty leap into the brave new welfare world of post-war idealism. There was much certainty about the institutions and practices which should be abolished. There was less certainty about the best long-term forms of provision to replace them.

All in all, perhaps, the Act should be applauded as the end of the Poor Law, the beginning of a new deal, however dependent on residential remedies, and the launch-pad for further legislative advance.

NOTES

1. E.g., The Dawn of Scottish Welfare, Thos. Ferguson, 1960; The Making of the Old Scottish Poor Law, Rosalind Mitchell, 1974; The Scottish Poor Law 1745-1845, Jean Lindsay, 1975; The Scottish Poor Law 1745-1845, R. A. Cage, 1981.
2. Peter Townsend, The Last Refuge, Routledge and Kegan Paul, 1962; Robin Means and Randall Smith, The Development of Services for Elderly People, Croom Helm, 1985.
3. Townsend, The Last Refuge, p. 17.
4. Means and Smith, The Development of Services, p. 23.
5. B. Gilbert — British Social Policy 1919-1939, Batsford 1970, p. 229.
6. Nuffield Foundation, Old People, Report of a Survey Committee on the Problems of Ageing and the Care of Old People, Oxford University Press 1947, p. 67.
7. Ibid., pp. 142, 143.
8. the Royal Commission on the Poor Laws and Relief of Distress, Report on Scotland 1909, HMSO Cmnd. 4922, vol. XXXVIII, pp. 117-122, 180-4, 232-4. Some of these parish homes continued after 1948 and indeed Moray and Nairn only closed theirs, near Grantown, in 1964.
9. Dr N. H. Nisbet, The Care of the Elderly, thesis in Department of Materia Medica, Glasgow University 1952, pp. 35-45.
10. Seebohm Rowntree, Poverty and Progress, a Second Survey of York, Longmans, Green and Co. 1941, p. 459.
11. Richard M. Titmuss — Problems of Social Policy, HMSO 1950, p. 515.
12. Sir William Beveridge, Social Insurance and Allied Services, HMSO, 1942, para. 236.
13. R. M. Titmuss, Problems of Social Policy, pp. 447, 448.
14. Ibid., p. 559.
15. Ibid., p. 334.
16. Age Concern, Second enquiry regarding hardships old people may be suffering owing to the present food restrictions, February 1944.
17. WVS   — Women's Voluntary Services, later Women's Royal Voluntary Services.
    BRCS   — British Red Cross Society.
    OPWC   — The National Old People's Welfare Committee was founded in 1941 and local OPWCs followed. In Scotland the SOPWC was a wartime offshoot from the Scottish Council of Social Service. In 1971 the title Age Concern replaced OPWC.
18. Isaacs, Livingstone, Neville, Survival of the Unfittest, Routledge and Kegan Paul, 1972, pp. 8, 9.
19. R. M. Titmuss, Problems of Social Policy, p. 68.
20. C. Morris, Public Health during the First Three Months of War, Social Work (London) 1940, pp. 186-190.
21. R. M. Titmuss, Problems of Social Policy, p. 501.
22. Public Records Office — PRO/MH/47.
23. Ibid.
24. Public Records Office — PRO/CAB/80/80/49.
25. Means and Smith, The Development of Services for the Elderly, p. 149.
26. Hansard, vol. 443, col. 1609.

27. J. Parker, Local Health and Welfare Services, Allen and Unwin 1965, p. 106.

28. Because residential homes were provided under Part III of the Act they were known administratively as Part III Homes until the Social Work Act of 1968, under which for the same reason they became Part IV Homes. In England and Wales the terminology remained Part III.

29. Nuffield Foundation, Old People, Report of a Survey Committee, p. 96. It is for speculation how far the armed services wartime chant 'You'd be far better off in a home', is attributable to this source.

30. J. Parker, Local Health and Welfare Services, p. 108.

CHAPTER 4

Separate Services 1948-1969
Welfare and Health

The post-war legislation established the Scottish social services, which, for two decades prior to the Social Work Act, were provided to individuals and families, through four separate agencies: Welfare, Health, Probation and Children's Departments. For this purpose, Probation excepted, the responsible local authorities were the four cities, the 33 counties — four of which were combined in pairs (Perth and Kinross, Moray and Nairn) — and the 21 'large burghs'.[1] While three of the last had populations over 70,000, 13 had less than 50,000. Moreover, eight of the uncombined counties had populations under 30,000. This was not a promising basis on which to establish modern personal social services.

A further factor, potentially inimical to new, independent growth, was the integration of welfare and health departments to a greater or lesser degree according to the policy of the different local authorities. This development was prompted by a Department of Health Circular (39/1948), advising local authorities that they could provide welfare services either through a new committee or through an existing committee, e.g., health. In the latter case, where the functions were discharged under the general oversight of the medical officer, a senior lay officer should be appointed to administer day to day services — the Welfare Officer.

This approach further emphasised the difference from the children's service, where the Act required the authority to appoint a Children's Officer, who should not be employed in any other capacity, and who must be approved by the Secretary of State.

Welfare Services

In the event, while 80% of local authorities in England set up a separate welfare committee, only 60% did so in Scotland.[2] The result was that a substantial number of health and welfare authorities appointed the medical officer to head the service. The Younghusband Committee even found that in 1956 seven Scottish local authorities still relied on a Medical Officer, or County Clerk for actual day to day administration of the welfare services. In this situation, where a large minority of authorities linked the two services, and there were common chief officials, the staff were also usually reckoned together. In general, welfare staff were also concerned with the mental health service, but a few authorities had separate units for this purpose. In these circumstances, the domination of welfare departments by the medical and nursing profession tended to obscure the importance of the social work element in the services. The emphasis was on the physical aspects of welfare problems. The ethos, influenced by medical authority and public assistance tradition, sometimes tended towards institutional and authoritarian practice. This seeming lack of vision and enthusiasm for new-style welfare services should be balanced by consideration of what actually happened in some of the large counties and cities immediately before and after 1948.

As early as 1943 Ayr County proposed to change the name 'Public Assistance Committee' to 'Social Welfare Committee'. In spite of the Department of Health's neutered response of 'no observations' on the proposals, the new title was assumed, and continued till superseded by 'Welfare Committee' in 1948. This was by no means unique, similar developments having occurred pre-war and war-time, in Glasgow and elsewhere. These authorities had started prior to 1948 their efforts to build up the new services of the future, mainly residential homes for the elderly. At times, when considering mansions for conversion, their intention for a small Home was inhibited by Scottish Office's cautions such as, 'a Home of this kind cannot be economically run unless it can accommodate a minimum of 25 persons'.[3] Fortunately, this advice was often ignored, particularly in rural areas.

Major factors in determining the quality and the direction of the new service were the quality of the new chairman and committees, and the philosophies of internal power groups, including the dominant county or town clerks. However, the calibre of the welfare officer appointed was crucial. These last were mainly the former public assistance officers re-designated. They usually carried extra duties such as authorised officer under the Lunacy and Mental Deficiency Acts, provision of boots and clothing for needy children, supervision of registrars in rural areas, and in a few places, supervisor of civic restaurants.[4] They were not strongly supported by assistant staff. Given the nature of the authorities, given the restrictions of finance, given the limitations of staff, it would be unrealistic to expect instant solutions or even dramatic changes in problems left so long unaddressed. Yet in many areas experienced and dynamic men, supported by interested chairmen, launched the new service with zeal and commitment to the cause of handicapped and elderly. There had been an Association of Welfare Officers with an annual conference since at least 1944, which had given much thought to future welfare services, as well as evidence to the Clyde Committee.[5] It would therefore be misleading to suppose, as often done, that the

Public Assistance era run unchanged right through till 1948 when new-style Welfare or Health and Welfare Departments sprang from the ground fully armed.

The main duties and powers of local authorities to provide welfare services were laid down under a mere two sections of Part III of the National Assistance Act. Section 21 required authorities to provide residential accommodation 'for persons who by reasons of age, infirmity, or any other circumstances are in need of care and attention which is not otherwise available to them,' i.e., for elderly, and handicapped persons, and those in need of temporary emergency accommodation. Section 29 gave power to authorities 'for promoting the welfare of — persons who are blind, deaf or dumb, and other persons who are substantially and permanently handicapped by illness, injury or congenital deformity'. The authorities were required to produce schemes which set out how they intended to discharge these powers and duties. They were also required to produce estimates of the numbers requiring services under these sections.

The Physically Handicapped

Services for the Deaf and Dumb were provided mainly on an agency basis by voluntary organisations with strong emphasis on religious and social activities. As regards blind persons, the main domiciliary service was provided by voluntary organisations through home teachers of the blind. Exceptionally, however, Glasgow, Stirling and Clackmannan Counties gave a service through their own home teachers. At 31 March 1957 there were 9,909 persons registered as blind in Scotland, and 78 home teachers employed to serve them.[6] These services, available also to partially sighted persons, consisted of advice and guidance on personal, domestic and financial matters, teaching in appropriate occupations, crafts and skills, arranging social and recreational occasions and providing practical facilities such as wireless and books. There were also five sheltered workshops for blind people in Scotland in the principal towns, four of which were operated by voluntary organisations. The Glasgow Workshop, the largest, was operated by the local authority.

The method of provision of services for the blind generated strong argument and feeling on both sides throughout this period. On the one hand the voluntary societies never ceased vehemently to question the local authorities' expertise in this sector. On the other hand political considerations entered to the extent of the STUC's Dunoon Conference of 1951 resolving 'Congress re-affirms its belief that welfare services for the blind should be under direct public control', after deploring the fact that 'these services continue to be almost entirely under the direction of local voluntary charities'.[7] This seems to be one of the rare occasions of the period when the Trade Union Movement expressed strong views on social services in Scotland.

As regards general services for handicapped persons, a circular was issued with the Act (Circ. 51/48 Department of Health). It stated that the guiding principle of the service should be 'to ensure that all handicapped persons whatever their disability should have the maximum opportunity of sharing in and contributing to the life of the community, so that their capacities are realised to the full, their self-confidence developed and their social contacts strengthened'. The National Assistance Act gave the local authorities wide powers to promote welfare in the following fields:

(a) compilation of registers of handicapped persons;
(b) assistance in overcoming the effects of their disabilities;
(c) advice and guidance on personal problems;
(d) instruction in handicrafts and diversionary occupations;
(e) the provision of social and recreational facilities;
(f) home visiting and practical assistance in the home;
(g) facilities for transport and holidays;
(h) assistance in securing open employment, provision of sheltered employment, and facilitating homeworkers' schemes.

It was not until 1962 that local authorities were given not only the power but the duty to provide the above.[8] Few new welfare departments were equal in resources or orientation to such massive demands in respect of large and widely differing client groups. Registration was carried out in a fashion, but, with the limited resources of the time, proved a massive and imprecise exercise, the value of which was questionable when not backed up by appropriate services. The following example from a city health and welfare department illustrates the problems and practice of dealing with mass caseloads without adequate staffing. In 1961 a visiting welfare adviser from the Department of Health, Scotland, was told by the health visitor in charge of the handicapped section, that of the 800 people on the register about 120 were housebound, who 'presented no particular problems'.[9] This kind of situation was neither exceptional nor typical. In many welfare departments in the 1960s a drive was being made to recruit occupational therapists to provide a domiciliary service.

The implementation of the wide powers to promote the welfare of the handicapped depended largely on the administrative/medical background common to most Principal Welfare Officers and Medical Officers. The main result was some new services to the handicapped as far as limited resources of staff and money would allow, in the practical form of occupational therapy, housing adaptations, aids to daily living, social and craft centres, and in a few instances, sheltered workshops.[10] There was inevitably much less emphasis on advice and counselling with personal problems. By the late 1960s, however, as seconded staff were returning from social work training, the balance was shifting as we shall see later when considering work with the elderly.

J. T. Gregory writing in 1965 on *Services for the Physically Handicapped in the UK* says 'Few social services could have had a more promising beginning than those for the physically handicapped that this National Assistance Act introduced. Until then there had been no statutory authority responsible for providing services for physically handicapped people other than the blind'.[11] In overall perspective there were no doubt some significant local advances, but the handicapped person was not suddenly smothered with the varied services detailed by Section 29.[12] Rather, such provision as became available tended to emphasise existing inadequacies, and to stimulate further demand. In this respect the position was not greatly different from that which obtained in the years immediately after the Chronically Sick and Disabled Persons Act of 1970. Now in the 1990s it is for consideration whether we have again taken our seats for a historical re-run, with the provisions of the Disabled Persons Act 1986 providing the latest feature.

Under Part III of the Act local authorities were also required to provide 'temporary accommodation for persons who are in urgent need thereof, being need arising in circumstances which could not reasonably have been foreseen, or in such other circumstances as the authority may in any particular case determine'. This temporary accommodation had been envisaged as only an emergency measure in case of fire, flood, etc. However, it soon proved to be mainly used by inadequate families, and by unsupported mothers evicted from their homes for rent arrears, etc. During the year ended 30 June 1957, 272 adults accompanied by 490 children were admitted to temporary accommodation.[13] Thus began the involvement of welfare departments with 'problem families', which we shall discuss further in Chapter 6. In passing it may be recorded that such accommodation was often noted more for its inferior and deterrent quality than for its suitability. In this particular provision some observers could detect a recrudescence of the old public assistance ethos.

Residential Care of the Elderly

We may now consider how the care of the elderly, by philosophy and legislation mainly residential, developed after 1948. Firstly, there was a major exercise to separate the chronic sick from the frail elderly, and to re-allocate the accommodation which had been used for both. Some of the old institutions passed to the new Health Boards as hospitals, some became 'joint-user/ establishments, while the remainder stayed with the local authorities to provide residential accommodation under Part III of the Act. Because of economic restrictions and competing demands for reconstruction resources, the pace of providing new Homes was slow. Necessary modernisation of the institutions was often delayed for the same reasons, and because of reluctance to spend on places later to be abandoned. The result was that the large institutions were slow to go out of service, and we have examples of some in the cities being nobly nursed along with necessary improvements for 40 years, such as Foresthall (Glasgow) closed in 1988 and Greenlea (Edinburgh) closed in 1987. In an introduction to his famous *Survey of Residential Institutions and Homes for the Aged in England and Wales*, better known as *The Last Refuge*, Townsend in 1960 aptly sums up the position 'So far as residential services for the aged and the handicapped were concerned, Britain appeared to have been going through one long tunnel of economic crisis between 1948 and 1958'.[14] From our present perspective that may seem an understatement.

Based on this survey Townsend produced a table showing numbers in former PAIs, other local authority Homes, voluntary and private Homes. On these he made the general observation, 'The four types of institutions tend to serve rather different purposes. The former public assistance institutions cater largely for the poorest social classes and for those who lack relatives, or have lost touch with them. The other local authority premises cater more often for women and those of middle or upper working class origin'. Without the benefit of specific research, the applicability of this to Scotland can only be a matter of opinion based on memory. What experience we have consulted suggests a roughly similar pattern in Scotland.

The table's figures are of interest showing that in January 1960 the distribution of places for England and Wales was 33% in former PAIs, 33% in local authority Homes, and 23% in voluntary Homes, while the comparable figures for Scotland were 34%, 25% and 37%. In England, even then, there was a substantial number (10%) in private Homes, few of which existed in Scotland. It is interesting to note that in Scotland in 1969, 27% of elderly in care were still accommodated in former PAIs, while the figure for voluntary Homes was still approximately 37%.[15]

The overall picture for Scotland of the period is slow development of new local authority Homes, continued heavy dependence on voluntary Homes, and little reduction of places in former PAIs. That over a quarter of the elderly were still so accommodated 20 years after the Act may be largely traced to the inability of the cities and some large burghs to dispense with the massive former Poor Law establishments on which they had invested and depended heavily. However, a study of the records of two of these recently closed institutions, Greenlea (Edinburgh) and Foresthall (Glasgow), suggest a picture somewhat removed from the crude pre-war poorhouse. Starting from such backward conditions as described in the previous chapter, and in face of great inherent difficulties, improved standards of care were achieved over the period. A short outline may illustrate the problems and some of the progress in both places.

Greenlea was built in 1870 as the Craiglockhart Poorhouse to cater for 600 females, 344 males and 36 married couples — about 1,000 in all. Additionally it had on site a lunatic asylum with some 230 places. Such was its size that the east-west corridor was said to run for a quarter of a mile. The original design separated the inmates by sex and behaviour category, and the architect's brief claimed thereby to provide a 'comfortable home for the aged and the poor' and a reformatory for 'the dissipated, the improvident and the vicious'.

During the second world war this institution was used as a hospital. After the war, faced with its unsuitability for modern purposes, Edinburgh Corporation embarked upon a 20-year programme of modernisation and refurbishment, as far as this was possible. Large dormitories were split into cubicles for two or four beds, but toilet and feeding facilities continued to present problems. In spite of major inherent difficulties an improved level of personal care was maintained for a much reduced population — 370 in 1980 — up until Greenlea's closure in 1987. This was made possible by the successor authority in 1975, Lothian Region, having completed a major replacement programme of nine new Homes opened between 1984 and 1987. The records of Greenlea are now available for study in the offices of the Edinburgh City Archives.

Glasgow's Foresthall is inevitably a bigger and more flamboyant story, of which the following outline roughly illustrates the massive problems inherited from public assistance days, firstly by Glasgow Corporation health and welfare department in 1948, then by the social work department of Glasgow (1969), and of Strathclyde in 1975.[16] As a local authority response to the population explosion of the industrial revolution, then overwhelming the existing care of the poor on a parish basis by the established church, Foresthall was opened in 1850 as Barnhill Poorhouse by the Barony Parish (Springburn, Maryhill and Anderston) and at its zenith was the biggest poorhouse in Scotland. In 1898, on the merger of the Barony and City parishes it became the sole poorhouse for Glasgow. From 1948 the renamed Foresthall was a 'joint user' institution under the control of Glasgow Corporation and the Western Regional Hospital Board. Since 1948 in fact it had developed hybrid medical and social work functions, and in the previous chapter we discussed conditions as found there by Dr Nanette Nisbet in 1949/50. As noted in Chapter 3, the residential standards at 1948, and for a few years thereafter, were in many respects backward if not primitive. Under the new regime the authority mounted a major programme of modernisation and improvements throughout the 1950s. The Convener of Glasgow's Health and Welfare Committee, Baillie John Mains (also a member of Clyde, Younghusband, and Morison Committees) described this progress as 'the transition from an oppressive building, which seemed drab and fearsome to a fully up-to-date modern welfare Home providing accommodation for the, elderly in need of special treatment, the homeless and distressed'. How far this interesting and interested claim was valid, only those resident or working there in the 1950s and 1960s could attest. It is probable, however, that the advances on the hospital side had considerable influence towards improved standards on the residential side, which were being fostered by progressive committee and officer attitudes. One of the recurrent problems was accommodating the homeless in the same building as the elderly, since at times in the 1960s as many as 100 'casuals' were being put up each night. Its last major service on this front came in 1969 when 400 people rendered homeless by the great storm were accommodated for several months. In such major crises the old institutions provided an essential service, and their present counterparts for such disasters are not at all apparent.

In 1969 Foresthall was still indispensable to the new Social Work Department, but was gradually run down over the next 20 years, with final closure achieved in 1988 through dispersal and the provision of more new Homes. It had lasted 140 years, and served three different regimes, Poor Law, Welfare and Social Work, while continuing in both hospital and residential roles.

Lesser residential anachronisms were more easily discontinued by 1948, as the following extract from Ayr County Welfare Committee minutes of January 1947 shows,
'Colmonell Sick House The Social Welfare Officer reported that Mrs D, aged 76, who has been caretaker of the Colmonell Sick House since 1931, has intimated her desire to terminate her employment as from 11 January. The Sick House, which consists of two rooms on the ground floor, and two attics with access by means of a wooden ladder, is most unsuitable for the purpose of a lodging house.'

The progress between 1948 and 1969 should be viewed with such early benchmarks in mind. We have now seen that some Scottish authorities, particularly the cities, saddled with an inheritance of massive 19th century institutions on the one hand, and bridled by increasing numbers and economic constraints on the other, were unable to make a rapid transition from PAIs to small Homes in the two decades following the 1948 Act. It is easy with hindsight to conclude that they should have abandoned these outdated, substandard institutions at an early stage, but their options were strictly limited. As it was, they improvised, ameliorated the worst, and even facilitated noteworthy developments.

Our brief survey of Greenlea and Foresthall can only raise the question as to whether the residential care of the elderly remained as encapsulated in a Poor Law time warp as described in studies in England and Wales. Obviously this field has been insufficiently explored in Scotland, and the availability of the records of these two places now closed should lead to further studies, which may, even from this distance, provide a clearer picture of institutional care of the elderly in the period concerned.

Generally during the period 1948-1969 provision of residential accommodation for the elderly, either directly or through voluntary organisations was a major pre-occupation of welfare departments. Most authorities in 1948 had taken the conscious decision not to provide special homes or hostels for the handicapped, but to accommodate them either with the elderly or through specialist voluntary agencies, such as the Red Cross or Cheshire Homes. In making schemes and plans in 1948 it was generally assumed that there would be a great increase in the residential places required. This assumption was based firstly on the increasing elderly population, and secondly on the reduced stigma when provision was no longer under public assistance.

Efforts were therefore directed towards rehabilitation of old public assistance institutions, purchase and conversion of suitable mansions, and building new Homes wherever resources for this became available. The Scottish Office rigorously controlled capital investment on building, and schemes submitted after great local effort and initiative often took years to gain approval. Conversion started earlier and proceeded more rapidly than new build, which was only gaining momentum in the Sixties. The opening of new Homes in most authorities scarce kept pace with the expanding elderly population and growing demand. Clearing the large city institutions was an Augean task in more senses than one.

In 1963 the Scottish Office issued its Circular 135/63 recommending 25 residential places per 1,000 of the elderly population. Provision as regards numbers and quality varied widely, particularly among the large burghs. Progress, however, was made in certain areas at an early stage. Even before the war Glasgow Welfare Committee had established at Crookston a complex of individual cottages next to a large residential home. These provided units for 72 single persons and 32 couples in a domestic setting. Mid-day dinner was served centrally, and arrangements were made to enable the elderly to cook morning and evening meals for themselves. This pattern was copied elsewhere, and some authorities well before 1948 had provided small Homes, e.g., Coatbridge with its two 'hostels', each of 16 places. The Crookston complex may well be regarded as one of the earliest bits of modern Sheltered Housing in Scotland. Similar voluntary developments were the Colinton Cottage Homes and the Whiteinch Home for Old People, with 31 and 39 houses respectively, both places mentioned as visited in the Nuffield Committee Report of 1947.

Ayr County in 1948 had agreed 'to establish small homes or hostels in as many districts as possible,' and by late 1949 had purchased three houses for conversion. Stirling County pursued a policy of conversions and new build, and by 1963 had produced a residential home at Grangemouth for 26 with 20 single rooms and separate toilets for each room. This was regarded as a peak in Scottish Welfare Departments provision, and other approximations followed. The fact that we quote such a case may be taken as an indication of the generally slow and limited progress.

The Rise of Geriatric Medicine

At this stage, however, it may be noted that Foresthall was of even more significance for the elderly on the medical side. As a hospital establishment in the 1950s it provided a test-bed for the treatment of the elderly, which under the pioneering leadership of the consultant, Dr Fergusons Anderson, was to contribute significantly to the development of the evolving discipline of geriatric medicine.

When considering the Curtis Report and the arrival of the Children Act, we emphasised the contribution of the new psychology led by John Bowlby and Anna Freud. The influence on the public care of the elderly from a related field, this time medicine, came a few decades later. Although the medical aspects of old age had been recognised in Europe in the 19th century as a special study, informed opinion usually dates the start of British geriatric medicine to 1935.[17] At that time Dr Marjory Warren on appointment to the West Middlesex Hospital found herself responsible for an adjacent Poor Law Infirmary and started up a geriatric unit there.

After the war developments began in Scotland, and were advanced in 1952 when the Western Regional Hospital Board appointed Dr Ferguson Anderson to a new post as consultant at Foresthall and regional adviser on diseases of old age. The problem was immense, the resources limited, limited virtually to beds in Foresthall, which still had the label and conditions described in Chapter 3. A plan was quickly drawn up dividing Glasgow and environs into five sectors of a quarter million, with a geriatric unit based on a general hospital in each.

To implement the policy, beds, staff, equipment and money were required on an unprecedented scale. With tuberculosis and other infectious diseases dramatically reduced through wartime public health measures, special hospital beds were released, and the Hospital Board scoured the city for building sites, supported by capital allocations from Scottish Office. Nurses and young doctors were attracted to work with old people in this new and developing specialism. Support services such as home help, occupational therapy, meals on wheels and residential places were provided as far as possible by an already hard pressed Glasgow Health and Welfare Department. By 1967 Glasgow had an organised geriatric service. On a lesser scale, similar services were developed in other Scottish cities. Not surprisingly, the World Health Organisation, when it came to sponsoring courses in geriatrics for European doctors, based the first in Glasgow (at Foresthall) in 1964. Consultants also travelled from Scotland to many countries to foster similar planning and teaching. Following these developments, the first Chair of Geriatric Medicine in the world was founded at Glasgow University in 1965. To this was appointed Dr Ferguson Anderson, who by his pioneering advocacy, gained for the subject and the cause of the elderly ready recognition in Scotland, the U.K. and further afield. Shortly thereafter a similar professorship was established in Edinburgh, and by 1976, there were 14 such chairs in the UK.

It needs to be emphasised here that until about 1950 old age and the care of the elderly had been seen largely in negative and hopeless terms, both by the doctors and nurses concerned because of their hospital experience and training. A great achievement of geriatric specialism was to reverse these attitudes, and to insist on adequate treatment and rehabilitation.

From various causes then, not least the close alliance of university teaching with practice in specific city hospitals, we have seen a vigorous innovative growth of special medical care of the elderly in Scotland in the years 1950-70. In places this interacted with and influenced the practice of welfare departments. At this stage on available evidence, it is not easy to estimate the extent of that influence. We may recognise, however, that inevitably the new knowledge and teaching brushed off on the attuned local authority medical officers, who were either running or close to welfare departments. Welfare officers in turn were exposed to these new ideas with their implications for the general care of the elderly.

Hospital or residential accommodation and community care

A major flaw in the 1948 legislation soon appeared. Under the National Health Service Acts hospitals were to provide for the sick; under the National Assistance Act, Homes were for the elderly and frail. But these were not discrete categories of people, and even the needs of individuals varied with time and health. Admissions had presented no great problem of definition in the omnibus Poor Law system, but after 1948, with restricted resources in both sectors, the question of hospital or local authority bed became a major issue, often with fierce debate between the welfare officer and the geriatrician, as they fought to preserve their scarce beds. Sometimes there was horsetrading and bargaining, sometimes there were good co-operative local agreements. The hospital boards made their representations to their ministers, the local authorities did likewise.

The government response was not in favour of amendment to the system. Neither was it for greatly increased hospital accommodation for sick old people, but rather for better use of existing places, coupled with expanded local authority provision and widened use of that. In official words with an almost Shakespearean ring 'The gap is not in the statutes but in the physical provision which they authorise'.[18] In the meantime the problem was to be treated on administrative lines, and in June 1958 the Department of Health for scotland issued its *Memorandum 61/58 'Care of the Elderly*. This defined inter alia the respective roles of hospital and Part III Home, particularly at the borderline. The latter's role was to include care during minor illnesses, care of the infirm who might need help in dressing and toilet, senile who did not require continuous care, and care of the terminally ill who would not benefit from hospital. All these now seem self-evident when residential establishments have moved into the care of the physically and sometimes mentally frail. Even with this regulation, some increase in hospital beds, and a great expansion of local authority accommodation, the problem did not go away. This serious dichotomy of service was left largely unaddressed for 40 years till the Griffiths Report of 1988, the full implications of which are yet to be realised.

The 1958 memorandum also gave advice on care in the community. Its wording and style are illustrative of its period and provenance. After an introductory statement that the family doctors and health visitor were in a favourable position to refer for services, the advice continues: 'A kind but brisk outlook is proper to welfare work for the elderly, and three principles are suggested:
    (1)   Keep them in their own homes
    (2)   Get them out of their own home
    (3)   Give them the feeling of security

Under the first head are included various measures to provide meals for old people who live alone and who cannot or will not cook for themselves. If old people do not receive regular and proper nourishment, they become liable to deteriorate physically and perhaps mentally, and thereby become a direct charge on the hospital or welfare service.'

In the 1990s we tend to date the origins of community care of the elderly to the early 1970s. Certainly in the immediate post-1948 period the main thrust of welfare departments was of necessity towards provision of good residential accommodation. The 1958 memorandum just mentioned, however, had been preceded in October 1949 by a significant initiative from the Department of Health — Circular 65/49, advocating the setting up of local ad hoc voluntary organisations and the general promotion of the welfare of the elderly in their own homes. In this connection it should be reiterated that the Scottish Council of Social Service had as early as 1943 launched the Scottish Old People's Welfare Committees.

The Circular's suggestions were readily taken up by many welfare authorities and other council and voluntary committees which they convened. This led to the expansion of local Old People's Welfare Committees throughout their areas in the early 1950s. A welfare committee chairman at one such promotional meeting listed possible activities as friendly visits, writing letters, and advice on benefit entitlements and adequate shares of available food, in a period of continuing shortages and rationing.

In these Old People's Welfare Committees was harnessed the developed wartime citizen action, with a new orientation towards the welfare of the elderly. While they enjoyed the support of the welfare committee and the encouragement of the Department of Health, their enthusiasm was sometimes frustrated by other local authority departments and on occasion by other ministries. Local education authorities would not grant the use of school kitchens, the Ministry of Food blocked attempts to gain parity of rations between meals for elderly and school meals from the same kitchens. Similar attempts to enable the elderly to purchase sufficient coal, the vital and scarce fuel of the time, were also blocked. Nothing daunted by difficulties the Old People's Welfare Committees, supported by Welfare Departments, continued their crusades for the welfare of the elderly in many areas of Scotland through the 1948-69 period. The Younghusband Report of 1959 estimated their number as 247.

These early tentative moves towards community care were described, perhaps optimistically by Dr Ian MacQueen, Medical Officer and Director of Welfare for the City of Aberdeen as a shift of emphasis, 'from simple support of the frail and diseases to counselling and casework for those not yet incapacitated, from hospitals to health visitors, from "hostels" to housing and home help'.[19] Also from the North East Dr I. M. Richardson, Lecturer in Community Medicine, University of Aberdeen, writing in 1964 noted change as follows: 'I believe the time has come to think seriously of a new welfare department, so staffed and organised that it would provide a counselling service to anyone in need, or likely to be in need, whatever that need might be'.[20] That great expectation, as far as the elderly were concerned, was not fully realised even by the new Social Work Departments in their first 20 years.

The Younghusband Committee

In June 1955 because of general concern about health and welfare services, and in particular the levels and appropriateness of staffing, the Minister of Health and the Secretary of State for Scotland set up a working party on the subject. Its remit was to inquire into 'the proper field of work and recruitment of social workers at all levels in the local authorities Health and Welfare Services under the National Health Service and the National Assistance Acts, and in particular whether there is a place for a general purpose social worker with an in-service training as a basic grade'. This was a small working party of ten people with direct practical experience of health services, welfare services, mental health, education and administration. Scotland was represented by Thomas Tinto, Principal Welfare Officer of Glasgow, and on the large Steering Committee by other three Scots including Councillor John Mains of Glasgow. The Chairman was the experienced and committed social work educator, Eileen Younghusband.

The Working Party produced its report, now generally referred to as the Younghusband Report, in 1959. It was a report of major significance for the Welfare Service, and even more so for the Social Work Services shortly to follow in Scotland and England. Its conclusions and recommendations included a definition of social work and social workers. Of the latter it says 'we use this term to denote those whose primary function is to carry out the foregoing activities by any one of the three social work methods—with individuals (casework), groups (groupwork) or communities (community organisation). Of these, only the first is at present systematically taught, or practised in this country'. The report proceeds to explain that the existing specialisation — welfare officers, mental health officers, almoners, psychiatric social workers — was mainly due to piecemeal historical development, and to suggest that the focus should be on the needs of individual or family rather than the categorisation of the presenting problems. It establishes the place for a 'general purpose social worker'. This function in the health and welfare services however was seen at three levels. The famous Younghusband three tiers were to include, firstly a graduate and professionally trained worker to provide a casework and consultant service. Secondly, social workers with two years general training to carry the normal run of work, and thirdly a new grade 'welfare assistant' with a short, systematic in-service training. To implement these, national qualifications in social work were recommended, and a National Council for Social Work

Training, which was established in 1962. Additionally, recommendations were made on caseloads, case records, recruitment and salaries.

The effects of Younghusband on social work and training are discussed further in Chapter 8. Here it may be observed that the report had a seminal influence on the development of generic social work and training for that purpose. The immediate effect on welfare departments in Scotland came from the setting up of two year 'Younghusband' courses, the first in 1961 at the Scottish College of Commerce in Glasgow. However, by the time these courses were established and producing more than token numbers, it was late in the Health and Welfare era, and the primary impact of Younghusband was on the thinking which lead up to the Social Work Act.

Assessment

A definitive assessment of the achievement of Welfare Departments between 1948 and 1969 would need a more intensive study than our outline history. We can however record some major trends and developments which took place under the administrative and other limitations described above, and in spite of at least a decade of economic restrictions following six years of a resource-draining war. The physically handicapped for the first time had statutorily recognised needs for services and the modest progress made to meet these, in a situation where demands exceeded resources, prepared the ground for further growth under the Social Work and the Chronically Sick Acts of 1968 and 1970 respectively. Residential accommodation for the elderly moved qualitatively into a new era, however continuingly imperfect in some of its provision and regimes. Quantitatively the accommodation moved from the 6,843 local authority and 4,660 voluntary and private places recorded by Townsend at the beginning of 1960 to 8,450 and 5,932 respectively in 1969, and this in spite of continuing closure in old PAIs.[21]

Because of responsibility for housing them in emergency, welfare departments became involved with homeless families, a development which featured in the move to joint social work departments. As noted above there was some promotion of community action in support of the elderly, and organisations such as Old People's Welfare Committees, Women's Voluntary Services, etc., were mobilised as partners. Councillors also became better informed on the conditions and needs of the elderly and handicapped, and often developed considerable personal as well as political interest in appropriate provision and treatment. Welfare, like Health and Education, was a cause with which Councillors could easily identify.

From inadequate bases staffing slowly expanded, and new disciplines such as Occupational Therapy were enlisted to the departments.

In the 1960s there was a gradual build-up of social work training for staff. Welfare departments benefit from this was limited. Firstly, their use of training was mainly by secondment rather than new recruits. Secondly, because of their minimal numbers of trained workers, it was difficult to provide supervisors for the necessary fieldwork training, hence a vicious circle. Moreover the combined health and welfare departments led by medical officers and influenced by health visitors who saw themselves as already performing the social work function, were not the most welcoming milieu for trained social workers. Nor were the welfare departments run by untrained welfare officers and senior staff, with their fixed and regulated systems, much more attractive to the newly trained. At September 1968 there was a total of 276 welfare staff, only 79 of whom had professional or basic qualifications.[22] In spite of all the constraints we have indicated, valuable services developed in certain areas — not least in Glasgow with all its difficulties of size and inheritance. The achievements of the welfare departments, while not so seminal as those of children's departments, nor so rapidly evolving as those of probation, should be seen against the 19th century conditions of pre-1948, and should be accordingly assessed.

Health and Mental Health Services

Parallel but not identical to the National Health Service (England and Wales) Act 1946, came the National Health Service (Scotland) Act 1947, which with certain alterations still obtains. Part II gave the Secretary of State powers to take over existing voluntary and local authority hospitals and cause them to be run by hospital boards. Part IV introduced free medical, dental, ophthalmic and pharmaceutical services for all, a major British ideal of the era, the regrettable abdication from which we have recently witnessed in all aspects of these services except the medical.

Part III required the setting up of new style local health authorities by counties, cities and large burghs to provide certain community services. The health committee so established appointed a medical officer, assistant medical officers and nursing staff. As discussed earlier, in 40% of Scottish authorities health and welfare committees combined to provide health and welfare departments. Apart from medical and dental care of mothers and pre-school children, health visiting for these groups and for the ill, the Act required the following social services — arrangements for the prevention and after-care in case of illness and mental deficiency; domestic help to a household with any person ill, lying in, expectant, mentally defective, and aged, or a child under school age; provision of suitable training and occupation for ineducable and untrainable children and for mental defectives over 16.

These were the powers and duties which formed the basis for the supportive services transferred to social work departments in 1969 such as day nurseries, home help, junior occupation centres and senior occupational centres.[23] They also led to work with 'problem families' by nurses who had become involved with children or young mothers.

During the war when large numbers of women entered employment, the earlier Health Departments had set up day nurseries for pre-school children. The Nursery and Child Minders Regulation Act of 1948 gave the health authority further powers to inspect and register childminders and those nurseries which they did not provide. The period 1948-69 saw the continued growth and development of nurseries under health departments. Social workers and educationalists might now regard this growth as dominated by diet and hygiene regimes, and insufficiently orientated towards child development. Yet the contribution of health department nurseries was a highly important one. Moreover in the 1940s some of them had provided an invaluable service to working mothers and their children on an almost Scandinavian scale, from early morning till late evening.

As regards the legislation on 'domestic help', initial emphasis by health departments was toward child-birth and young children. The service rapidly developed however, and by 1962 MacQueen reported that it rivalled the ambulance section as the biggest single spender in health and welfare services.[24] By 1969 on transfer to social work, home helps were an established major local authority service, with a useful organisation depending on the unrivalled local knowledge of the district nurse and health visitor.

At the time not all social work directorates appreciated the full worth or potential of the service they were inheriting. Nor in the early 1970s were home help sections with their wide client contact in the community always adequately recognised by social workers, pre-occupied as they were with their own massive problems of 'fieldwork'. This service has since seen a second great period of expansion and refinement, and in the 1990s is a major heading in social work budgets.

The health and welfare, and health departments of 1948-1969 laid the foundations on which social work departments were able to build in respect of home helps, day nurseries and some preventive work with young children. They also performed this function in respect of mentally handicapped persons through their after-care duties and the provision of junior and senior occupation centres.

Mental Health

As noted earlier, health departments had powers to provide care and after-care for the mentally ill and the mentally defective. It should be remembered that the principal legislation in this field up until 1960 was still the Lunacy (Scotland) Acts 1857 to 1913, and the Mental Deficiency (Scotland) Acts 1913 and 1940, only marginally amended by the National Health Service (Scotland) Act 1947. In the early stages much of what work was done was bravely carried by duly authorised officers, who were often the welfare officers with previous experience of this service from the public assistance days. As health departments found their feet, more work was taken on by nursing staff and the scope widened. The service provided was largely for the mentally defective. Social work with the mentally ill was restricted mainly to those receiving hospital treatment, and even after discharge was still carried out by hospital staff or voluntary associations.

The Mental Health (Scotland) Act 1960 gave impetus to this service. This Act like its English counterpart of 1959, signalled the end of the over-dependence on the 19th century hospital system. It aimed at reducing both numbers admitted and periods of detention, and like the Health Service Act emphasised the supportive community services to be supplied by the local authorities. As regards the latter, it conferred few new powers, but clarified existing, by removing restrictions, thus enabling local authorities to provide services under health, welfare, education or children's legislation as was most suitable.[25]

However, two new requirements are worth noting. Power was given to provide and run hostels for those with mental illness or mental handicap. Some health authorities made plans under this heading, including provision for 'elderly mentally confused', but little was actually achieved before 1969 — indeed scant provision existed for the latter group in 1989, and that little was due to the voluntary sector. As late as December 1971 in the whole of Scotland, for all mentally disordered persons there were only 12 hostels with 139 beds, which at that time catered for 65 mentally defective and 42 mentally ill persons.[26] The other power of note was to appoint mental health officers for the purpose of ascertainment and the supervision of mentally defective adults including those under Guardianship. A number of those appointed had a social work qualification, or became qualified in the 1960s, and brought over a distinctive contribution to social work departments.

The duty under the National Health Service Act to provide Junior Training Centres and Senior Occupation Centres was taken up conscientiously by most health departments, and considerable progress was made in providing such establishments in sizeable urban centres. This was an area in which many medical officers showed considerable interest and concern. These centres, though numerically still inadequate, and sometimes limited by premises, methods and staffing, were nevertheless proven assets to the new social work departments.

Other aspects of community care, however, for the mentally ill and handicapped appeared more on paper than reality, an aspect that continued for at least 30 years after the 1960 Act. The essential feature of the field-work Mental Health service, in its short life between 1962 when it really became operational, and 1969, was that, in spite of being under-resourced and hospital oriented, it was a useful specialist service. This expertise, like that of probation work, was soon diluted in the new social work departments, and only began to be restored through the specialist training of the late 1980s.

Before concluding on welfare, health and mental health services it is appropriate to consider some important features contemporary to that scene, all the more as approaches to the advent of social work have so far tended to concentrate on its child care origins. Two key figures in the local authority services of the time were the medical officer and health visitor. They certainly played a cardinal role in these services but their universal competence was perhaps somewhat over-rated. Dazzling images of these professionals were sometimes projected from the responsible Scottish Office division — The Department of Health — with an understandable, partial enthusiasm. The medical officer was described as 'essentially a sociologist with clinical insight', and the health visitor as 'a health teacher and medico-social worker dedicated to prevention in social work for the Elderly'.[27] This idealised central role of the latter was sustained by the Department of Health throughout the 1950s, and was conducive to the strong reservations among health professionals over the need for such innovations as social work departments.

Add to this the fact that medical officers were running or directing half the welfare services in Scotland and looking over the shoulder of the welfare officer in the remainder. It will be apparent that it could not be easy for ordinary welfare officers or emerging new social workers to establish a lead in the face of such highly endowed and qualified professionals. The only other small corps of qualified and articulate professions, medical social workers and psychiatric social workers, were mainly in hospitals outside the local authority ambit. Indeed, it must be recognised that the medical officers and staff were the main body of qualified personnel of the period here. Moreover some of the medical officers had that stature of recognised authorities and pioneers which had characterised the great public health advances of the first half of the century.

In 1960 an administrator seeking the all round family field worker might well have looked as much to the trained and qualified nursing service as to the less developed ranks of local authority functional services. For the leadership level, medical officers were well placed, enjoying great influence in St Andrew's House as well as authority in their own kingdoms. Certainly, some experienced and able medical officers, as the 1960s progressed, saw themselves as the natural potential directors of any new family service.

They had demonstrated their capacity to improve the environmental health of their communities, and to bolster family health and well being at the most vulnerable points. They were among the first to identify 'problem families'.

The incarnation of social work in its present form was always a near run thing, and the major question may not be so much why the new departments were not fostered on education, as recommended by the Kilbrandon Report, but why they did not end up in a health and social work stable.

NOTES

1. Counties and cities provided all their own public services. Large burghs provided all services except education, and, in some cases, police.
2. Younghusband Report, p. 345, table 36.
3. Ayr County Council Welfare Committee Minutes, January 1948.
4. Paisley and Glasgow.
5. The Association was the direct successor of the Society of Inspectors of the Poor for Scotland, formed in Glasgow in 1858 and praised by the Royal Commission of 1909 for their work and general influence on poor relief. Thus the Welfare Officers celebrated their centenary in 1958 by a conference addressed by the Secretary of State.
6. The Younghusband Report, paras. 336 and 273. The number of persons registered as blind was around 10,000 throughout the period — see annual SHHD reports on health and welfare.
7. Quoted from Ayr County Welfare Committee Minutes, October 1951.
8. National Assistance Act 1948 (Amendment) Act 1962.
9. SRO HH.61/83669, 26.6.61 notes on visit to Dundee by Miss M. M. McInnes.
10. In 1969 there were only three local authority sheltered workshops — at Hamilton, Motherwell and Falkirk (Stirling County/Falkirk Burgh).
11. J. T. Gregory, Services for the Physically Handicapped, p. 281 from Trends in Social Welfare, ed. J. Farndale, Pergamon 1965.
12. 'In the development of their welfare services for the disabled since 1948 Scottish Local Authorities as a whole have made only relatively slow progress' Report of Department of Health for Scotland 1958, HMSO, Cmnd. 697, para. 319.
13. Younghusband Report, para. 501.
14. Peter Townsend, The Last Refuge, Routledge and Kegan Paul 1962, p. 20.
15. Vera Carstairs and Marion Morrison, The Elderly in Residential Care, Scottish Health Services Studies No. 19, SHHD 1971.
16. On closure in 1988 the records were lodged with the Strathclyde Archivist. Since then Strathclyde Social Work and Education Departments have jointly produced a history for use in secondary schools, The Relief of Poverty 1989. This includes a chapter on Barnhill Poorhouse. Some of the Foresthall equipment, pictures and memorabilia are to be seen at the Heatherbank Museum of Social Work, Milngavie.
17. Isaacs, Livingstone and Neville, Survival of the Unfittest, Routledge and Kegan Paul, 1972.

William Ferguson Anderson, 'Geriatrics' from aspects of the Scottish Health Services, 1900-1984, ed. G. McLachlan, EUP.

18. Department of Health for Scotland Report 1950, HMSO Cmnd. 8184, p. 50.
19. Dr Ian MacQueen, A general view of services for the elderly, p. 181, from Trends in Social Welfare, ed. J. Farndale, Pergamon 1965.
20. Dr I. M. Richardson, Age and Need, A Study of Older People in North East Scotland, E. S. Livingston 1964, p. 113.
21. Social Work in Scotland 1969, HMSO Cmnd. 4475, para. 3.3.
22. Social Work in Scotland, A Report on the Social Work (Scotland) Act, Edinburgh University 1969, Appendix D.
23. The junior occupation centres were soon to pass from Social Work to Education following the Melville Report, HMSO 1973. See — The Education (Mentally Handicapped Children) Scotland Act, 1974.
24. Dr Ian MacQueen, A general review of services for the elderly, Trends in Social Welfare, ed. J. Farndale, Pergamon 1965.
25. Department of Health for Scotland, Mental Health (Scotland) Act 1960. Local Authority Services, notes on Part II of the Act, HMSO 1960.
26. SWSG, Scottish Social Work Statistics, 1971, Table 2.32.
27. Quotes from Department of Health Circular ECS 75A/1950 (for health visitor) and Sir G. K. Henderson, Health Bulletin, DHS(X) 3/43 (for medical officers).

CHAPTER 5

Separate Services 1948-69

Probation

'Probation used wisely is merciful and efficient; the same system used unskilfully brings the administration of the criminal law into public derision' Leo Page, The Young Lag 1950.

Probation, unlike Welfare and Child Care had no antecedents in the Poor Law, and was thus unaffected by the main legislation of 1948. The immediate post-war probation service was essentially that established in Britain by the Probation of First Offenders Act, 1887, and expanded by the Probation of Offenders Act 1907. To bring these dated provisions into the 20th century, the Scottish Office, following a Home Office lead, set up a departmental committee on probation, which reported in 1936. Its recommendations, delayed by the war inter alia, were finally implemented in the Criminal Justice (Scotland) Act, 1949. This largely followed the similar Act of 1948 for England and Wales, but retained distinctive features of the Scottish system, notably the ad hoc probation committees appointed by local authorities. By 1949 both legislation and practice in Scotland were, understandably, somewhat out of date.

Probation, like some later progressive treatment measures, seems to have had origins in Massachusetts. Notably, a Boston cobbler John Augustus in 1841 offered to stand bail and supervise a man charged with drunkenness. By 1859 he is said to have supervised 2,000 such persons, and by 1869 Massachusetts, New England, had set up a state agency for this purpose. However, it should be noted that back in Old England as early as 1820, the Warwick magistrates sometimes sentenced a man to a day's imprisonment followed by supervision from his parent or master. This practice was also followed from about 1841 by Matthew Davenport, Recorder of Birmingham, who added periodic checks by the police into the offender's conduct. By 1876 the Church of England Temperance Society set up its first Police Court Missions to reclaim drunkards, with the magistrates co-operating by release on bail. Their work was gradually extended to other offenders. Probation's origins therefore largely lay in voluntary religious concern for drunken offenders in the 19th century.

The first Scottish initiative on probation seems to have been taken by Baillie Murray in Glasgow in 1905. Aware of the practice in the USA and concerned about excessive imprisonment for fines failure in 1904, he persuaded the Chief Constable to assign plain clothes officers to supervise cases selected by the courts. It is noteworthy that such a reforming step should have come from a Glasgow Baillie's action to keep adults out of prison, just as a similar concern by Baillie Mack to avoid imprisonment for young children in Edinburgh, led to recommendations for industrial schools in the 1840s.[1] Esmee Roberts in her thesis, Social Work Education for the Probation Service in Scotland, develops the interesting proposition that the impetus for probation in Scotland came not so much from religious concern to reclaim drunkards, as from a need to find more efficient law enforcement systems in the Courts.[2] A UK departmental committee of 1992 mainly concerned with probation staffing was followed by the first specifically Scottish legislation, the Probation of Offenders (Scotland) Act 1931. This resulted in full-time probation officers being appointed in Glasgow, who took over the work pioneered by the police in 1905.

The Children and Young Persons Act 1933 (England and Wales), and the Children and Young Persons (Scotland) Act of 1937 made further demands on probation by providing for supervision in respect of care or protection cases as well as offenders. This latter Act contributed to the fact that the Scottish probation service up to the time at least of the Morison Report in 1962 was disproportionately concerned with juveniles.

The Criminal Justice (Scotland) Act 1949

By 1948/49 not only probation, but the whole criminal justice system in Britain was seen to require reform. There had been a substantial wartime and post-war increase in criminal activity, not least among the young. In Scotland the incidence of crimes made known to the police had remained static around 10 per 1,000 of the population from the beginning of the century to the mid 1930s. In the 1940s it nearly doubled and after falling back a little in the early 1950s, took off and reached nearly 30 per 1,000 in 1964.[3] The 1940s rise may be attributed partly to wartime conditions. It also followed changes in 1933 to the keeping of criminal statistics.

Correspondingly, public and parliamentary pre-occupation with crime ran high. The spirit of the age was one of reform, and this was ready to embrace criminal justice. In the face of new crime waves, the enlightenment and liberal concern of the 1940s was in stark contrast to the reactionary, punitive attitudes of the 1980s. Prisons and punishment were not seen as the simple solution to all crime. The Criminal Justice Act of 1948 (England and Wales), and the Criminal Justice (Scotland) Act 1949 were the response to those facts and this ethos. At this juncture in this context, it may be of interest to mention some general provisions of the historic 1949 Act which affected young persons and others. The abolition of the obsolete sanctions, penal servitude and hard labour, dates from 1949. The restriction of the death sentence on persons under 18, established by the Children and Young Persons acts of 1933 and 1937 (Scotland), was refined to apply to those under 18 at the time of the offence. Courts were debarred from imposing imprisonment on those under 17, and were required to obtain reports from a probation officer before so sentencing those under 21 as a last resort.

The ending of judicial corporal punishment, the legendary 'birching', was not due to this Act, but was contained in section two of the Criminal Justice Act, 1948, which provided that 'No person shall be sentenced by a court to whipping', and was applicable to Scotland as well as England and Wales.

To keep young persons out of prison the Secretary of State was empowered to establish remand centres and detention centres for those between 14 and 21. The section in both Acts on remand centres remained a dead letter for many years. In England provision was late and inadequate. In Scotland two genuine considerations affected action — or inaction. It was considered inappropriate to admit younger boys to penal establishments, and the small numbers involved made it difficult to justify provision in any one place. In the event a remand institution for those aged 16 to 21 was finally set up at Longriggend in the 1960s. The use of Longriggend for 'unruly' children has caused concern over the years and in general the adequacy of policies for remand of young persons in Scotland from 1949 to 1971 is open to debate, particularly in the light of an increase between 1965 and 1970 of 171 to 592 young persons certified as 'unruly'.[4]

As regards detention centres, while England set up junior centres for those under 17, Scotland provided this facility only for the 17 to 21 group, again on the principle of the inappropriateness of including young persons in the penal system. The only such sanction in Scotland for the younger group was detention for a limited period in a Remand Home under the Children and Young Persons Act, which was frequently if not very effectively used. Detention centres, with their service barrack regimes of parades, marching, and physical activity were based on the sanguine belief that a 'short, sharp shock' would deter, if not reform, potential young criminals. This belief strangely survives in certain quarters, in spite of research indications to the contrary, and the views of experienced observers, who see such veneer training as mainly a method of turning out more athletic and disciplined potential young criminals. Detention centres as such, disappeared with the amalgamation of the various penal treatments for young offenders under the Criminal Justice (Scotland) Act 1980. Some of their peculiar regimes, however, have survived in the successor custodial establishments concerned.

One non-custodial feature of the Criminal Justice Act 1948, which was not replicated in the Scottish Act was the provision of Attendance Centres. These were centres to which juveniles of 12-17 were required by the Juvenile Court to report on Saturday forenoon or afternoon, and take part in parades, physical training, crafts or hobbies for a few hours. They were usually conducted on police premises by police officers selected for their interest in youth work and delinquency. By 1960 there were some 50 centres in the principal English cities, and a success rate of over 70% was claimed for them. The system was researched by F. H. McLintock, who reported in 1961, 'attendance centres are quite effective when applied to a young offender with little or no experience of crime, coming from a mainly normal home or background'.[5] The Kilbrandon Committee, after receiving favourable evidence on the subject and making visits to some English examples recommended the setting up of a few centres for boys under 16 in the largest cities. This recommendation was not finally implemented, and Scotland has never experimented with attendance centres.

And so some of the novel measures of the Criminal Justice Acts — remand centres, junior detention centres and probation hostels, which we shall consider later — left Scotland largely untouched for at least two reasons. It may be that St Andrew's House and the academic and judiciary establishments wisely decided that such innovations did not meet the known needs of Scotland. If so, why, apart from the tandem principle, were these provisions allowed to be included in the 1949 Act?[6] On the other hand the grand illusion of our superior systems of education, law, and shipbuilding was still intact. In the late 1940s as opposed to the late 1980s, the Scottish Office as well as the Scottish people seemed less compliant to a London lead, whether it was in education or criminology. Perhaps the spirit of the time reinforced general Caledonian caution and complacency. We had survived a second major war with the feeling that, as in the first, Scotland had made a disproportionate sacrifice. 1949 may have been Holy Year in Europe, and ground-nut fiasco year in Africa, but in Scotland it was also the first fervent year of the new National Covenant. This was no time for wearing second-hand suits from the South — a comparable phenomenon to the 1990s witnessing renewed resistance to London diktat.

The Organisation and State of the Probation Service in the 1950s

The 1949 Act, which became operational in June 1950, was important for the development of the probation service in several respects. Firstly, ad hoc local authority committees were required, based on the usual administrative units of counties and large burghs, with emphasis on the possibility of combinations. This pattern, in contra-distinction to the court-based committees of England and Wales, was to prove crucial when it came to the question of including probation within the new social work departments.

Further, the probation committees of 1949 were given the power, but not the duty, to set up case committees. Their functions were to include general supervision over the work and records of probation officers, to the extent of seeing individual case reports, and support or discipline for the officer as required. Forty years on, in a more professional era, these may seem strange and dated provisions. At that time of transition to a trained service they may have been necessary, and where used were generally welcomed by probation officers. Official thinking also saw this as a means of promoting greater commitment in committee members. Their use however was more honoured in the breach than the observance.

The Act extended the probation officer's role beyond the simple duty to supervise, to one of 'assisting, advising and befriending'. The requirement from the probationer, laid down in the probation order, was to be of good behaviour, to conform to the directions of the probation officer, and to meet any other conditions such as residence or medical treatment. To these propositions he was required to express his assent. Arising from the Act, the Probation (Scotland) Rules of 1951 required that probation officers should have 'undertaken theoretical and practical training sufficient to qualify them for the efficient discharge of their duties'. Finally, there was provision for probation hostels for probationers in employment, or probation homes for others. We shall look later at the restricted use of these in Scotland and the reasons therefor.

In 1949, and still through the 1950s, not only was the probation service out-dated, it was thin on the ground, and used in a limited and geographically inconsistent way. many areas had no full-time staff, and relied on voluntary officers. The Far North was slowest to change, and as late as 1962 there were no full-time officers north of Aberdeen; in 1969 there were 9.[7] Throughout the 1950s the main use of probation was for the supervision of juvenile offenders, probation orders being made in about 30% to 35% of charges proved, while the use of adults continued low at 7.0% to 8.0%.[8] Again there were great variations of practice by areas. In the period 1946-50 Juvenile Courts in Perth used probation in 50% of cases and fining in 2%, while Lanarkshire put 12% of their juveniles on probation and fined 48%.[9] This restricted and varied use was made against a claimed success rate for juveniles and adults of at least 82% for the period 1946 to 1959.[10]

The question must be asked what accounted for the reluctance to develop the service in the early 1950s in contrast to the successes of the

1960s. How far was it official complacency with a cheap, old-time, semi-voluntary service, how far was it local authority parsimony, and how far was it due to limited professional guidance from senior personnel of the police court mission style, either at central or local level? The writer has heard all these adduced, determined by the stand-point of the observer. Discussions with experienced serving officers of the period have also pointed to the inhibiting effect of some untrained senior officers who feared change. This resulted in a system often characterised by authoritarianism and conformity, described as operating like a church boys' organisation.

At this point we need to look further at the ad hoc committees. The local authorities were required by the 1949 Act to appoint committees to include non local authority members, particularly people with experience of probation and delinquency. There was special emphasis on including burgh magistrates and JPs. The sheriffs and sheriff-substitutes of the area were ex officio members. From these provisions, and the requirements for case committees, one could have expected strong bodies with a high degree of involvement and commitment to service development. Further, whereas the welfare and children's services were controlled by over 50 authorities, some much too small, the device of combination ensured that responsibility for probation by 1960 was concentrated in 34 committees, and sharing of staff further reduced this effectively to 29 probation departments. Only one large burgh, Kirkcaldy, was responsible for a separate service.

Again, the Clerk to the Probation Committee was often the County Clerk, whose professional interest as a lawyer and contacts with courts were a potential bonus. He was also usually in direct contact with the central department. Reciprocally, the responsible Assistant Secretary in St Andrew's House knew the Clerks and Principal Probation Officers. Just as on the welfare side the prestige and influence of the great medical officers was important, so on this front there was a strong supporting battalion in the persons of the sheriffs, amongst the principal protagonists for probation in Scotland.

The sheriffs, however, even when they attended, were not effective committee men, when armed merely with an equal vote after debate. They only became fully alive to the major deficiency of the Scottish system after the Morison Report in 1962 and then their pressures were more directed to the remoter authority of St Andrew's House than the local stage where the action and decisions took place.

Yet in the early years these favourable factors do not seem to have produced proportionate results. The Morison Committee on the Probation Service reporting in 1960 was not at all impressed by the Scottish committee system. This was not surprising in the light of their fundamental, preconception 'we suggested that — the strength of the probation service in England and Wales lay in its administration as a court service by representatives of the courts. This source of strength is lacking in Scotland'. They then state that enquiries showed that probation in Scotland was regarded as one of the less important committees of the local authority, that the power to appoint non local authority members was little used, and that both the Scottish justices of the peace and the burgh magistrates had inadequate judicial experience for the purpose. As a result of these factors it was claimed that local authority members dominated, and 'when the balance has had to be struck between the need to improve the service and the increased burden on the rates — the latter consideration appears to have received more than its due weight'. This was probably true for some areas.[11]

Whatever the reasons for these conclusions, whatever their validity, the Scottish probation service, surprisingly enough, relative to its baseline, made a great leap forward between 1949 and 1969. The progress, slow and limited in the 1950s, became rapid and substantial in the 1960s. Even in the former period, however, the growth of staff numbers was remarkable. In 1951 there were 78 full-time officers, 170 in 1960 and in 1968 there were 336.[12] The main influences towards the rapid development of the 1960s seem to have been threefold — the Morison Report, a fresh and active lead from the Scottish Office, and pressures from the Sheriffs and the National Association of Probation Officers. We shall now consider these influences, which together produced the expansion of staffing and the inauguration of training.

Morison Report

A Departmental Committee was set up in 1959 by the Home Secretary and Secretary of State for Scotland. Its remit was to 'Inquire into and make recommendations on all aspects of the probation service in England and Wales and in Scotland'. It was also charged to examine the approved probation hostel system in these countries. Appointed chairman was Ronald Morison, a London expatriate Scot, who after a brilliant career as a Scottish QC and Sheriff, was repeating his success as an English barrister and chairman of industry in the south. The writer has heard from Scottish members of the committee and others closely involved that his conduct of the enquiry was much admited.[13] He was knighted in 1960.

The membership of 14 included three prominent Scots with relevant experience, Sheriff Aikman-Smith, T. A. Fraser Noble, later Sir Fraser Noble, Principal of Aberdeen University, and Councillor John Mains of Glasgow, who had served on both the Clyde and Younghusband Committees. A fourth Scot, the psychiatrist Dr J. D. Sutherland, was a member as Director of the Tavistock Institute, which at that time was involved in certain aspects of probation training. Miss Eileen Younghusband was also a member. Further, there were two experienced and able civil servants as assessors, from the Home Office the assistant secretary in charge of 'probation branch', and from Scottish Home Department the assistant secretary with responsibilities including criminal matters and probation. Altogether this was a strongly led and powerful committee which reported late in 1961, and made a second report in 1962.[14] The main report is generally referred to as the Morison Report.

The committee's findings concerning Scotland were that there had been a narrower conception of the functions than in England and Wales; probation was comparatively underused; the formal qualifications of Scottish officers were in general substantially lower; and that it was undesirable for Probation to share an inspectorate with the child care services. The main conclusions subsuming and explaining these findings were, not surprisingly, that 'The method of administration of the probation service in England and Wales is efficient, and has been of prime importance in the growth of the probation system'. 'The probation service in Scotland has not developed as it should have done, because it has been regarded as a relatively minor local authority service. Its administration by committees dominantly composed of local authority members is inappropriate but, in the circumstances of Scotland, direct local authority participation in the administration is required'.[15]

To rectify these deficits as perceived in the Scottish system, Morison made several recommendations. These were based on the Morisonian acts of faith — a court social service, the desirability of specialism, and the need for strong central government linkage and direction, as opposed to local authority administration. These were to emerge again a decade later at the time of social work re-organisation, and proved largely instrumental in keeping the probation service in England and Wales a servant of the Courts and a colony of the Home Office.

For Scotland, Morison considered three possible systems of organisation — administration by the Scottish Office, local probation committees without local authority representatives, and local committees with reduced local authority representation. Whatever their preference, they finally only backed the last. It was recommended that probation areas should be based on sheriffdoms, with the local authority appointing from their own numbers half the committee, the sheriffs and all sheriff-substitutes to be members ex officio, and the remainder to be appointed by the Secretary of State. The Secretary of State should prepare a scheme of administration for each probation area 'after consultation with the appropriate courts and local authorities'. The order of power and precedence here is significant.

To maintain specialism, it was recommended that 'A separate probation inspectorate is ultimately desirable, but impracticable in the foreseeable future. The Child Care and Probation Inspectorate should have an adequate proportion of members with experience of the probation service.' There was a recommendation that pre-entry training should be introduced as soon as possible, with a two years course being ultimately desirable. To broaden the scope it was advocated that it should include the after-care functions, which were then carried out for prisons and borstals by staff of the After-Care Council, and for approved schools by specialist welfare officers. This recommendation was made subject to the conclusions of the Scottish Advisory Council on the treatment of Offenders, then in session. There was also a mild recommendation to include matrimonial conciliation in a probation officers duties, which had previously been rejected by the Secretary of State when it came from the Royal Commission on Marriage and Divorce in 1956.

The main conclusions and recommendations of the Morison Report did not receive universal support. In England and Wales, while the County Councils Association was in favour — the voice of 'the shires' — the Association of Municipal Corporations suggested that probation should be a local authority committee because of the 'need for the fullest possible integration of the probation service and the local authority social services'. In this they do not seem to have had great clout either with the Committee or the Home Office, who were to receive the report. The Association of the County Councils in Scotland are not on record as taking a strong line.

However, Scotland found a voice in the person of Councillor John Mains, who in spite of earlier limited participation, produced a 'Dissenting Note', a title which does less than justice to a historic pronouncement. He vigorously refuted the central thesis that the weaknesses lay in the local authority composition of probation committees, and attacked the lack of guidance from the Scottish Office to officials and members. He indicated the illogicality of seeing a fundamental failure in the Scottish system when the success rate in all three countries was the same. He emphasised that the strength of any social service depends on its effectiveness as a community service, and pointed to the co-ordinating committees set up in 1950 to bring statutory and voluntary services closer together. Finally, he mounted an incisive attack on the retrograde idea of specialism, 'when the whole trend of social work is to generic training at all levels'.

It is strange that this significant pronouncement came from an elected member and not an academic or professional, and that it was made in 1961, well before the Kilbrandon Report of 1964 or the White Paper of 1966. We can perhaps detect the result of his experiences as a member of the steering committee of the generically oriented Younghusband Report, but his main inspiration probably came from close association with the Glasgow Probation Service.[16] Whatever the origins, this 'Dissenting Note' was of some significance not only for Probation, but for the impending re-organisation of Social Work in Scotland.

The Morison Report was duly signed in December 1961 and presented to Parliament in March 1962 as Cmnd. 1650. In England and Wales its effect was to confirm the status quo of a specialist service to the courts, administered largely by the justices of the peace, and effectively controlled by Probation Division of the Home Office. Some recommendations were common to Scotland such as 'The probation officer's report should be known as a social enquiry report' (Rec. 3), and 'The probation service is now a profession requiring professional training and skill' (Rec. 14).

In Scotland Morison's recommendations were affected by the fact that changes were already in the air. The Kilbrandon Committee on Children and Young Persons had been set up in 1961, and the awaited report of the Scottish Council on the Treatment of Offenders was not published till 1963. In considering the recommendation for after-care functions the latter, after some prevarication, concluded 'We should ourselves sum up the arguments in favour of a probation and after-care service by saying that it would be one step towards an integrated family case-work service'.[17]

And so in 1965 after-care for prisons and borstals became a probation officer's function. After much debate in the Scottish Office the after-care work for approved school boys and girls remained until 1969 with the specially recruited approved school welfare officers whose numbers were increased and work re-organised. As regards the major recommendations on the composition of probation committees, nothing was done, partly because the sentiments of the 'Dissenting Note' were gaining force, and largely because of waiting for Kilbrandon and its sequels. Similar considerations affected the recommendations on the inspectorate, although it was strengthened by recruits with probation experience.

This rejection of an overdue Departmental Committee's major recommendations, and refusal to ride in tandem with England was on this occasion not only an assertion of the independence of separate Scottish systems, but a major and significant step towards the re-organisation of social work that was to follow in six years. Yet Morison was not without some effect on the Scottish probation service. The criticisms of neglect and underdevelopment stimulated interest and action in the Scottish Office and the local authorities, and encouraged the sheriffs to be more outspoken. The emphasis on training was influential.

Probation Hostels

The Departmental Committee on the Probation Service was also commissioned to enquire into and make recommendations on the approved probation hostel service system in England and Wales and in Scotland. Their report was signed and presented to parliament in 1962 as Cmnd. 1800.

Probation hostels were hostels approved for the use of boys and girls between school-leaving age and 21, who were required to reside there as a condition of their probation. The young people went out to work, and from their earnings paid a nominal sum for their maintenance. The remaining costs of the hostel were then divided between the Treasury and the probation committee of the sending court. Residents in a probation home did not go out to work, but received training and performed duties within the Home. Hostel treatment was generally been regarded as having considerable advantages for the incipient young offender from a poor home background, or requiring temporary removal from a delinquent culture. It was of short duration, a year or less, relatively cheap, took place in small units and was treatment in the community. At the time of the Morison Report there were in England and Wales 20 hostels for youths providing some 400 places, and 12 hostels for girls with 249 places. It was generally thought by courts, the probation service and the Home Office that these provided suitable disposal for young persons, who might otherwise have been inappropriately placed in approved schools, borstals or prisons. Their value was assessed by a Home Office Research Study of 1966, written up as 'Hostels for Probationers' HMSO 1971, no more remarkable for its clarity of findings than its speed of production.

The Morison Committee found that the probation hostels were a valuable provision, that the voluntary organisations providing them were doing a good job, but this ought to be supplemented by hostels provided by probation committees. In England and Wales a need for some more hostels of between 15 and 20 places for both boys and girls was identified in the large conurbations and some smaller towns. The Committee also disapproved of the type of provision made in Scotland, and recommended that only such special hostels as described above should be approved for the future.

The history of probation hostels and homes in Scotland is quite different from that in England and Wales. In fact special probation hostels have never been adequately provided or tried, although identical legislation existed for that purpose. Some half dozen children's homes or hostels registered under the Children Act, notably one provided by the Salvation Army at Kilbirnie, were used for probationers with a condition of residence. Over all there were in 1962 only 14 in hostels, mainly male, 28 in probation homes, mainly female, and 20 in lodgings. The use of Homes increased by 50% in the next few years, the use of hostels scarcely at all. Most of the places in these hostels or Homes were occupied by children in care of the local authorities, and this was not an ideal mix.

Development between 1946 and 1966 was strongly inhibited by the doctrine of the Scottish Advisory Council on the Treatment and Reha-bilitation of Offenders in a report of 1946, 'Probation with a Condition of Residence'. It stated 'hostels to which probationers are sent should cater for other classes so that the probationer may not find himself a member of a group of individuals, all of whom have been before the court'. They recommended more use of such hostels for probationers, and further advocated lodgings or foster homes as the best though not the most practical solutions. In this the same voice or voices which were pressing the national panacea of boarding out before the contemporary Clyde Committee may be discerned.[18] This worthy but not entirely logical philosophy was in direct conflict with practical experience in England and elsewhere.

Against this background, consideration of the Morison Report on hostels in Scotland was protracted from 1962 till nearly 1969, by which time in the midst of a main upheaval it was too late to launch new initiatives.[19]

Re-organisation of social work was just round the corner. Probation officers and probation committees had other crucial concerns about their future. Local authorities faced with major new commitments and minimal resources to meet these, could not realistically have been expected to launch out on new sidelines like probation hostels. Yet the Scottish Home and Health Department made a brave 11th hour try. Proposals were mooted for a boys' hostel in Glasgow, and premises were investigated at Larbert for a girl's hostel, but both proved abortive ventures. The Glasgow proposal should not be confused with the hostel run by the WRVS in Pollokshields from 1963 to 1968. It was essentially for boys on after-care from Borstal, and attempts to mix probation cases were generally unsuccessful.[20]

The thoughts of the Mackenzie Report of 1969 showed no greater courage or decision on this subject for the new era 'We do not find it possible to make a recommendation. The problem of adolescents on their own in the community, not all of them able to cope with the stress involved, needs careful thought and experiment, especially in the cities'.[21] This was the sum of Scottish vision 20 years after the Act, and continuous debate and advice to the Secretary of State by the sundry bodies concerned in that time.

The end result of this 'auld sang' was that in a period when the time was ripe, resources were available and legislation enabled, Scotland failed even to experiment with a facility apparently used with success in England, Europe and elsewhere. The corollary was further heavy dependence on approved school and remand home committals.[22] The situation does not seem to have improved with the fresh powers given by the Criminal Justice (Scotland) Act 1980, and it remains to be seen whether the even more attractive financial proposals of 1991 for 'supported accommodation' will encourage developments.

The Inspectorate and Other Influences

The Morison Committee concluded that inspection by the Home Office Probation Inspectorate was an indispensable asset to the probation service in England and Wales. In addition to the routine confirmation of new officers, general assessment of casework, and advice to probation committees, Morison recommended that the practice of triennial full inspections should be adhered to. As regards Scotland, they accepted against their better judgment, the existence of a combined child care and probation inspectorate, if it were strengthened by inspectors with specific probation experience.

In the late 1950s this comparatively underdeveloped inspectorate was somewhat revitalised, and took a more active and progressive role in the 1960s. In 1958 a new Chief Inspector, was appointed, who had a decade's experience in the Home Office Child Care Inspectorate, including oversight of residential aspects of probation hostels.[23] His active and dynamic approach to principal probation officers, county clerks, committees and sheriffs brought the probation service somewhat more to the forefront, and stimulated the expansion of staffing and training. Much of this was achieved in the face of normal public and official antipathy to services for offenders, but he had engaged the collaboration and support from senior departmental officials, by this time, of the combined Scottish Home and Health Department. The Scottish Probation Service now had strong, if at times critical support in their areas, and favourable advocacy in St Andrew's House.

The other main influences in promoting progress were the Sheriffs and the National Association of Probation Officers. The Sheriffs as individuals, and the Sheriffs-Substitute Association now became strong advocates of expansion and improvement both at central and local government levels. The Scottish branch of NAPO became active in the 1960s, and was strongly supported by the general secretary from London in representations, and organising conferences, which had some impact on committee members and others. This activity reached a peak in 1968/69 when the principal probation officer for Lanarkshire was chairman of the National Association. By this time, however, the preoccupation was more with the Probation's future role than its current service.

Training

One of the main thrusts of the forces described above was towards an adequate supply of trained staff. The following is an outline of the development of training for probation in Scotland between 1949 and 1969. Those seeking more detail will find the subject dealt with at length in 'Social Work Education for Probation in Scotland', an Edinburgh University thesis of 1972 by Esmee Roberts.

Prior to 1949 there was no formal training, although oral tradition alludes to a part-time course set up in 1935 for its officers by Glasgow Probation Committee. In the 1930s and 1940s probation officers in or near the cities were encouraged to attend relevant extra-mural classes and other lectures. In 1945 a central register of those adjudged suitable for appointment by probation committees was established. The selection for and maintenance of this register was done by the then Scottish Central Probation Council, with the assistance of the inspectorate. Up until the end of 1959 officers were appointed from this register and given a minimal three weeks training after appointment. In England and Wales since 1949 special training preceded appointment and those under 30 were required to hold a social science qualification before acceptance for the course. The Scottish arrangement was due partly to the small number involved and partly to the lack of training courses.

The decade 1949-1959 saw a progressive sequence towards appropriate formal training. The 1949 Act had given the Secretary of State power to defray expenses incurred by him or any other body on the training of probation officers. The Probation (Scotland) Rules of 1951 stemming from the Act provided that the Secretary of State before confirming an appointment must be satisfied that the officer had undertaken appropriate theoretical and practical training. There followed pressure from various sources to implement these provisions, although the Morison Committee still gained the impression that 'some Scottish probation committees favour maturity at the expense of academic training — and look upon the university trained social worker as a person who is less likely to take a firm line with his charges than is 'a practical common sense' type of officer without an academic background' (para. 339).

In 1954, after specific representations from the National Association of Probation Officers and Glasgow Probation Committee, a Training Committee was set up by the Scottish Central Probation Council. By this time also the latter body included social work teachers from Edinburgh and Glasgow Universities. In 1959 the Council became the Scottish Probation Advisory and Training Council.

From 1951 to 1959 training took the form of a three week course for recently appointed officers. This was organised by the inspectorate, and consisted of some case-work, considerable law, and much background and theory of delinquency. This course depended heavily on psychiatrists, understandably so, as they had a general lead in this field at the time, and in Scotland they were the gurus of the delinquency scene.

After prolonged planning, a year's course with concurrent theory and practice was established in Glasgow in 1959, under a part-time director and deputy. This course continued to be administered by the Advisory Council through the inspectors, till taken over by Jordanhill College of Education in 1967. Before that however, in 1962, a leading social worker from the child care field was appointed as full-time director. The latter ably directed the course for its duration, and produced a continuous supply of trained probation officers up till 1969, the largest single contribution to social work education of the 1960s in Scotland.[24] She and other organisers of this course were leading protagonists in the move towards social work unification, and had considerable influence on the views of the new probation officers trained in the 1960s.

By December 1968 two thirds of full-time probation officers had at least completed a one year course, in contrast to the 1961 position where 66% had only the early three weeks course. This left about 100 officers unqualified. In 1963 the device of a 'Certificate of Recognition of Experience' had been developed for workers in Child Care, Health and Welfare, who had reached a certain age and length of service. This was applied to the probation service in Scotland, and so in November 1968 about 50 officers received the certificate. There were left a further 50 who did not meet the criteria, and for their cases a certificate of 'Recognition of Experience and Training' was further devised. This was achieved after a six weeks course based on the University of Edinburgh, followed up later by two residential weeks.

Training for probation was one of the success stories of the 1960s and thus it was that, in contrast to the earlier years, a rapidly developing probation service approached social work re-organisation in 1969 with some 336 officers, all of whom held some qualification either from the years training or from the certificate of recognition process, the largest complement of trained personnel of any of the separate services.

Summary

In 1949 probation in Scotland was a backward service. Outside the cities and larger population centres it was thin on the ground, and dependent on part-time personnel. Training, as in some other Scottish services of the time, was conspicuous by its absence. The use of probation across the country was varied and limited, concentrating mainly on juvenile offenders. Yet, in the ten years after the Criminal Justice Act staffing more than doubled.

The Morison Committee of 1959-61, however, still found an under-staffed, undertrained and underdeveloped service, for which they blamed, not entirely correctly a faulty and weak local authority commit-tee system. Their main recommendation of reducing local authority influence was, fortunately for social work if not for probation, not accepted. Yet their advice on the importance of the service, the need for training and widening of the scope seems to have been heard. The acceptance of their recommendation for special probation hostels was half-hearted, and delayed till too late for any effective action.

From unpromising beginnings, limited initiative, hesitations and parsimony, the 1960s saw significant developments, influenced to a greater or lesser degree by the considerations we have discussed. Staffing was expanded to give nationwide cover. By 1969 there were 336 full-time officers as compared to the 78 of 1951. The service also broadened to include fines supervision (1964), aftercare of offenders (1965), and parole in 1968. By 1968 two-thirds of the officers had at least a year's pre-service training. The remainder then acquired appropriate certificates of recognition of experience. And so at the inception of social work departments the probation service had a force of 336 officers with some form of qualification.

In conclusion, probation moved from a poor basis, slowly at first, and then rapidly in comparison with the other services, to the position of a relatively well developed and staffed service in 1969 immediately prior to the re-organisation of social work. While probation officers' initiative towards this re-organisation may have been comparatively limited, if not negative at times, their final contribution in terms of manpower and organisational capacity was a major one. Yet, not everyone shared the view of Councillor Main's Dissenting Note, 'No social service benefits from being held in isolation, least of all probation.'

NOTES

1. T. Ferguson, The Dawn of Scottish Welfare, Nelson 1947, p. 294.
2. Esmee Roberts, Social Work Education for the Probation Service in Scotland, Edinburgh University MSc Thesis 1972, pp. 75-77.
3. A. J. Arnott and J. A. Duncan, The Scottish Criminal, Edinburgh University Press 1978, p. 8.
4. SWSG Circular SW.6/1971, para. 9.
5. F. H. McLintock, Attendance Centres, MacMillan and Co. 1961, p. 99.
6. The 'Tandem Principle' is used to express the process whereby some Scottish legislation usually follows provisions for England and Wales.
7. Social Work in Scotland 1969, Cmnd. 4475, SED 1970, p. 34.
8. The Probation Service in Scotland, HMSO 1961, p. 13.
9. John A. Mack, Delinquency and the Changing Social Pattern, Charles Russell Memorial Lecture of October 1956, p. 3.

10. The Probation Service in Scotland, HMSO 1961, p. 13.
11. Report of the Departmental Committee on the Probation Service 1962, Cmnd. 1650, paras. 245/6.
12. Social Work in Scotland 1969, Cmnd. 4475, SED 1970, p. 34.
13. In February 1989, I was able to discuss the Morison Committee with two members, Sheriff J. Aikman-Smith and Dr J. D. Sutherland. Earlier, in November 1988, I had the opportunity of discussion with the Home Office permanent secretary of the time, Sir Charles Cunningham, who knew Morison well both in London and Edinburgh.
14. Report of the Departmental Committee on Probation 1961, Cmnd. 1650. Second report of the Departmental Committee 1962, Cmnd. 1800.
15. Cmnd. 1650, Conclusions (50) and (88).
16. This view was confirmed by conversations in February 1989, with Sheriff Aikman-Smith of the Morison Committee and David Keir, Principal Probation Officer, Lanarkshire and a leading NAPO figure of the time.
17. The Organisation of After-care in Scotland, HMSO 1963, pp. 14, 15.
18. W. Hewitson Brown, Secretary of the Clyde Committee, was also involved with the SACTRO Committee, and influential there and in the Scottish Office generally.
19. Probation hostels in Scotland: Final Report by the Scottish Probation Advisory and Training Council, SHHD, HMSO 1966.
20. Ann D. Smith, A Home for Young Offenders, Holmes, 62 Kelvingrove Street, Glasgow.
21. Social Work in Scotland: Report of a Working Party on the Social Work (Scotland) Act, University of Edinburgh 1969, pp. 72, 73.
22. Probation Hostels in Scotland; HMSO 1966, p. 12.
23. C. R. Corner, Chief Inspector of Child Care and Probation 1958-69.
24. Idris Phillips was the part-time Director. Kay Carmichael was the deputy. Vera Hiddleston was the Director appointed in 1962.

CHAPTER 6

Separate Services 1948-69

Child Care

'We shall get nowhere unless we stop confusing mothercraft with hospital sick-nursing — All children should be tirelessly noisy, playful and grubby handed except at meal times.'
George Bernard Shaw, Letter to *Times* of 2.8.44.

Shaw's typical over-simplification highlights a fundamental child care change of the 1940s, from the dominant hygiene and control regimes to the provision of good substitute family environments.

The Children Act of 1948 was not the first piece of Great Britain legislation specifically for the protection of children. In the 18th century children were seen as the chattels of their families. By the 19th, though still largely treated as miniature, subject adults, they were slowly being recognised as a separate category. That century initiated a proliferation of Acts and action to safeguard the interests of children in the spheres of employment, education and the courts. The last quarter in particular saw the foundations laid of our systems for protection and custody of the most vulnerable children. Between 1883 and 1885 voluntary societies for the prevention of cruelty to children sprang up in London and the principal cities of Britain, including Glasgow and Edinburgh. It was only a short step to the founding in 1889 of the National Society in England, and the Scottish National Society for the Prevention of Cruelty to Children. From Victoria's accession in 1837 to her jubilee in 1897 more than 100 Acts for child welfare came into force.[1]

The 20th century, which may in general terms be seen as the 'Children's Century', has been characterised by several great omnibus Children's Acts. Foremost among these was the Children Act of 1908 which encoded for the first time piecemeal legislation on children's rights. Having abolished the death sentence for children or young persons and restricted imprisonment, it provided the basis for places of safety and established the separateness of 'juvenile courts'. It laid down the legal foundations for child life protection and prevention of cruelty or neglect of children. Some sections — on begging, brothels and juvenile smoking — were clearly determined by the problems of the age. Even more revealing of contemporary customs are the prohibitions on giving liquor to children under five, except in cases of sickness, and the section on suffocation of infants in bed through overlaying by an adult under the influence of the said liquor. In the year of the Act there were said to be 59 recorded such cases in the eight principal towns of Scotland — presumably only the tip of the iceberg.[2] Section 107, which provided 13 different disposals for a child before the Court, would make modern Scottish panel members envious, although it must be pointed out that one was judicial whipping. Altogether this Act was the first major milestone in state child care, and merits more than others the title of the 'Children's Charter'.[3]

Great as it was, the 1908 Act was not an answer for all time. The social upheaval of the First World War and the not unrelated developments in public health, housing and education produced much preoccupation in the 1920s with child health and child protection. Departmental Committees on Sexual Offences against Young Persons were set up and reported, for England in 1925 (Cmnd. 2561), and for Scotland in 1926 (Cmnd. 2592). A major UK Departmental Committee on the treatment of Young Offenders reported in 1928 (Cmnd. 2831). The principal findings of these Committees were incorporated in the Children and Young Persons Act 1933, for England and Wales, and ultimately in the Children and Young Persons (Scotland) Act 1937. These two similar Acts preserved and extended the main provisions of the 1908 Act, and also codified protection for children in the employment and entertainment spheres.

They raised the minimum age of criminal responsibility from seven to eight, and defined a child as under 14 and a young person as 14 but under 17. They developed the separate juvenile court premises idea to include a separate 'panel of justices specially qualified for dealing with juvenile cases'. They replaced detention arrangements by the introduction of remand homes, and rationalised reformatory and industrial schools into 'approved schools'.

The essential spirit of these Acts is enshrined in the words of Section 49, 'Every court in dealing with a child or young person . . . shall have regard to the welfare of the child'. This concept in theory heralded the end of the era of punishment for the offence in favour of the welfare of the child principle. In practice attempts were made to combine both, not always an easy process, as discussed in Chapter 7.

These provisions, by-passed by the Children Act of 1948, were to continue as the avowed basis at least of juvenile justice till 1968 in Scotland. The means of effecting the welfare of the child, however, were still mainly seen as removal from family and environment to an approved school, or the care of the local authority or other fit person, until he was 18. This is understandable in the light of the widespread poor housing, ill health, unemployment and poverty of the 1930s, which provided a poor infrastructure for any ideas of family rehabilitation.

The Children Act of 1948, as discussed in detail in Chapter 2, required the local authority to receive into care any child who needed it and keep him so long as his welfare required, but otherwise to return to parent, guardian, relative or friend. The central duty, to be discharged preferably on the basis of boarding out, was 'to further his best interests, and to afford him opportunity for the proper development of his character and abilities'. This duty, and the return home provision, look revolutionary when compared to the pre-1948 Poor Law requirements, 'To set to work or put out as apprentices all children whose parents are not, in the opinion of the council, able to keep them.'

To discharge all these duties a local authority was required to set up a children's committee and appoint a well qualified children's officer.

The Monckton Report had proposed the children's officer idea to introduce the personal element of care into what seemed an institutional system — a children's friend if not a fairy god mother. Curtis had gone even further by pronouncing 'we desire to see the responsibility for the welfare of deprived children definitely laid on a children's officer. This may indeed be said to be our solution of the problem referred to us' (para. 441).

To carry out such a burden they produced the following prescription of perfection, 'The Children's Officer should in our view be highly qualified academically, if possible a graduate who has also a social science diploma. She should not be under 30 at the time of appointment, and should have had some experience of work with children. She should have marked administrative capacity and be able readily to grasp government procedure, and to work easily with local authority committees. Her essential qualifications, however, would be on the personal side — she should have very high standards of physical and moral welfare, but should be flexible enough in temperament to avoid a sterile institutional correctness.'

This then was the background and legal structure against which the children's departments of 1948 to 1969 were expected to develop.

THE IMPLEMENTATION OF THE CHILDREN ACT (1948) IN ENGLAND AND WALES.

Before detailed consideration of developments in Scotland, it is necessary for background and reference purposes to make an outline survey of the period in England, where between 1948 and 1963 the major development and innovations under the Act took place.

By July 1947 central responsibility had been placed on the Home Office, which in September issued a circular inviting local authorities to proceed with the appointment of children's committees and children's officers. As a result some authorities had their arrangements made well in advance of the appointed day, while a few ran over into 1949. The

Home Office was able to say that 'The transfer was carried out smoothly, and by the end of 1948 the new arrangements were taking satisfactory shape. About two-thirds of the children's officers are women, and most have university training,' by which they really meant education.[4]

Two major difficulties faced the new service — escalating numbers, and limited resources of staff and suitable accommodation. Curtis had estimated the number of children in care as 46,000. By the end of 1949 this figure was 55,255, in 1959 it was 61,580 and by 1968 was 69,358. The number of children received into care also climbed steadily to a peak in 1965. The rise in these figures was partly due to an increased birth rate, but mainly to a wider door and a more liberal interpretation of need. To meet these pressures there were urgent demands for more staff and more buildings. In the earlier years the former were in short supply, and the latter became the priority. In the words of Jean Heywood, 'The tradition of institutional care was a long one, administratively convenient, and largely understood. In a new service the children's homes provided immediate evidence of the quality of the work'.[5]

And so the new children's officers and their few assistants, including at times experienced office staff, embarked on the great enterprise of taking all the children into care who seemed to need it. To do this they had to find places by increasing boarding out, and maximising and improving residential facilities, while at the same time withdrawing from Public Assistance Institutions. This was the pattern of the first five years.

The development of boarding out, slow in the early years because of pressures of admissions and limited staff, quickened and broadened to include handicapped children and large families. But as the period progressed, as child care officers became trained and children's officers had more time to take stock, the limitations of boarding out as a panacea were recognised. The same was to happen also to family group homes as it became apparent that there was a role for the expertise of trained residential workers. In this process some of the influence came from American thinking and writing.[6] In the next decade we were to see from similar sources the questioning of the very principle of residential care. Be that as it may, between 1948 and 1960 in England and Wales the new children's officers and their staffs, while wrestling with inadequate residential accommodation, took on the dimension of boarding out as prime provision, advanced its use, broadened its application and raised its quality. Such speedy progress was of course not universal, and black spots remained.

The Ingleby Report

In less than ten years most new children's departments had set up a transformed system of substitute care for children deprived of a normal family life. They were conscious that many admissions might have been prevented, and they were aware of the many more children neglected in their own homes. They were wrestling with the problem of 'The Problem Family', but were limited in their powers to intervene by the legal provisions of the Act. In the words of a leading children's officer, 'Children's officers soon found that attempting to wipe the slate clean was rarely satisfactory and that substitute home care, however kindly, was but a pale shadow of the real thing'.[7]

Yet by the mid-1950s many children's departments were actively engaged in preventing the need for admission of children to care, although often subject to criticism of their role, and to doubts about their legal and financial grounds for such action. As early as 1952 the Association of Children's Officers decided to change their objects to 'further the welfare of children deprived of a normal home life *and to encourage and assist in the preservation of the family*'. Two well-known phrases were coined at this time; 'A fence at the top of the cliff is better than an ambulance at the bottom'; and 'The need to break the cycle of deprivation'. The former was a professional tag, the latter is usually associated with the Minister, Keith Joseph.

A concomitant of this was growing concern about delinquent children of similar origins processed through the different channels of courts and approved schools. Some children's officers, led by Barbara Kahan of Oxfordshire, clearly identified the delinquents as produced by similar families to the deprived, and developed capacities to deal with them more appropriately through fit person orders and varied residential child care measures. In this they carried their more progressive committee members and the young child care officers trained in new thinking. By 1960 the Home Office Child Care Inspectorate were recognising this Oxfordshire movement, and commended its success in a report on a full inspection of that county's provision.[8]

Alongside the child care service, further doubts were being expressed by progressive magistrates, agonising over the contradictions between the 'welfare of the child' and the 'guilty' concepts inherent in the juvenile court system. The Magistrates Association, aware that the subject had last been reviewed by the Departmental Committee on Young Offenders of 1927, suggested that fresh consideration was now due. And so the Committee on Children and Young Persons was set up in 1956 to consider the constitution, proceedings and powers of juvenile courts, and the remand home and approved school systems. Because of general concern about children neglected in their own homes, they were further required to consider the prevention of cruelty to, and exposure to moral and physical danger of juveniles. Two-thirds of the committee, chaired by Viscount Ingleby, were magistrates or lawyers, and neither the local authorities nor the child care profession were strongly represented. By remit and constitution Ingleby was necessarily court-oriented.

They produced their report in 1960 (Cmnd. 1191) with over 100 recommendations mainly on juvenile courts and disposals. They recommended that juvenile courts should be maintained, but the age of criminal responsibility should be raised from eight to 12, and that those under 12 should be brought to court only as 'being in need of protection or discipline'. On the wider front their major contribution was for a general duty to be laid on local authorities to prevent or forestall the suffering of children in their own homes, and for a local authority power to undertake preventive case-work and provide material needs that could not be met from other sources. Faced with the contesting claims of children's and health departments they did not venture to specify the department, but reiterated the importance of co-ordination of services. They produced their own peculiar device of local authority 'family advice centres' run by an independent officer to avoid rivalry.

In view of their composition and remit it is not surprising that on the central question of a family service they temporised, with the cautious pointer for the future; 'It may be that the long term solution will be in a re-organisation of the various services concerned with the family, and their combination into a unified family service.'

Even this was a considerable advance in 1960, but Ingleby's greatest contribution is to be found in the provisions enabling preventive work with families, contained in the subsequent Children and Young Persons Act 1963, and in its inspiration towards a similar enquiry in Scotland, Kilbrandon, which had more immediate and radical results.

Children and Young Persons Act 1963

To meet some of the recommendations of Ingleby the government prepared a bill, which amongst other things clearly allocated the new responsibilities to children's departments as a logical extension of their powers and duties. Parliament passed this in July 1963, and it became operational in October 1963 as the Children and Young Persons Act, generally applying to Scotland as well as England and Wales, with the exception of the parts specifically relating to juvenile courts and approved schools. Section 1 placed a duty on local authorities 'to provide such advice, guidance and assistance as may promote the welfare of children by diminishing the need to receive children into or keep them in care — or to bring children before a juvenile court'. To this end it made provision for giving assistance in kind, or in exceptional circumstances cash. In this we may see a forerunner of the famous Section 12 of the Social Work (Scotland) Act 1968.

This opened up for major development a field previously only partly cultivated. As with most new Acts the government had no idea of numbers involved, staff required or likely costs. There was the sanguine assumption that it might even effect an overall saving. Although there was a requirement in the Act for local authorities to make yearly reports to the Secretary of State on the new work under Section 1, there is no clear record of developments in England and Wales in the following six years. The position in Scotland, fortunately, is much clearer as we shall discuss later. Extensive developments there certainly were. Practical assistance in the form of clothes, furniture and household equipment was now given openly. It was possible to assist financially with electricity, gas and rent debts, but this was generally done sparingly. Staff were appointed on a domiciliary day care and even overnight basis for family preservation. Field staff expanded generally for the new remit. Family advice centres were indeed set up in a few cities, but did not spread.

Apart from its effect on practice, the 1963 Act had an effect on ideas and systems in England and Wales. It centralised in children's departments responsibility for first line action on abused and neglected children, as well as those received into care, and, to some extent, those manifesting themselves as delinquent. It also established a principle of practical and cash sustentation on the basis of assessed individual need rather than national scales for categories. The Act was a great advance, a substantial springboard for the next leap, and a major milestone in child care for Scotland as well as England.

General Assessment

In the first five years the new children's departments in England and Wales were struggling to contain a situation of escalating numbers matched by shortages of staff and appropriate places for children. In the first decade they moved from a system of large institutional homes to small family group homes, or retained the former on a reduced and upgraded style. An archaic and restricted boarding out system was greatly expanded and developed.

These achievements were facilitated through increased staffing, residential and field, deriving from training on a substantial scale established at an early stage. Progressive children's officers welcomed and indoctrinated a stream of new young recruits, attracted by congenial leadership and interesting ideas. In less than ten years a transformed system of substitute care for deprived children had been established in the best areas. This was not, of course, universal and in many places, not least some of the northern county boroughs, progress was slow and limited. By the mid-1950s children's officers had turned their attentions to the neglected child and the 'problem family', and through co-ordinating machinery, or in spite of it, were developing new approaches, practical as well as case-work. The late 1950s saw a major drive towards preventive work, and professional practice and philosophy finally achieved official recognition in the Children and Young Persons Act of 1963, towards which the main vehicle was the Ingleby Report.

From there it was no long step to the setting up of the Committee on Local Authority and Allied Personal Social Services (Seebohm) in 1965 and its report in 1968. The resulting Local Authority Social Services Act of 1970, while not so radical or comprehensive as its Scottish counterpart of 1968, achieved most but not all of the ideas for which children's departments had been striving. 'The rationalisation of the social services under the influence of the Seebohm recommendations has been directly influenced by the child care movement, and in the end history may see this as its most enlightened and important contribution.'[9]

Amongst the various factors contributing to the substantial and significant achievements of children's departments in England two may be noted here — the children's officers and the Home Office. The Home Office since the 19th century had carried wide central responsibility for the protection of children, and had built up an experienced and powerful inspectorate. In 'Children in Care' Jean Heywood says, 'In this development the unified central control was of great import. The Home Office, through the specialised understanding made available by the work of the Advisory Council and the Central Training Council, and the accumulation of field experience of its inspectors over the whole country, was able to promote an interchange of experience and dissemination of knowledge among local authorities and the voluntary organisations, and encourage the whole service to work towards a nationally accepted standard'.[10]

The role of the children's officers cannot be over-emphasised. They included a large number of able and informed graduate women, and to a lesser extent men, who were committed and crusading activists. Moreover, in the words of David Donnison, 'The creation of children's departments brought social workers to the chief officers' table in the town hall dining rooms'.[11] For the first time on the welfare scene these professionals were able to match up to the powerful education officers, treasurers and clerks, to attract resources, including well qualified staff, and even to exert strong influence on committees and powerful chairmen, through the combination of the intrinsic worth of the cause and their own demonstrated capacity to verbalise and advance it. As we shall see, there was no such parallel phenomenon in Scotland.

The enlightened implementation of the Children Act in England and Wales produced the setting there for the development of progressive social work with families as units. In the process it incidentally provided a number of Scots with the training and experience which they could not get at home. Even more importantly, it offered a pattern for future development, which was soon to be pursued more radically and speedily north of the border.

Child Care in Scotland before 1948

Until the late 19th century responsibility for child protection lay largely with the church or the burgh. The provision of the 1908 Children Act on suffocation of infants had been anticipated as early as the 13th century by a church ordinance forbidding mothers to take young children into their own beds 'by reason of the frequent dangers arising from this practice', and presbytery records of the 16th century show continuing concern with the offence of 'smooring bairns'.[12] Amongst the earlier identifications of need is a minute of Stirling Burgh of 1562 which reads 'The counsall haivand consideratioun that thair is certane puir bairns greting and crying nytlie under stairis for falt of lugeing, hes grantit that ulklie ane laid of colis be laid into thair almshouses for lugeing of the saidis puiris during this winter'.[13] In the same century the Scottish Poor Law Act of 1579, concerned with punishment of beggars as well as relief of the poor, allowed for beggars' bairns between five and 14 to be passed over by direction of a magistrate to any person of substance who chose them.

By the early 18th century child care in Glasgow was centred on the Town Hospital, but for a mixture of reasons the practice of boarding out for maintenance or employment grew through the century, and by 1819 there were only 58 children left in the Hospital, with 212 boarded out and visited annually, in theory, by the Hospital superintendent.[14] The Hospital now catered for abandoned or unwanted infants, mainly illegitimate. In the period 1802-1818 there were 197 such children admitted, of whom 113 died.[15] There were, therefore, cogent reasons to board children out of such institutions into the country to escape the endemic disease and food shortages of the time.

The fate of the deprived child of this period was either to be placed in a household with the possibility of exploitation, or to be retained in the institution with a high chance of early death. No better was the lot of the proletarian infant left in his own slum home in the care of young siblings or a feeble granny, while father, mother and all above ten years were, of economic necessity, away in cotton or other mills from dawn till dusk. As late as the 1881 census 25% of cotton workers' children never saw their first birthday. As a small experiment to combat such conditions, a public day nursery was opened in Glasgow to receive healthy children between 18 months and six years at a nominal charge.[16]

In the hungry 1840s the slightly older children not yet employed found food and survival in roaming the streets and on occasion sleeping there. In 1840 as many as 280 such were known to be maintaining themselves in Aberdeen. It was to meet this challenge that in 1841 Sheriff Watson opened the first industrial school to feed, train and educate. The feeding and minding were central to the regime, with breakfast, dinner and supper provided. Dr Guthrie, the Scottish Barnardo, advanced this cause by his powerful oratory, and in 1847 'ragged schools' were opened in Edinburgh for his 'city arabs'. These ventures gained recognition by an Industrial Schools Act of 1854 pre-dating similar English legislation by three years. And so the predeces-sors of Approved or List 'D' Schools were founded for basic physical child care, originally on a day basis.

Large scale provision of voluntary children's homes was soon to follow as a manifestation of late 19th century philanthropy in response to the continuing appalling conditions of life, death, hunger and morbid-ity in the industrial city slums. In 1878 William Quarrier opened at Bridge of Weir the nucleus of his village homes, which in 1945 catered for over 1,200 children. In 1875 Canon Jupp had started his village at Aberlour, which in its heyday cared for 500 children and later diversi-fied into small homes all over Scotland. The histories of both these large voluntary child care organisations make interesting reading.[17] The histories of the smaller voluntary homes opening at this time in the cities and towns of Scotland is more recondite or lost. Deriving from such foundations, the state of child care in 1945 is described in chapter two above.

Boarding Out

To complete the historical picture, it is necessary at this point to look at the main Scottish mode of child care, boarding out.

From the beginning of the century to the time of Curtis, and indeed up to 1969, over half the children in care were placed for a pittance in the community in private houses often remote in distance and culture from their own homes. The boarding out, particularly as practised by the cities, found a ready outlet for the children in the cottages and crofts of the Highlands and Islands. It seemed to promote the child's health and well-being, it removed the problem, it was relatively cheap and it supplemented the economy of crofter and cottar. Scottish administra-tors enthused over the system's merits, and English visiting Poor Law Inspectors commented favourably on the ample provision of basic foods, healthy appearances and the easy acceptance of substitute relations. The Chairman of the Board of Supervision for Scottish Local Authori-ties, Sir John McNeill, in a statement to a Select Committee of 1870 described the system's merits as 'they are treated as members of the family; they acquire the habits and feelings of the persons among whom they are brought up; they acquire a sort of domestic attachment to the father and mother, or to the old woman with whom they are boarding; they are well educated; and ultimately they melt into the population'.

This was the general philosophy of Scottish boarding out, which persisted well into the children's departments era, although by that time the idea of assimilation into the local population was no longer valid, but rather there was the problem of transplanting back to their distant urban culture on school leaving. The strong emphasis on good education, a reflection of national aspirations, was preserved throughout the period and was something that children's committee members could identify with and encourage for children in care, particularly if they showed promise in secondary or further education. An article entitled *Glasgow's Pride and Problem* from the Glasgow Herald records this attitude — 'The Children's Committee are proud of their former proteges who make good. Among recent successes are two who have become doctors, another is a Church of Scotland Minister; there are several teachers, one is now in charge of the school in the district where she was boarded out'[18]

The system enjoyed general support in the receiving areas, not least from the schoolmasters and doctors, whose stipends or practices might well depend on the pecuniary advantages involved. The only real detractors were such potentates as the factors of the Duke of Argyll (for Iona) or the Duke of Hamilton (for Arran) who forbade tenants to foster, partly through fear that independent revenues and loyalties might undermine their own power in the islands.

The history of boarding out in Scotland is a fascinating story still insufficiently explored and documented. One of the few systematic airings of the subject was given at a conference on public relief in Edinburgh in 1904. Papers delivered there were reprinted as *Transactions of the 4th International Home Relief Congress, Edinburgh 1904* and may be seen in certain libraries, notably the Mitchell in Glasgow.

On this occasion, for the benefit of visiting nations, the essential English and Scottish philosophies were debated with comparative rivalry. The English Local Government Board Senior Inspector, the experienced Miss Mason, who believed in the twin supervisory devices of voluntary local committees and thorough central inspection of the home, foster parents and child by 'lady' inspectors, first gave her famous opinion, 'The boarding out system is, in my experience, the very best or the very worst of systems, according to the manner in which it is administered'. In summing up later she even advanced as far as to claim that given the systems of supervision and inspection she advocated 'The

English system of boarding out beyond the union is, so far as I know, the best in existence'.

The ambivalence of her initial pronouncement, however, characterised official thinking in London and in the local authorities for the half century up till 1948 (contributing to a fostering rate of half the normal Scottish 60%) when the Act resolved the matter by prescribing boarding out as priority provision for England as well as Scotland.

Mr J. Patten Macdougall, advocate and member of the Local Government board for Scotland, produced an equally enthusiastic paper on The Boarding Out of Pauper Children in Scotland. He based his case on the three main aspects; that it was a spontaneous growth without statutory basis, that it was inherently an out-door system in the Scottish Poor Law tradition as opposed to the indoor English and Irish traditions, and that it aimed to remove Poor Law stigma as well as provide a suitable home life and background.

There was little change in this practice or philosophy of boarding out between 1904 and the Clyde Report of 1946. The latter, however, in spite of its continued general approbation, clearly criticised such limitations as remoteness from home area, the poor quality of after-care, and the use of crofts where 'the practice of taking children seems to be regarded as an industry, and the labour obtained therefrom often enables the guardians to maintain their crofts'.[19]

Establishment of Children's Departments in Scotland

The new reforming Children Act of 1948 was not received with great enthusiasm in Scotland. There was apathy if not opposition on the part of many councillors and officials, central and local. In the Scottish Office unified responsibility was easily transferred to the Home Department, following a minute to the Secretary, 'It seems difficult to justify a different line in Scotland from the one which is being followed in England and Wales'.[20] A brief 11th hour circular (SHD No. 6873) was issued on 29 June to await a proper introductory document on 6 August (SHD No. 6913), a month after implementation. This followed closely the Home Office Circular No. 160/1948 of 8 July.

The authorities responsible for the new service were the cities, the counties and the large burghs, many of whom had few children in care and minimal resources for welfare services. Only the four cities and the counties of Aberdeen and Lanark exceeded or approximated to the Curtis figure of 400 children, envisaged as a working load to justify a children's officer. Many authorities, failing to comprehend the need for change, wished to combine the children's committee with welfare, or to appoint a children's officer with the additional duties of registrar and burial ground clerk. For example, Aberdeen City in proposing the existing welfare officer as children's officer expressed the view that the children's committee would not be regarded in local authority circles as a very important one, and that 'the welfare of 300 or so children would not provide full time employment'. In Glasgow on the other hand, with some 3,000 children in care, the Director of Welfare in a letter to the Convener of Welfare (copy to Scottish Home Department) put forward the idea of five or six district children's officers resident in their areas, with a chief children's officer in charge.[21] Scottish Home Department officials, by early 1948 appreciating the real difficulties in the way of full time appointments, advised combinations, but realised that they would have to face up to authorising part-time appointments or the undertaking of other duties, a procedure discouraged by the Act. The idea that the appointment of children's officers might be left to the major receiving areas was even toyed with, but abandoned as unlikely of acceptance, 'as visits to the receiving areas are not unwelcome to some members of councils'.[22]

The failure to appreciate the central importance of the children's officer role should not surprise us too much if we recall the unanimous dictum of the Clyde Report, para. 69; 'We are strongly against any system under which the whole matter is referred to an official, who merely reports to the local authority committee, and under which the latter has no personal contact with children.' While Curtis saw the children's officer as the key to the problem of deprived children, Clyde's and Scotland's faith in the boarding out process as the great panacea was still unshaken.

A further limitation on the innovatory concept of able women as children's officers came from the all male Scottish Association of Welfare Officers, who according to the minutes of a meeting with the Scottish Home Department 'agreed that women should be employed, but in general would favour a man as children's officer with women assistants'.[23] On the local authority side there was general apprehension about costs, and serious concern was expressed at the level of salaries for children's officers being offered by municipalities in England.

In the event few combinations of authorities were effected, there was a substantial number of part-time appointments, and even without the Secretary of State's consent, child care functions were discharged by the welfare officer responsible to the welfare committee in the large burghs of Ayr, Airdrie, Coatbridge and Hamilton.[24] Even where children's officers were appointed the establishment could be seriously inadequate. In the early 1950s the city of Dundee had only a children's officer and one assistant to care for 500 children. These officers did not even have their own clerical or administrative staff, but were serviced by the welfare department.

These uninformed and parsimonious attitudes affected the development of child care in Scotland for the first ten or 15 years. Children's officers were commissioned with low pay, low staffing and the barest of accommodation and facilities, to set up the new departments and effect radical changes in child care. It is not surprising that as late as 1965 a list circulated from the Scottish Office shows that in the 52 departments only 11 children's officers had either a training or a university qualification, relevant or irrelevant. This was in strong contrast to the position in England mentioned above. Of the 52, 14 were part-time and 29 were men, some with a continuing public assistance tradition. The position is aptly described by an Association of Child Care Officers' publication; 'Initially child care in Scotland was a depressed service, starved of resources, both money and personnel. There was a tendency for Scots to travel South for better jobs and training'.[25]

It was left to the Scottish Advisory Council on Child Care to highlight these serious defects to the Secretary of State in 1963. Appointed in 1948, after a quiescent period, they played an active and important role in the 1960s under the chairmanship of the convener of Roxburgh County Children's Committee, later the life peer Baroness Elliot. Having in a short space produced reports on Voluntary Homes, Remand Homes and the Prevention of Neglect of Children (Cmnd. 1966 of 1963), they had become aware of the serious shortage and inadequacy of staffing. Their concern led them to produce a further report (*Staffing of Local Authority Children's Departments'* — HMSO 1963) which clearly dealt with the main issues. They identified the basic problem that many authorities lacked the size and resources to provide a proper service. Of the 52, 32 had populations less than 50,000. Forty departments had less than 200 children in care, some a mere handful, and employed only one or two field workers, although the total involvement and personal quality of the small authorities service was often urged in mitigation. The committee also found largely untrained staffs and a lack of suitable courses in Scotland, with even available places on existing courses not used.

Their recommendations included combinations of authorities into adequate service units, the setting up of a Scottish training committee, secondment of existing staff, improved salaries in line with those in England, and better accommodation and supporting services. The training committee was established that year, and in the six years up to 1969 the other recommendations began to have effect, except of course the size of units, which had to await the Wheatley Report and reorganisation in 1975. Many in the field felt that 'although this report gives some indication of the difficulties, it fails to convey the sheer desperation of the staffing situation in the local authority child care service in Scotland'.[26] Even at the end of the era, the Scottish children's departments were still relatively under-staffed and under-trained, with a total of 305 field staff in 1968, 60 of whom were professionally qualified, to cater for some 11,000 children in care as well as the related work.

Numbers in Care and Method of Provision

In 1960 central responsibility for child care services was transferred from the Scottish Home to the Scottish Education Department. The change proved fortunate as this department then deployed some particularly able and committed administrators, who saw the importance and the further potential of child care, and eventually nursed these through to the Social Work Act of 1968 and the consequent reorganisation, as will be discussed in the next chapter.[27] Before this, official information on the services was scant, as the Home Department published only a thin annual paper giving numbers in care and costs. The Scottish Education Department through the 1960s, together with its main report on education, produced a child care section as an annual report which discussed the position and the trends as well as supplying statistics.

From these sources we see that the total in care rose steadily in the first years from 9,068 in 1949 to 10,250 in 1952, thereafter declining till 1960. From 1963 numbers rose again from 10,162 to 10,797 in 1969 and 11,008 in 1970, the first full year of Social Work, and the last before the Children's Hearings system substantially altered the basis of reckoning. More significant is the rate per 1,000 of population under 18, which varied from 6.2 in 1949 to 6.9 in 1952 and averaged 6.6 thereafter. In 1968 the figure was 6.7 when the comparable figure in England and Wales was 6.3. The Scottish figure might have been even higher if it had included some of the excess concealed in the Approved School population, which in that year was 1.01 per thousand as compared to 0.56 in England and Wales. The rate per thousand is of course determined by various factors, and should not be seen necessarily as an index of poor field work. At the same period Oxfordshire, with one of the most developed services, had one of the highest rates per thousand. The Scottish figure of 6.7 was an average, and there was great variation from as low as 1.0+ in the smallest authorities to over 10.0 in the cities. When the city figures are extracted from the burgh tables, there is little difference between county and burgh figures, which on first sight seem high. Exceptionally Aberdeen County gives a remarkable rate throughout the period varying between 10.0 and 14.3 per thousand.

Throughout the period 1948-69 the traditional form of care, boarding out, was maintained for 60% of the children. In the early years the standard of placement was still as described by Clyde, 'in many cases is extremely low, and in some cases extremely fortuitous'. Yet in spite of lack of trained staff and some doubtful standards, boarding out on a large scale seemed to work in Scotland without known major tragedies or protests. Moreover the local authority child care scene of 1948-69 exhibited little evidence of florid child neglect or abuse. This seems strange in comparison to later occurrences in social services, and not least when one recalls the events which precipitated the enquiries of 1946 and the Children Act. There are several possible reasons which may be adduced here, but not established.

Firstly, until 1960 in the general population conditions of nourishment, clothing and housing were not high in comparative terms. Secondly, discipline and upbringing, in the homes from which children came and in their schools, was often harsh to severe, and popularly approved of as such. On the positive side foster homes were usually not in deprived areas and their smaller communities may have exercised a vigilance through school, doctor, minister and neighbours. This, however, may be a cosy picture of an earlier Scotland, and some experienced children's officers would say that the neighbourhood often exercised a silence to the point of collusion. That seems to the writer a fair conclusion.

Further, the idea of child abuse was not so developed as a professional, popular or media concept. Finally, child care officers were not yet concentrating on children in their own home, and when clear cases of abuse obtruded, children's officers tended to play incidents close to their chest, involving as few others as possible. This was the general position in the country areas. In the cities the matters were more the province of the RSSPCC, who usually contained it unobtrusively. The apparent lower incidence of 'non-accidental injury' or abuse, of the specialist child care period compared to the post 1969 social work era, merits further study, as indeed does the striking difference of publicised incidence in Scotland and England in the latter period.

Next to boarding out came placement in voluntary homes which accounted for some 15%. These were a mixture of large orphanages run by Quarriers, Aberlour and the Roman Catholic Church, or medium size homes run by Barnardos and the Church of Scotland, or smaller foundations. In the latter categories it was easier to effect change, as the following 'Woman's Viewpoint' article from the *Glasgow Herald* of July 1950 shows. 'The airy bedrooms, brightly painted by member of staff, have four or five beds, the children having their own lockers, and the older ones their own shelves for special books or treasures — in the dining room the children sit at small tables with the ages mixed.' This was probably not a typical voluntary home of the day, and it took longer to transform the usually large dormitories, dining halls and institutional regimes, but some homes showed creditable early pioneer work.

Overall numbers in the voluntary sector, including their own admissions, dropped from 5,578 in 1949 to 2,520 in 1969. In the first decade their local authority admissions dropped from 1663 to 1173, but then curiously rose between 1963 and 1969 from 1474 to 1976. It would be interesting to investigate these trends further. Local authorities in England and Wales by contrast initially depended on their own residential accommodation, overtaken in five years by boarding out. These two forms together accounted for 80% of children accommodated, and voluntary homes played a lesser and declining part there.

And so, in Scotland with three quarters of the children catered for by boarding out or voluntary homes, there was generally less concentration on provisions or standards of residential care, with some notable exceptions. Some of the burghs, for instance Hamilton with 67 children in care (1968), and Motherwell/Wishaw with 41, relied heavily on boarding out (81% and 71%), and had a few places in voluntary or county Homes. Exceptionally Ayr County Welfare Committee was early in the field by approving in 1944, 'separate accommodation pending boarding out for between 30 and 40 children', and opening for the purpose a converted mansion in April 1948. By advertising for a couple as caretaker-gardener at £225, and housekeeper at £120, they were accused of sex discrimination by the Ardrossan and Saltcoats Business and Professional Women's Association.[28] This was not without deeper justification as the same committee, later reconstituted for the purpose of the National Assistance Act, consisted of provosts, ministers, captains, colonels and an occasional earl or working man, but resisted the admission of women members from 1949 to 1952.

Whatever the priorities, local authority children's homes expanded from 37 in 1949 to 83 in 1958.[29] The number of children so provided, however, only increased by a quarter, as the new homes were mainly for replacement or reduction of older provision. It should be added that most of these were medium size establishments, although in 1950 Aberdeen Children's Committee were described as progressive in the Glasgow Herald because they were 'planning to open a series of small family homes instead of one or two large omnibus homes, which other local authorities are starting'.[30] This was in line with the Clyde Report (paras. 87, 88) which specifically opted for cottage homes of 12-15 children, and accepted large homes with dormitories reduced — also to 12-15. Perhaps this was realistic for the circumstances of the restricted building and investment priorities of the time. In the event few children's departments built family group homes, a provision that had to await the Social Work era in Scotland.

One area of child care remained largely untouched by the reforms — residential care of babies and pre-school children, particularly those of poor physique. In the early years of the century Glasgow, Paisley and other authorities had converted castles or villas on the Clyde coast for children who for health or other reasons could not be boarded out or placed in voluntary homes. In the 1930s and the 1940s health departments, meeting an urgent need of the day, had set up residential nurseries for short term nursing and care of debilitated, disadvantaged or poorly housed children, and these were maintained after the Children Act and after the health and hygiene needs had declined. In 1964 there were fourteen such residential nurseries in addition to seven run by children's departments and seven by voluntary organisations. Many of these continued till the end of the era.[31]

In England there were the children who lingered on in Public Assistance premises condemned by Curtis as mass minding establishments run on institutional hygiene lines. Lady Allen, describing such a nursery containing many children who could not talk at three, reported the matron's explanation as, 'They do not need to talk, everything is done for them'.[32]

The problem in Scotland was only different by virtue of scale and fewer and smaller establishments, but was even more chaotic. In the preparation of an SHD circular in July 1949 to clear up responsibilities between children's and health departments, replies from authorities had indicated that illegitimate children were placed in nurseries run by the children's committee in Dumfries, the health committee in Ayr County and by health and welfare in Aberdeen. In Coatbridge the welfare committee ran a nursery for abandoned and neglected children.[33] These arrangements prolonged the serious division of responsibilities which the reforms had been introduced to prevent, a prolongation due to the power and undoubted efficacy of medical regimes, long tradition and reluctance to spend on funding the children's department in new ventures whether by staffing or premises. Young children often lingered in such institutions, physically and hygienically well protected, but deprived of the emotional and social contacts necessary for development which might have come from a foster mother and older children in a boarding out or small Home setting.

It is of interest to note in passing that during this period an earlier form of child care, emigration, was scarcely used in Scotland, with only single figure numbers being approved by the Secretary of State in the years 1963-69. Initiated in East London in the 1860s by two women, one of them Annie McPherson, a Glasgow philanthropist, it was used by William Quarrier in the 1870s and taken up by Barnardos on a large scale not least in the inter-war years. Schemes were interrupted by the second war, but between 1947 and 1955 some 2,320 children from the UK were emigrated to Australia alone. This aspect may be studied in *Child Migration to Australia,* HMSO Cmnd. 9832 of 1956 or Anna Magnusson's *The Village — A History of Quarriers* 1984. The local authorities and voluntary organisations still have powers to arrange emigration under the sections on child care transposed into the Social Work (Scotland) Act from the Children Act 1948.

Remand Homes

Under the 1948 Act children's departments acquired responsibility for remand homes which catered for a strange and difficult mixture of children between eight and 18, either awaiting court appearance, a vacancy in an approved school, a place in a mental hospital or requiring a place of safety. Superimposed was the difficulty of providing a separate regime for those committed by the courts to 28 days detention, and of coping with various children dumped during the night, apparently to suit the convenience of police or courts. The strange mixture might include apparent babes of eight on place of safety order, and young men of 17 charged with serious crimes.

Established as 'places of detention' under the Children Act of 1908, they became 'remand homes' under the Children and Young Persons Acts of the 1930s, and were finally re-labelled 'assessment centres' under the Social Work (Scotland) Act of 1968. In these 60 years, though constantly criticised, they changed little, and with untrained and inadequate staff were quite unsuitable for their supposed purposes in the period 1948-69.

In 1961 at the request of the Secretary of State, the Scottish Advisory Council on Child Care examined the five main homes in urban areas, as well as overnight accommodation elsewhere, and produced a report *Remand Homes*, Cmnd. 1588 of 1961. Their central finding read, 'Your committee have been dismayed by the inadequacy, both in quantity and quality of staff employed in some of the remand homes visited, and by the conditions under which they are required to work'. They recommended improved high levels of staffing, reduction of overcrowding, a special remand home for girls over 12 and the use of children's homes for those aged eight to 11. Finally they recommended that direct responsibility should be transferred to the Secretary of State for provision on a regional basis.

This last recommendation, unlikely to be accepted at any time, was, with Kilbrandon on the horizon, a non-starter. The other recommendations had some effect, in as much as new remand homes were opened in Dundee, Edinburgh, Dumbartonshire and Lanarkshire, as well as an extension to facilities for boys in Glasgow. New regulations, the *Remand Home (Scotland) Rules 1964*, were also promulgated.

There were brave efforts to improve an overloaded and essentially unworkable system, but the poor staffing, repressive regimes and bad traditions persisted. In spite of physical improvements the remand homes continued throughout the period as a small semi-slum backwater of child care in Scotland.

Training

In 1948 in England amongst those who launched Children's Departments there were, even including children's officers, few trained staff, and this continued as the single greatest lack of the first decade. The need had been anticipated by Curtis to the extent of issuing an interim report on training early in 1946. In July 1947 the Central Training Council in Child Care was formed, which came to be serviced by a team of Home Office inspectors ably lead by a member of Curtis, Miss Sybil Clement Brown, a former LSE teacher and associate of Miss Eileen Younghusband.

Courses of a year's duration were set up for boarding out visitors, soon to be re-christened child care officers, at four universities and by 1948/49 at six. These were open to persons under 40 who were graduates and/or qualified in social science, teaching or health visiting. By 1960 these courses had produced 681 women and 67 men with the Certificate in Child Care, but the Home Office in its report of that year was still concerned that the lack of qualified child care officers was hindering preventive work and the finding of more foster homes.[34] On the residential side, which had been the main concern of Curtis, initiatives were even faster. Courses of six months in college and eight months work and study, for young persons with no pre-entry qualification, put the first trained personnel in post by Spring 1949. By the end of 1960 about eight different courses run by authorities and voluntary organisations had produced over 2,000 house parents.

A further training influence on the development of child care, particularly as a family service, was the 'Carnegie Course' set up in 1954 as an experiment at LSE to train graduates as social workers in child care, medical social work and probation, on a generic social work basis. This had an influence out of all proportion to its numbers.[35] In spite of the proper reservations of the Home Office, the 1950s saw a major assault on the problem of training, and trained personnel continued to enter child care in the 1960s in England and Wales, who had considerable influence on the changes of that decade.

The history of training in Scotland was 'too late and too little'. While some of the universities had been running degree or diploma courses since the end of the war, the first course of professional training in child care only started in Edinburgh in 1960, prior to which training had to be gained on the English courses mentioned above. Students found a welcome there, and in many cases stayed on where work and salaries were attractive. In 1960 there were less than 20 trained child care staff in Scottish local authorities, and even in 1968 out of a total of 305 only 60 had professional and 57 basic qualifications.[36] The position was worst in the large burghs, where in 1962 only one, Greenock, had any qualified staff. The Clyde Committee had given a clear recommendation — 23 — 'that a training committee should be set up to prepare the necessary schemes of training and examinations for the staff of Homes, and for persons engaged in child care work'. The Scottish Home and Health Department cannot escape the major blame for the failure over 15 years to have this central recommendation implemented. As mentioned earlier, action had to await the initiative of the Scottish Advisory Council's report of 1963, *Staffing of Local Authority Children's Departments*, immediately after which the Training Committee was set up and undertook a study of needs.

Even after that the establishment of courses was difficult and slow, not least because of the scarcity of tutors and supervisors for practical work. The difficulties were further complicated by the question of the adequacy for child care purposes of the pilot Younghusband course started in Glasgow in 1961, and the movement towards generic courses at LSE and elsewhere. Yet new courses proliferated in 1967, 1968 and 1969 — 20 years after the Act — of one year, two years and three years for the different types of needs, graduates, experienced workers and less mature students. Residential child care was expanded in these years by preliminary courses in Edinburgh and Glasgow, basic courses at Langside and an advanced course at the University of Glasgow. By 1966/67 there were almost 30 students in fieldwork courses in Scotland, much effort was put into training and generally high standards were achieved. Overall it was too late to have a major impact on child care in Scotland, but it was an important investment for the future.

CHILDREN NEGLECTED IN THEIR OWN HOMES AND CO-ORDINATING COMMITTEES.

The Children Act had scarce become operational before it was realised that it only dealt with part of the problem of family breakdown, which earlier intervention might alleviate or prevent. In fact at the committee stage of the Bill, Dr Somerville Hastings had sought an amendment to put the local authorities under a duty to assist in the rehabilitation of the parents of neglected children. This had to wait a further 15 years till section one of the Children and Young Person's Act of 1963. The Home Secretary resisted by suggesting that such powers already lay with the health, education and probation services, but promised to draw local authorities' attention to the need.[37] This was done in the introductory circulars to the Act, Home Office 160/48 of 8 July and the Scottish Home Department Circular of 6 August 1948. This latter reads, 'While the provisions of the Act relate only to children who have had the misfortune to be deprived of a normal home life, the importance must also be kept in mind of doing all that is possible to save the children from suffering this misfortune. Where a home can be so improved that it is unnecessary to remove a child from his parents or that a child who has been taken away for a time can properly be restored to his parents care, the advantage is of course unquestionable'. At this stage however, the local authorities, already hard pressed by having to produce staff and buildings to implement as yet unmeasured new commitments, had neither the resources nor the stomach to pursue too seriously this sanguine exhortation, which amounted to willing the ends without providing either the legal of financial means.

Yet the dilemma would not go away. A powerful and perspicacious report by the Women's Group on Public Welfare, *The Neglected Child and His Family*, Oxford University Press 1948, brought the issue back into the public arena. Discussion in parliament ensued, and a working party of officials from the Home, Health and Education Departments in England and Scotland was set up. They reported against further statutory measures, which would then have been an embarrassing admission, in favour of administrative measures to fully co-ordinate existing services. The necessary circulars were issued in 1950 suggesting that each authority should designate an officer to be responsible for co-ordinating the work of the statutory and voluntary agencies concerned with the welfare of children in their own homes.[38] Apart from children's departments these included Welfare, Health, Housing, Probation, RSSPCC and the National Assistance Board. The Younghusband Report of the Working Party on Social Workers (1959), tabulating the implementation of co-ordinating arrangements, shows that in Scotland 30 areas had set up both designated officers and committee machinery, 13 had designated officers only and nine had taken no action. As in England and Wales, children's officers were the designated officers in half the areas concerned. For many of the small Scottish authorities co-ordinating machinery was artificial and superfluous, as the officials were already in close working relationship, or indeed discharged duties for various departments under different hats.

The working of co-ordinating committees was reviewed both in the report of the Younghusband Committee of 1959 and *The Neglected Child and the Social Services* by David Donnison in 1954. Both these studies are concerned with how the co-ordinating machinery was working as an administrative and professional device, and at that stage did not draw any general conclusions. Co-ordination became a major industry in the local authorities of the 1950s, but failed to make any significant impact on the problem. This was due to various factors such as inter-departmental strife, particularly in housing matters, lack of confidence in the training and expertise of other disciplines, and the reality that effective power and decision making lay not with officials but with committees, who were not empowered or even generally motivated to intervene. Even where it functioned well, there were not always staff with sufficient time or training to implement the decisions.

The Problem Family

The problem for which co-ordinating machinery proved inadequate was *The Problem of The Problem Family*, as expressed by the title of the work by A. F. Philp and Noel Timms of 1962. This is a critical review of the writing on the subject up to 1956, starting from the classification points of (a) the failure of families to attain certain minimal standards, and (b) their failure to benefit from social services. They suggest that the actual term 'problem family' was first specifically used in 1948 by the Women's Group on Public Welfare in their *The Neglected Child and His Family*, mentioned above.

Even in the decade up to 1948 there were at least six written works by medical officers of English cities, concerned about infant mortality and maternal welfare, or the failure to take up welfare foods and to use the services of nurses and sanitary inspectors. This concern soon spread to housing managers, school welfare officers and others. Donnison showed that many of these families were known to at least six agencies, and quotes an instance of a probation officer arriving at a house to find a mother already being interviewed by other three officials and a councillor.[39]

In the 1950s 'problem families' because of welfare state provisions and rising standards became more obtrusive to baffled officialdom and obvious to a puzzled public. Where in the past it had gone unnoticed or accepted as the inevitable lot, the blatant persistence of these unreformed disadvantaged now stood out as a monument to the welfare revolution's failure. The new children's department's involvement, direct or through co-ordination, was the final lever to prize the 'problem family' out of the Poor Law penumbra direct on to the centre stage of the welfare state.

To meet this problem beyond the resources of their standard staff, the various services experimented with a variety of aides. These included NSPCC women visitors, special visitors for unmarried mothers, home advisers and residential housemothers. The emphasis of the time was on the bucket and brush technique as opposed to the notebook and pen. Perhaps the most notable and effective contribution was made by the Family Service Units starting in Liverpool in 1947 and expanding to at least a further six English cities. These derived from wartime Pacifist Service Units, and were mainly untrained amateurs living locally in groups, who on a religious basis believed in the worth of each individual and the power of love expressed through practical help and care. They offered supporting friendship and gave practical help with home-making, domestic activities and child care, all of which provided a basis for sympathetic discussion and advice. They had the merit of not being concerned with service to particular individuals or special needs, and were an early form of total family service. A more formal and institutional approach were the mother-craft training homes. These mainly derived from Brentwood, Lancashire, an experimental pre-war residential centre for mothers in need of recuperation with their young families. In 1948 the Salvation Army opened a training home in Plymouth, the Mayflower, for mothers convicted of neglect and put on probation. This was followed in 1952 by a Quaker foundation, Spofforth Hall, Harrogate, and St Mary's Mothercraft Training Centre, Dundee.

These centres received mothers with their young children and tried to train them in basic domestic skills, home-making and child care. One of the great needs discovered incidentally was for simple companion-ship and social life, of which many of these immature women were chronically starved. Apart from training in isolation from community the other major weakness was the non-involvement of fathers. Yet these training homes saved many from the prison sentences of the time, effected some real and temporary improvements in their family life, and were a practical though limited contribution to a major problem of the period.

The literature on this subject as it affected Scotland is sparse. Out of the 154 works listed by Philp and Timms as written up to 1956 there is nothing of substance in the Scottish context. This was not because it was not manifest or undiagnosed. Such families were legend in the records of health, housing, education, welfare and children's depart-ments. The staff concerned knew their 'problem families' well, having struggled with them for years. Perhaps it was because they accepted the phenomenon as a natural perennial that they did not attempt to systematise or jargonise. Exceptionally John Mack, Stevenson Lecturer in Citizenship at Glasgow, submitted in 1953 a private report to the Carnegie United Kingdom Trust entitled *Family and Community*. However, this erudite and wide-ranging work, discussed in the next chapter, contributes little to our understanding of Scottish child care practice, as it is essentially delinquency oriented, and draws its mate-rial mainly from England. The problem began to receive general attention in Scotland a decade or so later than in England. One of the few clear pictures of thinking on the subject is given in a report of papers presented to a conference in Peebles 1963, *Working Together: Problem Families*, organised by the Royal Institute of Public Administration. Apart from a call for increased practical help, soon to be legitimised by the Children and Young Person Act of 1963, the main emphasis was on early identification and a trained family case-work service.

By this time a few smaller authorities, mainly counties, were recruiting staff for the purpose, and the children's officer of Angus in evidence to the Kilbrandon Committee claimed intensive family case-work in an attempt to treat the problem and not the symptoms.[40] Additionally, in Aberdeen and Edinburgh the Councils of Social Services were, on a small scale, building up case-work services for families. Paisley Burgh had responded to the problem on the housing front as early as 1942 by setting up 'Supervised Dwellings' on the Dutch model, and followed this by establishing a lightly staffed Home Service Unit in 1960. Glasgow Health and Welfare Department also tried various minor 'family welfare units' in a few deprived housing areas in the 1960s, but the Family Service Unit movement as known in England never took root in Scotland. There was no strong lead from the Scottish Office who pleaded lack of trained social workers to account for lack of activity of this type.

It was in Dundee, with its strong voluntary tradition of supplementing deficient public services, that the only major residential approach was developed. A bishop's wife, Mrs Graham, while local chairman of RSSPCC, was shocked at seeing inadequate young mothers sent to prison for child abuse and neglect. Together with like-minded people from statutory and voluntary services she found a large house in the town, and launched St Mary's Mothercraft Training Centre, an expression of religious caring run on interdenominational lines from 1952 to 1972. This was a further example of an enlightened individual in Scotland giving a lead for new policy departures to avoid imprisonment, as we saw Bailie Mack do in the 1840s in Edinburgh with juveniles, and Bailie Murray in Glasgow for probation in 1905. Registered as a probation home it catered mainly for young mothers sent by the courts on probation, although it also admitted cases from health and children's departments. From limited beginnings it expanded, and at its peak was catering for up to 20 mothers per year and 48 children, mainly under school age, eight mothers and families at any one time. After early trial and error with admissions, they found that their greater success was with cases characterised by poor health, over-frequent child bearing and poor housing, but less where low grade intelligence, alcoholism or promiscuity were features. The regime was one of training in domestic skills and child care along with caring for the mother and some counselling. As with other such centres mentioned above, the major weakness lay in its limited influence, apart from during weekly visits or the monthly overnight stay, on the immature or ineffectual fathers who were a central defect in the family functioning.

There has been no major study of this pioneer work, and little record remains beyond the series of annual reports from 1952 to 1970. It is interesting to note in the report of 1962 that there were fewer such mothers appearing in court, and the local authorities seemed more able and willing to treat them in their own community. This was probably due to some improvements in children's departments staffing and functioning, and also to considerable field activity by health departments constantly exhorted by the Department of Health to deploy their health visitors and domiciliary service to this end.

The Committee on the Prevention of Neglect of Children 1961-63

(The McBoyle Committee and Report — Cmnd. 1966)

The Ingleby Committee was appointed by the Home Secretary in 1956 and reported in 1960 (Cmnd. 1191). The Kilbrandon Committee was appointed in 1961 by the Secretary of State for Scotland and reported in 1964 (Cmnd. 2306). Sandwiched between these was McBoyle — 1961 to 1963 — a committee of the Scottish Advisory Council on Child Care, originating in a request from the Secretary of State to advise him 'whether local authorities in Scotland should, taking into account their existing statutory responsibilities and powers, and the activities of voluntary organisations, be given new powers and duties to forestall the suffering of children through neglect in their own homes'. This remit was included as an extra feature of Ingleby but not of Kilbrandon, both commissioned primarily to consider the powers of the courts affecting juveniles.

The McBoyle Committee, consisting of five Advisory Council members and five Secretary of State nominees, were closer to local authority services and this specific child care issue than their Ingleby counterparts. Not least was this true of Mr J. McBoyle under whom the committee functioned with commitment and precision.[41] The resulting report is logical and decisive. After outlining events leading to recognition of the problem, and the setting up of co-ordinating machinery, it identifies the origins of neglect cases and the nature of 'problem families'. It concludes that the two major weaknesses of existing services were the barriers of communication and the absence of sufficient trained case-workers. McBoyle was more direct than the Younghusband or Ingleby Committees in recognising the failure of co-ordination, and ascribed it to the fact that co-ordinating officers and co-ordinating committees had not been directly answerable to any local authority committee.

The main recommendations were that local authorities should be given powers to provide a comprehensive service for the prevention of neglect, which would include the giving of practical help in kind or cash, family advice centres and the provision of training centres for families who could not be rehabilitated in their own homes. The report was presented to Parliament in March 1963, by which time the Children and Young Person's Bill, inspired largely by Ingleby's similar findings, was at second reading and soon to receive royal assent in July.

In October of that year the Children and Young Person's Act 1963 became operational, and under section one, local authorities in Scotland, as well as England and Wales, were given the long awaited duty to undertake preventive work with families and the power to give assistance in kind, or cash where necessary, to promote the welfare of children by diminishing the need to receive them into or keep them in care. In the event McBoyle came too late to have much impact on the Act. It did however have the effect of awakening Scottish local authorities to the importance of the issues, and, as a forerunner to Kilbrandon, registering the fact that Scotland was capable of some independent thought on child care and social work matters, and need not blindly follow the patterns of the South.

Preventive Work

For reasons already explained there was little serious rehabilitative work in the first 12 years. In the early 1960s it started in a modest way in children's departments. Health departments too had become more active on this front after a Department of Health circular (DHS 73/1954) drawing attention to the ill effects on children of family break-up, and exhorting them to deploy their health visitors and domiciliary services as far as possible. Some light on preventive work of the period is provided in a study by Tom Burns and Susan Sinclair of Edinburgh University on the use of professional time in seven children's departments in 1960. The results of this are contained in a report to the Scottish Advisory Council on Child Care, entitled *The Child Care Service at Work*, HMSO 1963. It shows an average of 12% of professional time spent on preventive work as compared to 41% on supervision of children in care. In the six remaining years after the 1963 Act preventive work got under way, as can be seen from the reports *Child Care in Scotland*, presented annually by the Secretary of State to Parliament. Casework with families not involving children coming into care increased until in 1969 it included 12,980 families and 40,735 children. At the same time the figures for reception or committal to care were 1,373 families and 3,323 children.[42]

Measures other than case-work were family aides, specialised home helps and use of foster mothers for day care. There was increased sharing and co-operating between departments, with the setting up of registers of 'problem families', passing of information on impending evictions, and even bringing social service departments together in one building. Under section one of the Act, the forerunner of section 12 of the

Social Work Act, there was a rapidly increasing use of cash support on rent and fuel arrears, which for the former doubled between 1966 and 1969, and for the latter nearly tripled. In these years much work went into obtaining repayments, an surprisingly enough at least a third was recouped under both headings.

Children's officers might point to the considerably greater expense avoided by these payments, but not all were convinced. In many areas treasurers and members of all political complexions, anxious about subsidising what to them was fecklessness, continued to be critical and unreasonably demanding. Committees habitually insisted on loans rather than grants and were sometimes niggardly and short-sighted.

Assessment

The account of Scottish child care to this point may seem to some unduly critical or at least less generous than warranted by the prevailing tradition of the superiority of children's departments in the social work stakes of the period. However, it must be realised that this was a relative claim, somewhat enhanced by the high profile of child care officers at the time of re-organisation, and the fact that they were the professionals best prepared to educate, train and influence the first generations of new social workers.

To correct any overall apparent imbalance, two major positive, progressive influences of the period need to be further adduced. The first of these is the Advisory Council, particularly in the years 1956-65 under the influential leadership of Lady Elliot. This consisted of members eminent in child care in its widest sense, together with some from medicine, the universities and the churches. They received secretarial support and close attention from the senior civil servants responsible for child care. In the few years 1961 to 1963 they produced the valuable reports already mentioned on Remand Homes, Staffing of Children's Departments and the Prevention of Neglect of Children (McBoyle). They also sponsored from Edinburgh University *The Child Care Service at Work*, HMSO 1963, which analysed the use of professional time in children's departments.

The second major positive influence came in the 1960s from a small group of child care officers, some of whom had seen service in England. In default of strong initiatives from the children's officers, they formed the Scottish regional branch of the Association of Child Care Officers, a leading organisation in the promotion of professional work with children and families from 1948 to 1970. At the inaugural meeting in 1954 there were 22 people, and in the last Scottish year of 1969 there were 194 members, with always a good and influential proportion from voluntary organisations. They held some joint conferences with the

Scottish Children's Officers Association, but close working relations unfortunately never developed. The Scottish branch exercised a great influence on ACCO and through this on major developments at UK level. In Scotland they were listened to by sympathetic ears in Scottish Education Department, and were also influential latterly on staffing and training, through the medium of the Advisory Council's discussions and reports. Their greatest achievement was in their campaign between 1964 and 1968 for an integrated social service, of which they, among all the separate services, were the foremost and most effective espousers, as will be seen in the next chapters on the re-organisation of social work.

The overall picture of the child care service produced by the 1948 Act is varied. In England, after early pre-occupation with merely finding places in a situation of escalating numbers and unsuitable accommodation, there was an early move towards preventive work with families, pioneered by a corps of able children's officers. This was by no means universal, and there were areas in England and Wales where this progressive pattern did not obtain. The pioneering work led on through Ingleby to the Children and Young persons Act of 1963, which legalised and promoted preventive work. In spite of this early, remarkable progress, the final steps towards a re-organised family service were slower, less certain and less radical than in Scotland.

Here the early problem of accommodation for children in care was largely solved by the long-standing, however unsophisticated, practice of boarding out most children, which was indeed the answer prescribed by the Clyde Committee. The first responsible central authority, the Scottish Home Department, gave a less certain and inspired lead to child care than the Home Office for England and Wales. The position improved from 1961 under the stewardship of the Scottish Education Department, where the administrative side, even more than the professional, gave a positive and progressive lead. The local authorities failed to appoint new style children's officers of high calibre, and generally starved the service of staff, building and resources. A situation report on nine of the large burghs by the Chief Inspector in July 1967 refers to the handicap of size in most cases, and in others 'extreme cheese paring', shortage of staff, and children's officers untrained, poorly paid and lacking in local authority status.[43] One of the greatest defects was the failure to establish training facilities until a late date, for which the Scottish Office must bear the major blame.

In the first ten years there was only limited development in fieldwork practice or residential provision, and the service remained static and inadequate for changing needs. The year of awakening was 1963, and if there were a golden age of child care in Scotland, it was the last five years 1964 to 1969. From a low base line, staffing, general provision and practice improved, while philosophies developed for the advance to an integrated service on a scale which the other separate services were not able to match.

From antiquated attitudes and poor provision, there was a slow and unenthusiastic move to implementation of the Children Act in Scotland. The last lap however, if not distinguished in comparative terms, was a laudable professional push to match progress elsewhere, and ended by providing a major plank for the edifice of the Social Work Service which followed.

NOTES

1. Sir W. Clark Hall, The Queen's Reign for Children, T. Fisher Unwin 1897.
2. Brian Ashley, A Stone on the Mantlepiece, A Centenary History of the RSSPCC, Scottish Academic Press 1985.
3. 'Children's Charter' was first used to describe an Act for the Prevention of Cruelty to and Better Protection of Children, 1889. It has also been occasionally used of The Children Act, 1948.
4. Sixth Report on the Work of the Children's Department (Home Office) HMSO, May 1951, p. 6.
5. Jean S. Heywood, Children in Care, Routledge and Kegan Paul, revised 1978 p. 161.
6. For instance 'Love is Not Enough', Bruno Bettleheim, Glencoe 1950, and 'Group work in the Institutions', Gisella Konopka, New York 1954.
7. Sylvia Watson, The Children's Departments and the 1963 Act — services for children and their families, Pergamon Press 1972.
8. Jean Packman, The Child's Generation, Basil Blackwell p. 109. The writer had a hand in that inspection and report.
9. Jean S. Heywood, Children in Care, Routledge and Kegan Paul, revised 1978, p. 195.
10. Ibid. p. 153.
11. D. V. Donnison, chapter 5 of Trends in Social Welfare edited by J. Farndale, Pergamon Press 1965, p. 41.
12. Thos. Ferguson, The Dawn of Social Welfare in Scotland, Nelson 1948, p. 285.
13. Keeper of the Records of Scotland, vol. B66/15/5, Stirling Burgh Court Record, 9 October 1562.
14. Thos. Ferguson, The Dawn of Welfare in Scotland, Nelson 1948, p. 288.
15. Ibid. p. 288.
16. Ibid. p. 292.
17. The Village — A History of Quarrier's Homes, Anna Magnusson, Quarrier's Homes 1984.
The Aberlour Centenary Year — Aberlour Trust 1975.
18. Woman's Viewpoint, Glasgow Herald 21.7.50.
19. Report of the Committee on Homeless Children (Clyde) para. 73, HMSO 1946, Cmnd. 6911.
20. Scottish Record office ED 11/293, Minute of 1.5.47 signed C.C.C., to Mr G. H. Henderson.
21. Ibid. ED 11/357, letter from Chief Welfare Officer, Glasgow dated 31.3.48.
22. Ibid. ED 11/357, Minute of 28.5.48 signed R.S.A.
23. Ibid. ED 11/357, undated Minute on Meeting of 10.5.48.
24. SWSG K/19/4, 10.6.67 Social Work staffing.

25. Alan A. Jacka, The Acco Story 1973. Distributed by BASW.
26. Letter to the *Scotsman* of 7.10.63 from Julia Robertson and Ruth Ross, Senior Child Care Officers, Midlothian.
27. These included Nigel Walker, later holder of posts in criminology at Oxford and Cambridge, Andrew Rowe, later academic and MP, and most notably J.O. Johnston, first director of Social Work for Glasgow.
28. Ayr County Council Welfare Committee Minutes, January 1948.
29. Scottish Home Department, Children in Care of Local Authorities in Scotland 1958, HMSO Cmnd. 779.
30. Woman's Viewpoint, *Glasgow Herald* 4.8.50.
31. Babies and Young Children in Residential Nurseries, Interim Report of the Committee appointed by the Scottish Advisory Council on Child Care — accompanying SWSG Circular 18/1971.
32. Lady Majorie Allen, Whose Children? Favil Press Ltd., 1945.
33. SHD Circular No. 7183 of 19.7.49. Children Act 1948, National Health Service (Scotland) Act 1947 — Children's Homes and Nurseries. Summary of replies from Town Clerks.
34. Eighth Report on the Work of the Children's Department (Home Office) HMSO 1961, para. 99.
35. Alma E. Hartshorn, Milestone in Education for Social Work, Carnegie United Kingdom Trust 1982.
36. Social Work; Report of a Working Party on the Social Work (Scotland) Act, Edinburgh University 1969, Appendix D.
37. PRO HH 61/44 letter from Mr Younger, Home Office to Mr Edwards, Minister of Health, 22.7.48.
38. Home Office Circular 157/50, Scottish Home Department Circular 7497 of 1950.
39. D. V. Donnison, The Neglected Child and the Social Services p. 74.
40. SWSG REcords CYP (62) 19, Appendix B. The Future of the Child Care Service.
41. J. McBoyle was a former County Clerk of Midlothian, who had shown interest in 'problem families', and had presented a paper at the RIPA conference in Peebles 1963 RIPA — Working Together: Problem Families 1963.
42. Social Work in Scotland 1969, HMSO Cmnd. 4475, 1970.
43. Report to Mr Rowe, signed by C. R. Corner 24.7.67, SWSG Records K/6/42.

CHAPTER 7

The Kilbrandon Report, Children's Hearings and Sequels

'If, towards the end of the 1960s, some United Nations official expert in comparative social statistics had been asked to compile a short list of countries in which an original and forward-looking system of juvenile justice was likely to become firm rooted, it is unlikely that he would have ranked Scotland high amongst his priorities.'
Martin and Murray, Childrens Hearings, 1976, p. 233.

Kilbrandon and Kilchattan is the name of an Argyll coastal parish south of Oban, from which Charles James Dalrymple Shaw (1906-1989) took his title on becoming a Scottish judge. Shaw was involved, either as a member or chairman, of at least three other important committees or commissions of the period — the Scottish Law Commission, the Scottish Standing Committee on the Youth Service, and last, but by no means least, the Commission on the Constitution, which preceded the referendum of 1979 on devolution for Scotland. For our purposes, the common term Kilbrandon Report refers to the recommendations of the Committee on Children and Young Persons set up by the Secretary of State for Scotland in May 1961 and presented to Parliament as a report (Cmnd. 2306) in April 1964. Lord Kilbrandon was Chairman.

Up to this point, as noted in earlier chapters, the literature on personal social services in Scotland is exiguous. By contrast much has been written about Kilbrandon, mainly as a prelude to extensive descriptions and investigations of the Children's Hearing System. More notable general works include *The Scottish Juvenile Justice System* edited by Martin and Murray 1982, *The Creation of the British Personal Social Services* by Joan Cooper 1983, and *Martin, Fox and Murray, Children Out of Court*, S.A.P., 1981. Most recently in 1988, a detailed and authoritative 'administrative/political' study, entitled *The Emergence of the Scottish Children's Hearings System*; has been published by the Institute of Criminal Justice of Southampton University. This fine exposition of Kilbrandon and its immediate sequels is the work of D. J. Cowperthwaite who, for most of the time, was the Assistant Secretary leading the Division of Scottish Home Department, which launched Kilbrandon and saw developments through to the establishment of the Social Work Services Group in 1967. This chapter owes some debt to all these sources, particularly to the last, but the emphasis and direction here is quite different, being concerned more with the origins of the whole social work service rather than the children's hearings aspect in particular.

The Ingleby Committee, which had been set up to advise on the law and procedures in respect of juveniles in England and Wales, achieved little in this respect, but under its secondary remit on children neglected in their own homes, produced effective recommendations to legitimise preventive work with families under the Children and Young Persons Act of 1963. Ingleby established in October 1956, reported in October 1960.

It was a consequence of Ingleby that the Secretary of State, responsible for similar Scottish services, had become committed as early as 1958 to some form of enquiry following pressures from professional interests and a question raised in parliament in that year.[1] At this point senior civil servants in the Scottish Office advised that enquiries might be facilitated and made more effective by separating the two main remits with which Ingleby had laboured. Acting on this, in January 1960, one committee under the Chairmanship of Mr James McBoyle was set up to enquire into the neglect of children in their own home. The McBoyle Committee reported in January 1963, largely confirming the Ingleby findings on this aspect. (It also ensured the incorporation of Scotland into the 1963 Act.) The second, a more high-powered committee, was established in the same year under Lord Kilbrandon to concentrate on a remit similar to Ingleby's prime task, 'to consider the provisions of the law of Scotland relating to the treatment of juvenile delinquents, and juveniles in need of care or protection, or beyond parental control, and in particular, the constitution powers and procedure of the courts dealing with such juveniles, and to report'. This was the apparently simple directive which resulted in the major transformation of juvenile justice, and which, even less predictably, carried the seeds of the reorganisation of personal social services, realised through the provisions of the Social Work (Scotland) Act of 1968.

If Ingleby was the main event that precipitated the Scottish enquiries, we still need to look at the underlying factors that conduced to both Ingleby and Kilbrandon. As explained in the last chapter, two converging paths led up to the enquiry for England and Wales. One was the concern of child care professionals that both deprived and delinquent children came from similar backgrounds, but were treated differently by the mere accident of which law delivered them for public action. The other was the dilemma of the lay magistrates trying to reconcile two conflicting principles — the theory of the welfare of the child, and the criminal concept of guilt and punishment.

These concerns were being rehearsed against a background of the following sociological trends. During the war, for a variety of reasons, delinquency had escalated in England and in Scotland, and for that matter in Germany.[2] To meet the flood with which juvenile courts could barely cope, the official practical response in England was to open extra remand and approved school places, including classifying schools. The latter were to assess the character and the needs of the boys concerned, to regulate the flow, and to study the phenomenon of delinquency. After the Criminal Justice Act of 1948 these measures were further supplemented by the expanded use of probation, probation hostels and attendance centres, as discussed in chapter five. Yet all this had little obvious impact on the overall pattern, and the 1950s and the 1960s in England were decades when juvenile delinquency became a major preoccupation of psychologists, sociologists and criminologists, including such authorities as Bowlby, Wooton and Mannheim. With parliament and public concerned, academics and administrators occupied themselves seeking causes and solutions. Scotland, with age-old memories of serious disorders and lawlessness, remained relatively impassive and philosophic over apparently minor juvenile troubles. Despite eighteenth century overtures by Adam Ferguson and other Scots, the sociologists had scarcely arrived here, and there were limited resources and time for such fringe activities in the serious study programmes of the four ancient universities.[3]

Throughout the period in England, grandiose ideas proliferated but were never realised. As early as 1945, at a Howard League Conference, a leading woman magistrate was proposing the replacement of juvenile courts by child welfare councils, while a former Home Office chief inspector was advocating a ministry of child welfare.[4] The Scandinavian panel system continued as a distant aspiration of various theorists until superseded by Ingleby and events in Scotland.

Ingleby, because of its remit, but even more because of its composition, was never open to such radical ideas, as is abundantly clear from the report (para. 83) 'In our view the question is not whether there should be legal proceedings in respect of children before any particular age, but what kind of proceedings would be most suitable — The change that we recommend is essentially one of procedure.'

In June 1964 the Labour Party in opposition produced a pamphlet *Crime, A Challenge to Us All*, which diagnosed the correlation between delinquency and deprivation, questioned the anachronism of juvenile courts, and expressed a belief in a comprehensive family service based on social work. On arrival in power, the new Labour Government had to convert this into an official White Paper — *The Child, the Family and the Young Offender* — Cmnd. 2742 of August 1965, which advocated informal 'family council' procedures based on consent to treatment by children's departments, or, where compulsory measures were required, through 'family courts' under civil proceedings. England was not ready for such radical reform, and this progressive White Paper had to be dropped after much opposition from powerful lobbies of magistrates and others, who believed in the need to preserve the difference between the guilty offender and the innocent non-offender. It was followed in April 1968 by a new White Paper, *Children in Trouble*, Cmnd. 3601, which proposed the retention of juvenile courts with powers to make 'supervision orders' for treatment in the community or 'care orders' for those requiring to be committed to care. This led, after major opposition and minor amendments in parliament, to the Children and Young Persons Act of 1969.

The passing of such large responsibilities to the Social Services Departments has given rise to conflict between juvenile courts and local authorities ever since, and various adjustments have been made in the law and otherwise. At the best, the Children and Young Persons Act 1969 proved unsatisfactory for England and Wales. At the worst it may be described as an ineffectual compromise which settled nothing.

In Scotland, as elsewhere, the incidence of juvenile delinquency, i.e., for ages 8-17, increased markedly during the war years 1940-46. After a temporary lull and fluctuations, it rose steadily between 1956 and 1962. While illustrating this in Appendix A as a rise from 2.1% to 2.9% of the population at risk — amounting to over 6,000 cases, the Kilbrandon Committee, in para. 8 of their report, made the somewhat cautious conclusion 'The figures suggest that in relation to the total child population, juvenile delinquency in Scotland has remained over the post-war period at a surprisingly steady rate, which is not greatly in excess of the pre-war rate (1.8% in 1938)'.

A contemporary Scottish authority, John Mack, commenting in 1953, gives a less complacent and more balanced assessment of the post-war position. On the basis of looking at trends he says 'By this test the post-war movement of crime is thoroughly disquieting in England and Wales, while in Scotland it gives ground for moderate concern. And that, broadly speaking, corresponds to the actual state of public opinion in the two countries'. Looking at the actual figures and even allowing for higher rates of reporting by the Scottish Police, he concludes 'The perplexing fact remains that in the field of juvenile crime the remarkable post-war increase in England and Wales still leaves that country (sic) comfortably below the level maintained by Scotland, and maintained in that country with a comparative degree of equanimity'.[5]

Whatever the interpretation, charges proved against juveniles increased from 15,329 to 21,912 between 1956 and 1962.[6] These were dealt with under the Children and Young Persons (Scotland) Act of 1937, and the general pattern of disposals was as follows. In about a third of the cases there was 'no action'. A similar number were put on probation, and about a sixth were fined. Some 5% were committed to approved schools and an even smaller number were sent to remand homes for 28 days detention. In a very small number of cases, parents were fined or required to find caution.[7] Comparatively few offenders were committed to the care of the local authority as a fit person, and even as late as 1961-62 children's departments colluded in a substantial number of care or protection fit person cases, mainly older children, being committed to approved schools. How much action or inaction was due to underdeveloped professional child care practice, or an overdeveloped local authority sense of economy, or simply a lack of resources, is difficult to determine.[8]

Thus, while over 80% were dealt with by relatively undemanding non-custodial measures, the problems did not obtrude too dramatically at local, central or public levels. The places where pressures mounted were behind the walls of the remand homes and the approved schools. Numbers admitted annually to the former increased over the period to reach a post-war peak of 6,681 in 1969. As explained in the last chapter, both premises and staffing were quite inadequate for normal running, even more so at peaks, and little was done to remedy this till after the Advisory Council Report, *Remand Homes* of 1961.

Numbers in approved schools having soared during the war, declined in the 1950s and schools were closed. In the 1960s numbers again increased, and, with relative speed and at no little expense, the Scottish Education Department responded by opening eight new schools.[9] These served not only to increase provision, but to replace barrack buildings, improve the basis for physical care, and generally to supplement an all round deficiency of residential places in child care, special education and mental hospitals. If, as suggested in the last chapter, the remand homes were a slum area of child care, then approved schools were often a disposal bin for the failures or rejects of somewhat narrow child care and education systems.

One group which could not share the detached philosophical view of increasing delinquency were the chief constables and the police, particularly in Glasgow and the West, where the problem was most severe. During the 1960s a long established practice of police warning was developed into a system of 'juvenile warnings', whereby first offenders were formally warned in the presence of their parents by a senior police officer. Of the several thousand warned annually — over 4,000 in 1962 — it was claimed that 90% did not come to police notice in the immediate future. The other measure strongly promoted at this time by Chief Constables was police 'juvenile liaison schemes'. Originating in Liverpool in 1952, they were established in Greenock, and spread from there to Stirlingshire, Coatbridge, Kilmarnock and Paisley. This was an extension of 'juvenile warnings', whereby a selected 'juvenile liaison officer' exercised a period of supervision over a boy by visits to his home, and with parental consent, to school. Great claims were made for these schemes which were assessed from time to time in considerable detail by John Mack.[10]

The discipline of the period most concerned with deviant juveniles was psychology. Prominent in this were the psychiatrists based on the Douglas Inch Forensic clinic in Glasgow, who influenced teams of psychiatrists, psychologists and social workers operating in borstals and approved schools. Amongst these, and in some educational and legal circles, a Scottish Scandinavian tendency developed which showed interest in the child welfare and panel systems of these countries. This interest, nourished by the Director of the Danish Institute in Edinburgh, culminated in a grand tour to Denmark in 1964, undertaken by psychiatrists, psychologists, probation officers, police and senior personnel from relevant branches of the Scottish Office.

Another important, though less publicised, focus of progressive thinking on child care, deviance and family problems was the child guidance movement. This had developed strongly in the Glasgow area in the 1930s and 1940s, and owed much to Sister Marie Hilda, who founded the Notre Dame Clinic in 1931 and directed it until 1951.[11] Local education authorities, notably Glasgow, followed this initiative with child guidance departments ably led by experienced psychologists, mainly women, in contrast to the English arrangement where the psychiatrists were dominant.[12] It should be noted here that none of these experts gave evidence to Kilbrandon as individuals. No doubt their voice was heard through the British Psychological Society, an improvement on the Clyde Committee procedure when, if they were heard at all, it was through the hierarchy of the directors of education. And so, by 1961, child psychology and psychiatry working from a family-centred approach, were relatively well developed in the cities of Scotland.

At an academic level, interest in and study of delinquency was mainly concentrated in the University of Glasgow. John Mack, Stevenson Lecturer in Citizenship, pursued the subject with an emphasis on the criminal sub-cultures and police juvenile liaison systems. D. H. Stott, a psychologist, approached the subject from an individual basis with emphasis on psychological and biological factors. His *Delinquency and Human Nature* was published by the Carnegie UK Trust in 1950. The Professor of Public Health and Social Medicine, Thomas Ferguson, took an epidemiological look at a sample of 1,349 Glasgow school leavers from the angles of physique, intelligence and school records. This study was published by the Oxford University Press in 1952 as 'The Young Delinquent in his Social Setting'.

The children's officers and children's committees played a relatively minor part in concern for or treatment of delinquency. It was not seen as their business. Acute problems were removed from the local authorities and the community by committals to approved schools, while the less acute were passed to probation. Children's officers saw approved schools as backward institutions controlled by powerful, dogmatic headmasters, of whom they were generally in awe. The headmasters, graduate, trained teachers, secured by the esteem of their managers and the Scottish Education Department, regarded children's officers in the main as unqualified and backward minor local authority officials, not to be compared to directors of education. These were two separate systems which seldom met, and had little direct converse or communication.

Such was the background of the years which spanned the Ingleby Committee (1956-60), and Kilbrandon (1961-64). The decision to launch Kilbrandon as a sequel to Ingleby was at Scottish ministerial level, but the immediate trigger-mechanisms were the minutes and discussions between Scottish Home and Scottish Education Departments in late 1960.[13] The fingers on the triggers were those of the assistant secretaries of these departments, amply illustrating the Hall, Land, Parker and Webb dictum, 'The principal to deputy-secretary grades of the civil service are the source and the graveyard of many ideas, initiatives and issues'.[14]

The final advice given by these officials was that Ingleby-type enquiries should be undertaken completely afresh for Scotland, and that this could best be done through two separate committees, the aspect of children neglected in their own home first being delegated to a strengthened committee of the Scottish Advisory Council on Child Care. In view of the failure of Ingleby to recommend radical changes for England and Wales, it was hoped to field a really strong and effective committee in Scotland to review the main issue of juvenile justice. To this end, on 16 March 1961, the Secretary of State announced in Parliament the establishment of a Committee on Children and Young Persons under the chairmanship of Lord Kilbrandon with the remit, 'to consider the provisions of the law of Scotland relating to the treatment of juvenile delinquents and juveniles in need of care or protection, or beyond parental control, and, in particular, the constitution, powers and procedure of the courts dealing with such juveniles, and to report'. The committee was appointed in May 1961, and so became operational five years after its English counterpart, Ingleby.

In the light of the conduct of committee and the subsequent report, most commentators agree that Kilbrandon was a fortunate choice as chairman. As indicated in the Introduction, judges are de rigueur for Scottish enquiries, and the nature of this one confirmed that tendency. Alternative suggestions included another judge, and, most adventurously, Barbara Wooton, who was soon ruled out because of her strong identification with English juvenile courts.[15] No doubt Kilbrandon was well known to the Secretary of State, as both Shaw and McLay, born at roughly the same time, originated from relatively nearby West of Scotland families, and were both prominent on the post-war Scottish scene. Kilbrandon's leadership of the Scottish Standing Committee on the Youth Service, however, made him the obvious choice.

Kilbrandon apart, there were 12 members of the committee, including a chief constable, a headmaster, a child psychiatrist and four lawyers. Of the latter, two were then sheriffs (Allan Walker and Margaret Kidd), and two were to become sheriffs. One of these last, Ronald Ireland, was at the time Professor of Scots Law at Aberdeen. This group of four, 'the sheriffs', had an immediate interest in, and practical concern for, the problems of juvenile law. The headmaster, Norman Murchison was recognised for his work with underprivileged and less able pupils. Dr Fred Stone directed the department of child and adolescent psychiatry at the Glasgow Hospital for Sick Children, later held the associated chair at Glasgow University, and was a member of the Scottish Advisory Council on Child Care.

Amongst the remainder there was experience of local authority work and juvenile courts. Mr W. Hewitson Brown, recently retired Chief Inspector of Child Care and Probation, brought in a long experience of the Scottish systems. As secretary of the Clyde Committee in 1946, he had exercised considerable influence, mainly to preserve the status quo, but conversations with surviving Kilbrandon personnel suggest that by this time his power had waned.[16]

The servicing of Kilbrandon was different from Clyde. Though less dominant, a competent and independent secretariat, Mr A. T. F. Ogilvie of the Home Department, assisted by Mr R. J. Edie from Education, made an important contribution to the workings and the report of the Committee. Mr Ogilvie at the time was a Principal in the Criminal Justice Branch, who had also worked in branches dealing with probation and child care. Further, he already had relevant experience of secretariat procedures in the major commissions on Marriage and Divorce, and on Scottish Affairs. In contrast to the Clyde Committee position noted above, he had less immediate involvement with the services being investigated, although he had a working knowledge of their activities.

At the time of Kilbrandon the historic ad hoc evolution of social reform had resulted in two separate codes governing the care and protection of children in the UK. The Children Act of 1948, examined in the last chapter, regulated the care of children deprived of a normal home life. The Children and Young Persons Acts of 1933, and 1937 (Scotland) legislated for the protection of vulnerable children, and regulated their treatment by the courts whether as offenders or in need of care or protection. For the purposes of these Acts, a child was a person under 14, and a young person was aged 14 but under 17. There was a requirement for selected persons to constitute special juvenile courts, dating, for Scotland, from an earlier Act of 1932.[17]

In England and Wales these provisions had been implemented, and magistrates' special juvenile courts had become the appropriate forum for children. For a variety of reasons there was very limited development in Scotland. The local authorities at county level were apprehensive of a change that might, inter alia, cost money, and one county, Fife, resisted through the courts up to the House of Lords. The burgh magistrates, jealous of their powers in burgh courts, also strongly opposed the new ideas. The sheriff courts, buttressed by their antiquity and prestige as leading Scottish institutions, continued their extensive business with juveniles. Faced with powerful opposition on all fronts, including the legal profession, the Scottish Office could take no strong line, and by the outbreak of war in 1939, little progress had been made after seven years of circulars, dispute and negotiations.

This is not surprising in the light of the views of the Lord Advocate of the time, as quoted by D. J. Cowperthwaite in chapter one of his work, 'It is useless to attempt to move too fast or too far in advance of public opinion — Scotland will never be reconciled to the alien institutions of the JP for the native institution of the Magistrate and the Sheriff'. And so it was that rural reluctance, municipal pride, and legal chauvinism frustrated the growth of an organised system of juvenile courts in Scotland.

The bulk of court work with juveniles continued to be transacted in the burgh and sheriff courts, and 30 years after the Act there were only four areas with specially constituted juvenile courts — the counties of Ayr, Renfrew, Fife and the City of Aberdeen. The Kilbrandon Report (para. 45) gives the distribution of activity in 1962 as follows:

Burgh Police Courts	45%	Sheriff Courts	52%
Special Juvenile Courts	15%	Ordinary JP Courts	7%

No one body had any great expertise. By the same token there was no powerful body, such as the lay magistrates in England, who held juvenile courts as a special vested interest.

The Kilbrandon Committee, appointed in May 1961, operated for almost three years, receiving and considering written and oral evidence from associations and individuals concerned with children, education, the law, and public administration.

It may be useful at this stage to compare the general approach of Kilbrandon with that of Ingleby, both charged with similar tasks through similar remits. At an early stage Ingleby had concluded 'It is the situation and the relationships within the family which seem to be responsible for many children being in trouble, whether the trouble is called delinquency or anything else. It is often the parents as much as the child who need to alter their ways, and it is therefore with family problems that any preventative measures will be largely concerned'. Having diagnosed the need for family preventative work, however, Ingleby maintained the need for a separate system of legal sanctions, 'We do not suggest that an element of compulsion can or should be eliminated. There are circumstances in which legal proceedings should be taken against parents, and, however successful preventative measures may become, there will continue to be children who should come before juvenile courts'.

Within these parameters it is not surprising that the Ingleby Committee, two thirds of whom were active in juvenile courts, concentrated largely on the powers, constitution and procedure of these courts, and reached a central conclusion that 'the juvenile court should be retained, but in its dealings with younger children, whose primary need is for care or protection, it should move further away from the conception of criminal jurisdiction' (Ingleby Report, Rec. 6).

Unlike Ingleby, Kilbrandon did not get bogged down by their remit's emphasis on 'the constitution, powers and procedure of courts'. The ambit of their consideration was mainly determined by two headings 'The Basic Problem' and 'The Underlying Principles'. Under the latter they disposed of the age of criminal responsibility as 'largely a meaningless term', and declared that 'the crime — responsibility — punishment concept — may inhibit the court in ordering the treatment the offender needs'. Under the former, by looking at the essential function of juvenile law before considering machinery, they declared 'The object must be to effect so far as this can be achieved by public action, the reduction and ideally the elimination of juvenile delinquency'. This may be taken as a measure of the radicalism and idealism of the Committee.

Working from these bases they established that 'The basic similarity of underlying situation far outweighs the differences, and, from the point of view of treatment measures, the true distinguishing factor, common to all children concerned, is their need for special measures of education and training, the normal up-bringing process, for whatever reason, having fallen short' (para. 15).

This diagnosis of the needs of the child, the failure of the upbringing process and the requirement of special measures of education, formed the foundation of Kilbrandon's recommendations. Congruent to these propositions was the assertion of 'the usefulness as a practical approach to the problem of juvenile delinquency, of regarding the child as an individual within a system of family relationships' (para. 17). While this may now seem a self-evident truth, at that time, when the emphasis of the law was on the child as an individual, it was a major break-through, if not a discovery. Having established the family as both the prime source and basis for action, Kilbrandon was clear that 'we must reject proposals for placing parents under supervision', and 'equally the practice of fining parents for their children's misdemeanours seem to be open to serious objections' (para. 22). Whereas Ingleby had recently pronounced, 'There will be circumstances in which legal proceedings should be taken against parents', Kilbrandon had leaped ahead to 'Compulsory supervision of the child can, and often will, take the shape of family case-work' (para. 21).

It might seem difficult to explain how two almost concurrent committees given the same problem under similar remits reached such divergent conclusions. Familiarity with the mores of the two systems of children's services would have suggested quite reverse results. In England under the Children Act of 1948 child care had dramatically developed and progressed to the point of widespread preventative work with families, including delinquency intervention. In Scotland as we saw earlier the service for the most part operated on its basic role of substitute care under the 1948 Act, leaving offenders and the older care or protection children to be dealt with through the courts, approved schools, and probation service. There were seen to be two categories of children, two codes of practice, and two separate agencies, ordained to operate in their own separate spheres.

Not could Scottish cultural attitudes towards inadequate families be regarded as the source of the Kilbrandon enlightenment. In child care, policies of deliberate segregation of children from their families were by no means unknown, and the authorities who genuinely practised family involvement and preventative work were by their very paucity notable, and therefor quotable to the Kilbrandon Committee.[18] In the education service, parents, particularly those of deviant children, were not generally welcome in schools, and at official level were often relentlessly prosecuted when their children failed to attend. In many housing authorities punitive politics of eviction were practised, often at the insistence of the same councillors who sat in judgment over defaulters in the education sub-committees.

It was still an age when corporal punishment of children and legal prosecution of parents were seen as the main effective measures for the reform of recalcitrant, inadequate, and back-sliding families. Though a few progressives, mainly in child care, might think otherwise, these were the general attitudes of establishment and public. The families concerned, by tradition expected such treatment, and, with or without resentment, generally acquiesced. The existence and the writ of the deity might be in doubt, but the power of the 'corporation' or 'the council' over the daily lives of the proletariat was not a matter for serious debate. It was therefore against the mainstream of Scottish tradition and practice rather than with it, that Kilbrandon had to swim.

If the explanation of the Committee's radical approach lies neither in prevailing professional practice nor in cultural attitudes, it is necessary to look elsewhere. The likeliest area for exploration would seem to be the quality of evidence or the composition of the Committee or the interaction of both. In the matter of evidence, the associations speaking for local authorities, police, the law and the courts, were generally, as might be expected against major change. The child care and the approved schools associations favoured limited change in the form of a court system more adapted to the needs of children. In this their thinking was largely conditioned by the Ingleby Report.

While it is true that the more peripheral medical and psychological professional associations espoused the ideas for radical change, it would be wrong to attribute much weight to them for the origins of the panel proposals. It is clear from discussion with the secretary and others that at an early stage the Committee had before them written information from the three main Scandinavian countries.[16] For this the secretariat made particular use of Kai Larsen the Director for the Danish Institute in Edinburgh and Professor Ola Nyquist of Uppsala University, whose writings on these systems had came to the notice of the secretary. It should be added also that a member of the Committee, Professor Ireland, had a general interest in Scandinavian culture, and took the opportunity when on holiday to inform himself on Norwegian practice.

On the balance of probability, for the prime source of the panel system, it is to the composition, transactions and leadership of the committee that a student should look, rather than to written or oral evidence of external bodies or individuals, which in the main did not suggest any radical change. The secretariat's early briefing action, and Professor Ireland's visit to Oslo may be seen as cardinal points here. As suggested above, this was a strong Committee, with a wide view of children's needs and considerable practical experience of the problems involved. Unlike Ingleby with its majority of juvenile court practitioners, there were no strong interests nor sharp professional allegiance. The 'sheriff' members took an independent line which later did not find favour with their associations. The justices of the peace were not unduly protective of juvenile courts. The education, child care, and child psychiatry members were open to new ideas.

Additionally, there were some shared common beliefs; firstly that the existing problems of delinquency and child protection were serious and related questions; secondly, that the Scottish haphazard system of courts was inappropriate; and thirdly, the idea, whether officially inspired or otherwise, that Kilbrandon must 'do a lot better than Ingleby'. These were sustained, nurtured, and directed by Lord Kilbrandon, who in the process exercised a firm but acceptable leadership. It is quite clear from discussion with those involved that Lord

Kilbrandon's own clear logic on the one hand, his receptiveness to new ideas on the other, and his great capacity of persuasiveness were paramount factors in the final unanimous decisions.

Having diagnosed the nature of the basic problem and established the principles on which it should be treated, the Kilbrandon prescription thereafter came in two parts — 'A New Machinery' and 'The Matching Field Organisation'. Under the former heading it was recommended that with the exception of cases involving a serious public interest, all children under 16 should be removed from the jurisdiction of criminal courts. Instead, in the case of offenders, truants, children beyond control, and those requiring care or protection, jurisdiction should be transferred to a system of juvenile panels. The right of the police, local authorities, and the RSSPCC, to bring proceedings at their own instance would be abolished. Instead, referral to the panels should in every case — irrespective of the basis or the source of the information — be through an independent official to be known as 'the reporter', who must be satisfied that the child fell into one of the categories listed above, and required special measures of education and training. The panels were empowered to proceed only where the basic facts were admitted or agreed, or alternatively after they had been so determined by a sheriff. Provision was included for appeal against a panel decision to the sheriff, and ultimately to the Court of Session. Unlike the once and for all procedure of the juvenile courts, the decisions of the hearings would be subject to review at set intervals.

The duty of carrying out the decisions of the children's panels or hearings as they came to be known, would rest with the local authority. For this purpose, the Kilbrandon Committee proposed a reorganisation of the social services for children and families to be known as the social education department — 'The Matching Field Organisation' — which would subsume the local authority's various responsibilities for children under the Children Act of 1948 and other legislation. This new department under the overall control of the Director of Education would be headed by a depute director to be known as the 'Director of Social Education'.

The reasons for proposing a department of social education rather than social work may now seem strange, but had then some rationale. The education authorities of Scotland, the main public agencies for dealing with children, were the largest and most prestigious local authority departments. By comparison, the newly arrived children's departments were under-resourced and under-developed. Moreover, the Clyde Report of 1946, as explained in chapter two, had carried a minority recommendation against special new children's departments, but favouring education. Indeed, the idea that child care should be taken over by the education service in both England and Scotland had an even earlier precedent in the Minority Report of the Poor Law Commission of 1909 (Part I, pp. 523, 553), signed by such progressives as George Lansbury and Mrs Sidney Webb. It may also have been in the minds of some of the Kilbrandon Committee that a new dimension of responsibility for underprivileged children might have been conducive to more child-centred attitudes in the formal Scottish education system of the time. Nor must it be forgotten that a basic Kilbrandon conclusion was 'their common need for special measures of education and training'.

As explained in the next chapter, a social education department was not to be. Later even Kilbrandon himself graciously conceded the inevitability of this departure in his foreword of 1976 to Martin and Murray's *Children's Hearings* — 'I do not regret that the Committee's idea of attaching the children's panels and the supporting field organisation to education authorities was rejected in favour of the social work system, as we know it'. This rejection of the social education department was to prove only a temporary setback. The full impact of Kilbrandon's two-pronged recommendation is sometimes overlooked because of the concentration on the revolutionary part one, the new machinery of the panel system. In the event, the initially rejected second part, which clearly registered the corollary need for a reorganised supporting agency, proved even more important by providing the first draft in the planning exercise, that was to lead to a much wider and more radical reorganisation of related services than originally envisaged.

A major discussion on juvenile justice or the merits of the children's hearings system as it has developed since 1971 is beyond the scope and period of this book. These issues are dealt with at length in such works as *The Scottish Juvenile Justice System 1983*, edited by Martin and Murray, *Juvenile Justice?* 1978 by Morrison and McIsaac, and *Juvenile Justice in Britain and the United States* 1978 by Phyllida Parsloe. However, some limited comment on the embodiment of Kilbrandon principles may be appropriate here, since oral tradition and some written commentary of the earlier years may have given the appearance of uncritical acceptance, while later events following cases in Orkney and elsewhere have attracted fierce criticism of parts of the process, which have by implication affected the whole.[19]

The great debate is between the offence — responsibility — punishment criminal court system of Europe, England, and Scotland up until 1971 on the one hand, and the welfare approach of Scandinavia and America, and Scotland post 1971 on the other. Since 1969 it is not so easy to place the mixed economy of England in this spectrum. The welfare systems have become increasingly open to the objection that they give unfettered discretion for over-zealous officials or panel members to prescribe measures out of all proportion to the needs of the case, which may well deny the civil liberties of the child and family. Kilbrandon had recognised this danger with the caution (para. 80). 'It must finally be a matter of judgment how far in relation to juveniles and their parents, the application of an educative principle in this way would in fact and in practice represent an appreciable inroad into family life amounting to a loss of liberty or freedom from interference such as to be unacceptable to our society.'

These issues are explored by Sanford Fox in Martin and Murray's 'Children's Hearings'. He states that 'by the early 1960s it had become apparent that in American juvenile courts, discretion had achieved a near complete dominance over law' in the face of 'the overpowering belief by juvenile court judges and their staff that they could do some good for children, and that it was therefore quite unimportant whether the particular charges were or were not true'. Referring to his experience of observing Scottish hearings, he illustrates this tendency by the case of a boy who was cajoled by the hearing 'into accepting that he had committed a crime that did not exist under the law'. While hesitating to generalise from this case, his conclusion on the American and the Scottish scene is one that can only be accepted 'there is an important, though concededly non-utilitarian value in according to children the dignity of not being required to incriminate themselves, and in otherwise recognising them as autonomous beings who are not merely pawns in the adult game of crime prevention'.[20]

Martin, Fox and Murray are more emphatic with their view, 'There is very strong evidence that a significant proportion of children's hearings fall short of the by no means excessively demanding standards laid down in the 1968 Act and Hearing Rules.[21]

More major doubts and criticisms of the Kilbrandon-inspired hearings system are expressed in the book *Legality and Community, The Politics of Juvenile Justice in Scotland*, Aberdeen University Press 1979, by a group of academics from law and psychology, who tend to see the hearings as a mechanism for imposing conformity to standard middle class norms of family behaviour. The chapter by Terry Bloomfield *Delinquency and Social Control* gives a useful exposition of the history, philosophy and theories of delinquency. On this platform, he argues that punishment versus treatment is a bogus issue; that the basic intention has always been control; and that the Kilbrandon style change is simply a movement from one type of control to another. In earlier days this control was exercised through discipline, work training, and physical regimentation, but 'now we have the specialist areas of psychology, psychiatry and social work, which provide theories to dictate and justify the mode of intervention'. That most approaches to the problem of delinquency have had the basic purpose of control would be difficult to deny, and indeed the same intention could be ascribed to many education systems, including the

Scottish until most recent times.

Martin and Murray, two Glasgow academics, who were closely involved in the early stages of the panel system through training activities, study and writing approach the central problem perhaps understandably with a different emphasis. In the chapter *Achievements, Issues and Prospects*, from their *Children's Hearings*, they recognise the danger of 'welfare totalitarianism', which may lead to serious inroads on civil liberties through measures taken outside of a judicial system. They suggest that if this happens it is not because of lack of safeguards provided by the legislation, but rather that 'panel members and their advisers are gravely at fault'.

It must be observed here that while such human error cannot, of course, be entirely controlled in any system, it may be regarded as a greater danger in an operation depending largely on lay people, often enthusiasts, rather than on professionals. However, in this respect the system is not greatly different from the lay juvenile courts which preceded it, and which continue in England. In fact it may be argued that both the selection and training for children's hearings is much more systematic and careful, aspects given considerable weight by Martin and Murray.

Whether we accept their general line or not, there can be little dispute about the concomitant advantages which they cite — the informal, unhurried consideration, the practical involvement of parents, and the education of public opinion through wider participation. Their conclusion that 'any such set of procedures for dealing with children who have broken the law must, in our view, necessarily involve a series of compromises which may be unacceptable to those for whom philosophical consistency is more important than viability' is logical, but the price of such compromise is open to debate.[22]

What may be observed with some certainty is that for the first 20 years the system dealt carefully and sympathetically with a large number of children — some 20,000 annually — with little evidence of serious complaints from parents,[23] public, police or other agencies in a field where, given cause, both press and public are known to be vociferous. It is worth nothing that the sheriff to whom the Orkney cause celebre was referred in March 1991, after being highly critical of procedures, felt constrained to describe the system as 'justly admired through the world as a quick, fair and sympathetic way of dealing with child care'.[24]

An even more authoritative pronouncement was made by Sanford Fox when he delivered the Kilbrandon Child Care Lecture at Glasgow University in 1991 — 'The Children's Hearings System has for two decades embodied and made operational child-centred concerns that are only now being recognised as goals round the world.'[25]

But in 1964 such critical approaches had not yet developed. The report was clear, firm and unanimous, and, to informed opinion, appeared constructive and impressive. Its panel system recommendations were received with enthusiasm by the agencies mainly concerned, except the sheriffs, some of whom on the Committee had given them full support. The unusually sympathetic reaction among senior officials in the Scottish Office is best conveyed by the words of one centrally involved; David Cowperthwaite — 'Divisional Officers found the Report exciting in its arguments and proposals; whether or not the latter could or should be implemented, the former had a novelty and persuasiveness that deserved to influence and perhaps transform the long-running and international debate on arrangements for dealing with juvenile offenders'.[26]

The ministers of the government, Conservative at the time, reacted cautiously by announcing in Parliament in April the publication of the report, and their intention to seek the views of interested bodies and the public. For the purpose of consultation, opinion was sought under the two separate aspects of a panel system and the reorganisation of services dealing with children. By both facilitating consideration, and giving the opportunity for partial or total acceptance, this proved a crucial step in the Kilbrandon sequels.

The press generally welcomed the proposals. The Glasgow Herald's leader comment contained the enthusiastic statement 'The Kilbrandon Report on juvenile delinquency has been worth waiting for. Few departmental enquiries have left so convincing an impression as having said the last word on their subject'.[27] When the Scottish Grand Committee debated the issue in July 1964, there was solid support for the Report from members, and even the minister, Lady Tweedsmuir, seemed to indicate approval of the diagnosis of the problems. The only major reservations expressed were about the 'Social Education Department'.

In June of 1964 (as mentioned above), a Labour Party study group published their pamphlet 'Crime a Challenge to Us All', which correlated delinquency with deprivation, and proposed for England and Wales a system of new non-criminal family courts to deal with children under school age. When the Conservative government fell in the autumn of 1964, it was replaced by a Labour administration containing ministers who had been members of the study group. The concepts of the Scottish enlightenment, however laudable and acceptable at this stage, would still need support from London, especially if they were to lead to legislative change with inevitable financial implications. The developments in thinking in England ensured political predisposal to such support.

Yet, even with general enthusiasm in Scotland and political commitment in London, there were still major hurdles in the way of implementation. These are clearly and cogently detailed in chapter four of

Cowperthwaite's book. The main difficulties were that, for England and Wales, the recommendations were just a party document. They dealt with only some of the problem — juvenile courts, and not social work reorganisation, and they would inevitably involve a time lag vis-a-vis Scotland. Scotland's proposals were cut and dried, came with the authority of an independent, but government commissioned Committee, and already enjoyed the support of the new ministers in an omnibus Scottish Office relatively free of Whitehall departmental disagreements and difficulties. 'It was for the government as a whole to judge whether two such different sets of proposals, even if appropriate to the different circumstances of the two law districts, could be negotiated through a unitary United Kingdom Parliament'.[28]

Two new ministers, who were determined that they could be, had arrived at the Scottish Office, Mr William Ross and Mrs Judith Hart. The former was a strong and determined Secretary of State, an Ayrshire man, who believed in Scottish institutions, the rights of man, and the importance of the family. The latter, a product of the London School of Economics, was already imbued with current sociological thinking as well as socialist principles, and had the vision and the drive, as well as the supporting networks, to initiate, pilot and implement major reform. With ministers urging, a combined official ministerial operation was mounted in Edinburgh and London to overcome the remaining difficulties. On 23 June 1965, in Parliament, the Secretary of State announced the government's intention to establish juvenile panels on the lines recommended by the Committee, and the acceptance of the consequential need to reorganise social services in Scotland, not necessarily on an education authority basis. he also promised a further statement on how 'the comprehensive casework service recommended by the Kilbrandon committee' would be provided — 'implemention of the children's hearings proposals could hardly take place in Scotland without social work reorganisation'.[29]

In four years from commissioning therefore, the Kilbrandon Committee achieved the spectacular result of seeing its principal recommendation on juvenile justice officially accepted, and its corollary prescription for reorganising family services used as a pointer to even greater reform. The Kilbrandon Committee were therefore the prime architects of social work reorganisation in Scotland, even though their prototype was not in the event accepted. The reasons for such a steady, successful outcome are not far to seek. As indicated earlier, the Committee was a potentially strong group of progressive and open-minded individuals with a variety of relevant experience. As important as the composition, was the leadership by an outstanding respected lawyer, less conservative than his fellows, who effectively led the Committee by his natural dignity, easy authority, and quiet persuasiveness. Additionally, there was a clear general will for change, and limited vested interests. The retarded development of the juvenile court system provided further impetus.

Yet in other such causes, even such potent factors have not always ensured a successful outcome in legislation. The major guarantors of realisation here were two-fold. In the first instance the senior civil servants of the Scottish Office were active initiators, encouragers and facilitators of this programme of social change. Secondly and crucially, the ministers concerned were interested, active and powerful enough to carry through to fruition in their province of Scotland, ideas which chimed with their party's aspirations, so far unachievable in the South.

And thus it transpired that 'an original and forward-looking system of juvenile justice' was unobtrusively and unexpectedly brought into the world by Scotland, which as Martin and Murray rightly observed, could not have been tipped as a front runner in such matters by an independent observer in the 1960s.

The Kilbrandon Committee was the vehicle for that unexpected achievement, and for the even more momentous move to a family social work service, as explained in the next chapter.

NOTES

1. Question from Mrs Jean Mann, M.P., Coatbridge, to Secretary of State 24.6.58.
2. Waite, R. G., Juvenile Delinquency in Nazi Germany 1933-45, PhD Thesis, State University of New York 1980, pp. 44-60.
3. McCrone, Kendrick and Straw, Understanding Scotland: The Making of Scotland, EUP. 1989, p. 2.
4. The Howard Journal 1945-46, Vol. VII — No. 1.
    Papers by Cicely Craven and Dr Arthur Norris.
5. John A. Mack, Family and Community, A Private Report to the Carnegie UK Trust, Department of Social and Economic Research, Glasgow University 1953, p. 50.
6. Children and Young Persons, Scotland, Cmnd. 2306, 1964 (The Kilbrandon Report) Appendix A.
7. T. Ferguson, The Young Delinquent and His Social Setting, OUP 1952, p. 102.
    A. J. Arnott and J. A. Duncan, The Scottish Criminal EUP, 1970, p. 105.
8. Children and Young Persons, Scotland, Cmnd. 2306, 1964.
    (The Kilbrandon Report), para. 9.
    The Scottish Region of the Association of Child Care Officers in their memorandum to Kilbrandon, para. I.V. suggested that 'parochial considerations' might affect the making of FPOs.
9. This action was seen by the Scottish Education Department as urgently necessary to avoid serious overcrowding and the associated disturbances that had arisen in similar situations in England. The author bears some responsibility, having been closely involved in the establishment of five of these schools.
10. For instance, John Mack, British Journal of Criminology, april 1963.
11. Bowlby, Spock, Stone et al, rediscovery of the family, Sister Marie Hilda Lectures, AUP 1981.
12. Leading amongst these was Catherine McCallum of the Glasgow CG Department. A

paper by her, Child Guidance in Scotland, printed in The Bulletin of the British Psychological Society, vol. xxii, June 1952, gives a definitive outline of the service. Supporting and influencing Scottish developments were the prestigious departments of child and adolescent psychiatry in the Children's Hospitals of Edinburgh and Glasgow.

13. D. J. Cowperthwaite, The Emergence of the Scottish Children's Hearings System, University of Southampton 1988, chapter 2.

14. Hall, Land, Parker and Webb, Change, Choice and Conflict in Social Policy. Heinemann 1975, p. 66.

15. Cowperthwaite, p. 20.

16. The meetings and discussions referred to here and later were with Dr Fred Stone in Glasgow 12.3.90 with Mr A. T. F. Ogilvie in Edinburgh 6.6.90, and with Sheriff Principal Ronald Ireland in Edinburgh 28.7.90.

17. The Children and Young Persons (Scotland) Act, 1932, had the intention of introducing special courts in all areas to take over such functions from the sheriff and juvenile courts. This was to be effected by an order from the Secretary of State when the local authorities signified their readiness. For detail see Cowperthwaite, Chapter 1.

18. A typical example of this is in the evidence given by the Children's Officer of Angus, contained in SWSG Records CYP(62) 19 Appendix B.

19. Des Browne, A System that has Lost its Way, The Scotsman 6 April 1991.

20. Sanford Fox, Juvenile Justice Reform, some American Scottish Comparisons. Martin and Murray, Children's Hearings, SAP 1976, pp. 216-219.

21. Martin, Fox and Murray, Children Out of Court, SAP, 1981, p. 270.

22. F. M. Martin and Kathleen Murray, Children's Hearings, SAP 1976, p. 26.

23. Martin, Fox, Murray, pp. 233, 234.

24. Sheriff Kelbey as quoted by Professor Sheila McLean, The Scotsman, 12 April 1991.

25. Professor S. J. Fox, Boston College of Law, 'Children's Hearings and the International Community', p. 4. HMSO C2.5 6/91 13129.

26. Cowperthwaite, p. 26.

27. Glasgow Herald 23 April 1964. The Scotsman of that date (p. 7) noted its welcome by the Howard League, Church of Scotland and National Association of Girls and Mixed Clubs.

28. Cowperthwaite, p. 32.

29. Ibid., p. 31.

CHAPTER 8

Social Workers and the Social Work Act

'Social workers became increasingly aware as they thought through the Kilbrandon proposals, that as guests in a powerful and very traditional host system, their social work roles and functions would remain peripheral, and they were unlikely to exercise significant influence.'

This sentence from *The Creation of British Personal Social Services, 1962-74* by Joan Cooper, former Children's Officer, and Chief Adviser to the Department of Health and Social Security, encapsulates the central action of this chapter. In the last chapter we saw how major reform was accepted through the agency of a powerful committee enjoying the encouragement of the senior civil service, with sympathetic ministers at one remove taking the critical decisions. In this chapter we shall consider the parts played by interested professionals to inform and influence the Scottish Office, this time with the relevant minister actively involved on centre stage. Two trends emphasised and reinforced this tendency. Whereas in the 1940s and 1950s Scotland almost invariably moved in tandem with England and Wales, by the early 1960s there was a development towards independence and the application of Scottish solutions to the problems of Scottish social services.

Secondly, at a UK level, whereas post-war reforms, in creating new social service departments, created as a by-product new kinds of social workers, in the 1960s these very social workers united to promote the creation of new services in which they would play a dominant role. Following the Secretary of State's announcement on 24 June 1965 of his intentions to establish a panel system and to consider further the complementary reorganisation of social work services, there was inevitably an urgency about the latter, without which the former could not proceed. These pressures were further reinforced by the realisation that the political climate and the parliamentary timetable would wait for no man.

To hasten the process it was announced on 4 August 1965 that three expert advisers would be appointed to work with civil servants and local authority associations on plans for the new service. This novel decision appears to have been that of the Minister responsible, Judith Hart, although there were parallels under the new Labour Government. Work was split between three groups. The 'study group' consisted of three consultants: Richard Titmuss, professor of Social Administration at the London School of Economics, Miss Megan Browne of the Department of Social Study at the University of Edinburgh, and Mrs C. Carmichael of the School of Study, Glasgow University, together with Mrs J. Hart and officials. A second group was referred to as the 'Joint Working Group', and consisted of representatives from the three local authority associations of the time along with Departmental officials.

The make up of the 'study group' was of crucial importance. Richard Titmuss had taught Judith Hart sociology at the LSE. In April 1965 he had delivered a speech at Eastbourne calling for Departments of Social Services, and had formed a working group to consider the case against a narrower 'family service'. He was perhaps the least involved of Judith Hart's advisory group, although Kay Carmichael said he played a very powerful part, especially in her thinking.[1]

Kay Carmichael was a friend and political associate of Judith Hart, and her direct link to the social work profession. From 1960 she had been involved in the training course for probation officers at Glasgow, and she was linked through PSW training with Megan Browne. The professional advisers worked closely with a new administrative unit set up at the Scottish Office to process the wide consequences of the Secretary of State's accepting the Kilbrandon recommendations. This unit was initially fostered in SHHD and headed by D. J. Cowperthwaite, but when, in the spring of 1967, the reorganisation aspects began to outgrow the original consideration, the reform of juvenile law, it was transferred to SED as Social Work Services Group (SWSG) under an assistant secretary, J. O. Johnston, and his principal officer, A. J. B. Rowe. Johnston's role was to prove particularly significant, but the whole department seem to have approached the project with unusual enthusiasm and commitment.

A third group, internal to the Scottish Office and the Crown Office, had the task of planning the detailed operation of the children's hearings system and the legislative provisions that would be needed to establish it. The local authority associations took a back seat in the development of ideas by the Joint Working Group. Judith Hart and her advisers shared a common orientation, and their ideas were well ahead of the local authority representatives. The political coincidence, which placed a sociologist in the relevant ministerial seat, was matched by the involvement of a particularly able and interested senior civil servant in J. O. Johnston. Some debate seems to have occurred within Judith Hart's Department between Cowperthwaite, who broadly supported the Kilbrandon proposals, and Johnston who was persuaded by the social workers' arguments against social education. However, all concerned appear to have been motivated by genuine concern to solve an identified problem, rather than by civil service vested interests.

The social work influence was considerable. Those civil servants who supported the proposals for social education — or even expanded health and welfare services — felt that these were criticised more because of social workers' anxieties about being ancillary to other professions than because they would have left rump services for adult probation and the care of the elderly.[2]

The Social Work Profession

The Kilbrandon Report's proposals for the establishment of a Social Education Department had amongst its effects that of unifying the emerging social work profession in Scotland. As we have seen, social workers in Scotland were divided by specialist employment into child care officers (CCOs), probation officers (POs), welfare officers (WOs), mental health officers (MHOs), psychiatric social workers (PSWs) and medical social workers (MSWs), with their professional organisations split along similar lines. In Britain there was a proliferation of professional social work bodies, which from the 1930s were combined into a loose federation, the British Federation of Social Workers. However, each organisation retained its own sovereignty and had markedly differing orientations. Service based associations concentrated on the individual social services rather than the particular needs of the client. On the other hand the psychiatric social workers emphasis was on individuals, but they had joined the BFSW because of a concern with social policy. Their interest in individual freedom and social service was taken up at a special session organised by the British Association of Psychiatric Social Work in London in 1938, where the question was whether to adjust the client or the environment.

The professional organisations most directly affected by the Kilbrandon proposals were those representing the child care and probation services. As we have seen in Chapter 6, even by the mid 1960s only a small minority of the staff of children's departments were professionally trained. In 1963 there were 37 full-time children's officers and 97 child care officers, plus 41 part-time officers. No formal qualifications were prescribed for children's officers nor for their subordinates the child care officers. Burns and Sinclair in *The Child Care Service at Work*, 1963, pointed out the problem of the overlapping roles of the children's officers and the child care officers who were organised in two separate professional organisations: the Scottish Children's Officers Association (SCOA) and the Association of Child Care Officers (ACCO).

As discussed in Chapter 6, the Scottish Region of ACCO was founded in 1954 with 22 members. By 1969 it had grown to 194, including members from voluntary organisations, staffs of training courses and

CCOs from most (not all) local authorities. At first, activities were confined to conferences, but gradually more work was undertaken, preparing evidence and discussion papers for committees and government departments, culminating in contributions to the Kilbrandon Committee. Because of Scotland's separate child care system, with its own inspectorate and Advisory Council, the Scottish Region of ACCO was independent of England. With its own battles of fight, the Scottish branch grew into a vigorous and active body.

There were many attempts to negotiate with SCOA, but the two organisations never formed a strong working relationship. ACCO was a much more political organisation, concerned with training and salaries, and conditions of service. Before 1960 the only training in Scotland was for houseparents at Langside College. Those seeking professional training had to travel to England until 1960, when a one-year child care course for those with a social science qualification was established at Edinburgh University, eventually providing six places. The following year a pilot two-year Younghusband course was set up in Glasgow at the Scottish College of commerce. Throughout the 1960s ACCO's Scottish Region and SCOA lobbied for alternative training courses and better salaries to combat the tendency for Scots to travel South to find these. Their activities bore fruit in the later 1960s when ACCO was able to claim credit for courses such as that at Moray House. In 1963 ACCO was one of the eight professional organisations to join the Standing Conference of Organisations of Social Workers. SCOSW superseded the Joint Training Council for Social Work which had been set up in 1959 to coordinate social work training. However, ACCO's generally low standards of professional qualifications tended to lead to polarisation between it and the better qualified associations in SCOSW.[3]

ACCO's Scottish Region was one of the first groups to produce a memorandum on the Kilbrandon Report in August or September 1964. In their evidence to the Kilbrandon Committee they had merely suggested that 'consideration be given to the idea that there should be an amalgamation of the separate services which are at present at the disposal of the Court'. Otherwise they had concentrated on Ingleby-style alterations to the law relating to the treatment of juveniles. However, they were quick to recognise the potential advantages and pitfalls in the Kilbrandon proposals. In their memorandum on the Report they argued that a Social Education Department was an unsatisfactory solution, since 'social work goes much beyond the bounds of social education and cannot be embraced by it, even considered in its widest sense', and that the Committee's findings implied lack of confidence in the children's departments in Scotland, largely justified, since, 'Child care in Scotland is, in general, sadly under-developed'. ACCO rejected the view that the proposed Social Education Department would provide a satisfactory service for children and their families, and proposed instead the introduction of a Department of Social Work, arguing that the fragmentation and over-lapping of the social services was not only unhelpful to families but highly wasteful of the few caseworkers available. They believed that social work must be concerned with the individual in his family, and that this led logically to the establishment of a family-centred service. They therefore recommended measures more radical than proposed by the Committee: that 'all the social services should be concentrated in one department set up on a regional basis'. The ACCO memorandum also advocated reorganisation in the Scottish Office, and that priority should be given to training arrangements. It concluded: 'Since the war, Scotland has lagged behind in the social work field, but we believe that a progressive scheme such as we have outlined gives Scotland the opportunity to lead the way.'[4] S.C.O.A were also to support proposals for reform based on the concept of an integrated social work department.

In 1962 there were about 250 probation officers (mainly male) in Scotland compared with 200 of all other types of social workers, of whom the majority worked in children's departments. Like ACCO, the National Association of Probation Officers tended to operate as a trade union as much as a professional association. This caused some conflicts when, in October 1967, a Scottish Standing Conference was set up. Members of NAPO did not regard themselves primarily as social workers, but rather as court officials, a position confirmed by the Morison Report. Probation officers were not very involved in case conferences with local authority social workers about individual cases, but ad hoc co-ordinating committees operated in some areas to prevent overlapping. Local authorities in Scotland were more influential on probation committees than those in England, and could occasionally shape events, although they were generally seen as reacting to court initiatives by the Sheriffs. As explained in Chapter 5, after the establishment of the one-year training course in 1959, Probation became the best-trained service outside the hospitals. From 1960 onwards all new probation officers (still mostly mature men) were exposed in training to the ideas of evangelical Scottish social workers such as Kay Carmichael and Vera Hiddleston (of ACCO), who stressed the common social work method. It was among the newer probation officers that the opportunities inherent in a new service were most widely recognised.

NAPO, as to some extent ACCO, was slow to realise the radical potential of Kilbrandon, initially regarding it as concentrating on legal rather than social work reforms. The Kilbrandon Report's recommendation that children under 16 should be supervised by the new service implied splitting the Probation Service in two, and came as a major shock to NAPO, which had not contributed many proposals to Kilbrandon.

However, once the Kilbrandon Committee had accepted the argument for 'social education' it was inevitable that at least half the probation service would be integrated into the new department.[5]

The situation of social workers in the other main services, Health and Welfare, was less clear. As we saw in Chapter 4, they were professionally poor services. In 1951 the Committee on Social Workers in the Mental Health Services (the Mackintosh Committee) highlighted the severe shortage of trained social workers in these services, and the Report of the Working Party on Social Workers in the Local Authority Health and Welfare Services, 1959 (the Younghusband Report) found that the situation had not improved greatly. By the 1960s the increasing development of the social services was making the shortage of trained social workers a major problem, and the deficiencies identified in Health and Welfare Services throughout Britain led to Younghusband's proposals for 'General Purpose Social Workers'.

During debates on the resulting Health Visitors and Social Work Training Bill, APSW views were heard in Parliament (through J. Hart, then an MP) supporting the provision of professional training under a Council of Training in Social Work, which was created in 1962 to award the Certificate in Social Work for those completing a two-years generic training. Another Younghusband suggestion, the National Institute for Social Work Training was formed in the same year.

These developments in the poorly-trained welfare, health and mental health services were of great interest to social workers generally, including the better-trained hospital social workers. During the latter half of the 1950s proposals were made for the extension of community care in both England and Scotland. In Scotland the Government published a White Paper in 1955, which was followed in 1957 by a Scottish Health Services Council Report on Mental Deficiency in Scotland, and a review by the Scottish Advisory Council for the Welfare of Handicapped Persons. The English Mental Health Act of 1959 was matched by the Mental Health (Scotland) Act of 1960, which envisaged the development of community care to reduce or eliminate the need for care in hospital unless intensive care or supervision was required. The role of local authorities had become more important, as the benefits were realised of keeping mental patients or mentally handicapped persons in the community wherever possible. Because of the number of patients who were able to return home after comparatively short periods in hospital, there was increased emphasis on the provision of community facilities required for their continuous support and after-care. No specific recommendations were made regarding the type or qualification of local authority staff to be employed in the Scottish mental health services, but, so far as social workers were concerned, the needs to be met, and the proposals for further development implied the employment of fully trained staff. The Younghusband Report estimated that if there were to be an increase in community care Scottish local authorities required about 40 PSWs.[6]

The British Journal of Psychiatric Social Work reflected these developments during this period. A.P.S.W's major focus was on training, and it was in that connection that they first took an interest in generic social work. By 1956 Noel Timms was writing of 'the melting pot into which parts of the social and welfare services are now being cast', and concluding: 'I think what we should aim ultimately (and this does not necessarily mean slowly) at a unity of social work in training and organisation.'[7]

MSWs had similar attitudes to training, and in fact there was always close co-operation between two associations. In 1944 a joint meeting was held between the two groups to attempt to define their respective roles, and agreement was reached that a common basic training was required.

The publication of the Kilbrandon Report had a major impact on these less-directly involved hospital social workers. By June 1965 IMSW had completed their memorandum on the Kilbrandon Report. Their conclusions were similar to those of ACCO, but probably based to a rather greater extent on questions of professional status, trained manpower, etc. They considered 'that the aims of the Report could only be fulfilled by a department serving not only these children but all members of the family at every stage'. They did not think that the service could function effectively from the education department of a Local Authority, but required a department where social work was the primary function. Following the Secretary of State's acceptance of juvenile panels and the consequent need to reorganise social services, the advisory group of three was appointed, as mentioned above. PSWs were, perhaps, the first social work group to be given an opportunity to air their views on Kilbrandon, when Judith Hart addressed the national meeting of APSW in Glasgow in September 1965. APSW had not given evidence to Kilbrandon, but at this meeting PSWs apparently made clear to Mrs Hart their hostility to the suggestion that the new departments were to be headed by directors of education.[8]

Acting as a unifying force for all these disparate professional associations was the Association of Social Workers (ASW). It was created between 1949 and 1951 from the old British Federation of Social Workers, and developed into a professional body composed of individuals committed to the pursuit of a unified profession. During the 1950s several attempts were made to explore the possibility of affiliation with other social work organisations. However, these generally foundered on the vexed question of standards of qualification for registration. The foundation of the Standing Conference of Organisations of Social

Workers (SCOSW), in 1963, representing ACCO, the Association of Family Caseworkers, the Association of Moral Welfare Workers, APSW, IMSW, NAPO and the Society of Mental Welfare Officers, was followed by a revival of ASW, which concentrated on attracting members from all specialisms, and was active in promoting the discussion of the proposals to reorganise the social work services. SCOSW had wider interests than the purely training remit of its predecessor, the J.T.C.S.W., and was eventually to become, in 1970, the British Association of Social Workers which superseded all SCOSW's constituent organisations (with the exception of NAPO) and was open to all qualified social workers.

In November 1965 ASW organised a conference at Stirling on 'Integration within the Social Services'. The principal speakers were Mrs Judith Hart and Mr R. Huws Jones, first principal of the National Institute for Social Work Training. Representatives from virtually ever social work service in Scotland attended — voluntary or statutory — and from other interests such as medical officers of health and county clerks. Those present seem to agree that Mrs Hart was making a genuine attempt to use the conference as a two-way process, and was, thus, adapting her proposals to the demands of the social workers. Among her main points was the need outlined in the Kilbrandon Report for an effective 'case-work service' to serve the lay panels for children under 16, and it was accepted that such a service must be capable of further growth into fields not directly concerned with juvenile delinquency. In the same year SCOSW published a discussion paper on the Re-organisation of Social Work Services. Although social work organisations were not officially invited to present their views on reorganisation until after the publication of the White Paper the following year, some views were made known, formally or otherwise, to the Joint Working Group. Organisations such as the Council for Training in Social Work, the Scottish Association for Mental Health, NAPO (Scottish Branch) and APSW contacted the SHHD, as did the Society of MOHs (Scottish Branch), the Scottish Churches Council and various other bodies. Moreover, many of the Civil Servants involved had close links with social work profession, partly through the professional advisers to their departments, such as Miss M. M. McInnes, Welfare Officer, SHHD, a persistent advocate for social workers in the health and welfare services. The members of the advisory group were, of course, well known figures in social work circles — Kay Carmichael was Scottish representative on the National Executive Committee of APSW, and a delegate of the Scottish Branch of SCOSW, as well as being involved with central government through the Probation Training Course. It was the Study Group, with its strong social work bias, which concentrated on the argument for social work reorganisation, largely leaving officials to set out the measures required to implement the children's hearings proposals.

In contrast, the local authority representatives on the Joint Working Group made a minimal contribution. Glasgow Corporation was said to have been unaware that they had a representative on the Working Group, who had only attended two or three times, an old local authority custom, common but not exclusive to Glasgow. The local authority representatives were advised to consult with their officials, and were aided by a memorandum produced by SHHD on *Attitudes of Professional Social Workers*.

The Joint Working Group's Review of Services

The Joint Working Group produced a review of social work services, which it felt should be included in what was now definitely to be a social work department. It was agreed that certain services must be included if the Kilbrandon proposals for children were to be effectively implemented. Judith Hart had stated at the Joint Working Group's first meeting on 19.11.65 that:

'In considering the necessary reorganisation the Government had decided that it should not be limited to social work for children as the Kilbrandon Committee had been, but should aim at a wider and more efficient integration of all the social services. The Working Group should not feel themselves inhibited from considering services at present beyond the scope of local authority responsibility.'

Thus, in a way, by the end of 1965, Judith Hart had already pre-empted the debate by placing the Government firmly behind a process leading inexorably towards a broad social work department, with the unifying element of social work as its central principle, rather than a narrow family service or social education department.

The Minister's rationale was expressed in a note by SHHD and SED on Consultation and Planning. This stated that on publication of Kilbrandon all interested parties had been invited to state their views and the majority had supported the concept of children's panels. A 'Social Education Department' had evoked less support, most agreeing that some reorganisation was needed but not through social education, because, firstly, the service should be centred on the family and community, and not the child, and, secondly, education authorities were not the best setting for the service. The Secretary of State was also aware from these and other sources, that social workers felt that present services were ineffective and gave insufficient scope for developing skills. It, therefore, seemed wise to review all social work services with a view to bringing them more closely together. Reorganisation would affect professional interests, shaping developments for a generation. It was felt it would be best if all concerned had an opportunity to make observations on a coherent set of proposals published in an early White Paper.[9]

The review therefore considered over a dozen services which contributed to social work functions. It was agreed that some should remain separate. Others made considerable use of social workers, but could function at least as well if the new service made social workers available on an agency basis. The two services which had to be integrated if the Kilbrandon proposals were to be implemented were Child Care and Probation (at least the section of Probation concerned with children). The first service which the Joint Working Group considered was Child Care.

After outlining the history and duties of Children's Departments, the review concluded: 'we should accept the social worker's view that the interests of those children can be best served by an organisation which is concerned with children as members of families and of society, as well as with children as individuals.'

Equal in importance to the integration of Child Care was the integration of probation, although probation officers were far from unanimous in supporting the proposals. The Joint Working Group agreed that it was desirable that social workers who undertook the supervision of children under the Kilbrandon proposals should be part of an organisation responsible for deprived children generally. Rejecting the suggestion of stigma from the mixing of penal and non-penal functions, the Joint Working Group emphasised the need for probation workers to operate in a family setting, and the fact that the new service was more likely to attract good recruits.

The JWG touched on social training establishments for adults, and family service units, and then turned to Approved Schools. The Kilbrandon Committee, envisaging a social education department, had recommended that the term 'approved school' should cease, and that they should become part of a range of residential schools catering for a wide variety of children, whose needs were not met under normal education provision. They also proposed the abolition of approved school managers in loco parentis powers, and of the approved school after-care service.

The JWG accepted the Kilbrandon proposals that children placed within such schools should remain within the jurisdiction of the juvenile panels, and that on their return to the community they should be supervised by a local authority social worker under the direction of the panel. This, they felt, would go a long way towards assimilating the work of the approved schools with the local social services. However, they concluded that opportunity for experiment enjoyed under voluntary management outweighed the advantages of the local authorities taking over full responsibilities for the schools.[10]

Similarly, the Kilbrandon Committee had proposed that the social education department should have responsibility for the 15 residential and 61 other special schools run by the education authorities in Scotland. The Joint Working Group recommended that the education authority should retain responsibility for these schools, but that panels should be able to use them as a method of treatment for children brought before their sessions. School Welfare and Attendance was a responsibility of education authorities, who employed about 250 school attendance officers and 50 welfare officers for this task. The Joint Working Group proposed that education authorities should continue to make initial inquiries into truancy, but that social workers should do any follow-up work required.

The Joint Working Group were unable to resolve the future of the assessment of children which involved two services; assessment centres and child guidance and assessment. The Children and Young Persons (Scotland) Act 1937, required each local authority to provide secure remand home accommodation for their area, for those detained pending appearance, those awaiting a vacancy in an approved school, and those undergoing a sentence of less than one month. There were, in 1966, eight remand homes in Scotland, managed by six children's departments. The Kilbrandon Committee had recommended that remand home detention as a form of punishment should be abolished, and that the residential homes in the cities should become the main regional assessment centres for children aged 12-15, operating as an integral part of social education service, with specialist assistance from the child guidance, school medical and hospital psychiatric services. Child guidance services were the responsibility of education departments. If the service were to be given to a social work department, not only the psychiatrist but the educational psychologist would still have to be 'borrowed' from another department. Not surprisingly, the JWG were 'unable to reach a view'.[11]

The Joint Working Group considered Welfare and Mental Health in four parts: the welfare of the aged; the welfare of the handicapped; the welfare of needy households; and mental health. Local authorities had no general responsibility for the aged, but they had duties under the National Assistance Act, 1948, which required the provision of residential accommodation for the elderly in need of care and attention. The care of the elderly in their own homes was encouraged by central government in the Department of Health for Scotland Circular 61/1958, which drew attention to the need for close collaboration between welfare departments, voluntary organisations and other services.[12] The Joint Working Group 'agreed that the provision of these services to old people involves a very large element of social work', and that, although the elderly required only a small element of casework, those working with the elderly should be under the supervision of those trained in casework. 'It would therefore be appropriate to give responsibility for the welfare of the aged to a social work department of the local authority.' However, the Joint Working Group feared that this might give the new department too many responsibilities. They concluded: 'We think that it would be appropriate for a social work department to be given this responsibility eventually, but we have been unable to decide whether it should have it at this stage.' Welfare of the handicapped was regulated by the National Assistance Act 1948, which gave local authorities wide powers to promote welfare. The Joint Working Group recognised the social work role in this service, but, as with the welfare of the aged, opted to postpone the final decision on if and when this service should join the social work department.

Welfare Departments also had a responsibility for needy households, although the principal statutory authority concerned with financial needs was the National Assistance Board. Under Part III of the National Assistance Act, 1948, local authorities had a duty to provide temporary accommodation for those in urgent or unforeseen need. The Joint Working Group considered this service along with the powers possessed by the local authority through the children's committee to give assistance to families in need under Section 1 of the Children and Young Persons Act, 1963. They agreed that these services should become the responsibility of the new social work department, as should social work advice to the National Assistance Board.

Under the National Health Service (Scotland) Act, 1947 and Part II of the Mental Health (Scotland) Act, 1960, local authorities had powers to provide a range of mental health services. While the Joint Working Group were aware that this service was not merely a social work function, since clinical responsibility lay with the medical profession, they thought that the social work element in this service should eventually become the responsibility of the social work department.[13]

The Joint Working Group's proposals, as outlined above, were considerably influenced by social work lobbying of the Study Group and civil servants in the period prior to the publication of the White Paper, and these views were generally incorporated in the White Paper itself. Most of this lobbying was fairly uncoordinated, but the Study Group spoke to several professional organisations and ACCO held a meeting for Glasgow MPs to enlist their support. However, the die was probably cast against a social education department by September 1965, when a SED draft paper echoed the social work associations arguments that 'there is now wide acceptance of the view that the social work services are not properly organised for the functions they are called on to carry out', and suggested it would be possible to 'attempt to remove the overlaps and difficulties between them by setting up 'a comprehensive social work service'.[14] This trend was reinforced by the fact that the 'Study Group' proved considerably more influential than the local authority working group in determining the White Paper published in October 1966.

One decision which caused surprise was the Government's determination to press on with reorganisation so close to the likely date of the Report of the Royal Commission on Local Government. The Secretary of State's explanation was that the likelihood of a delay in the programme following the publication of the Royal Commission's Report was formidable, and to wait until an agreed policy for local government reorganisation was achieved would mean an unacceptable delay for the social work services.[15]

The White Paper — Social Work and the Community

'Social Work and the Community' (Cmnd. 3065 of October 1966), followed broadly the line, expounded earlier by ministers and the JWG Report, that there was a need for social work reorganisation to bring together services with substantial social work content into a single local authority social work department. It was proposed that: 'the local authority should in future have power to provide all citizens, of whatever age and circumstances, with advice and guidance in the solution of personal and social difficulties and problems'.

The argument for a new department was developed in paragraph 8, covering the fact that families in trouble were liable to be involved with and visited by a number of services employing social workers with basically the same skills. These services had to compete among themselves for the limited number of trained staff, and it was difficult to ensure that their efforts were deployed in the most effective and economical way. Moreover, the White Paper pointed out that families in need of help often did not know which service to approach — a unified service was to be seen as a 'single door'.

The White Paper acknowledged the efforts of both social work organisations and local authorities to co-ordinate specialisms, but pointed out that these were rarely satisfactory and always costly in working time. The argument, again, was that reorganisation would not only benefit clients and social workers, but also provide better value for money. It was in the context of the provision and development of better services that it seemed 'necessary that the local authority services designed to provide community care and support' should be brought together. These were now to include services for the handicapped, mentally and physically ill, and the aged. Social workers arguments had borne fruit in that the 'responsibilities of this organisation would therefore be wide, but would be homogeneous, in that they would all be based on the insights and skills of the profession of social work' in a new Social Work Department.[16]

The White Paper did not necessarily envisage generic social workers, anticipating that use of specialist skills would continue. However, specialisms need no longer be bound to statutory requirements. It was hoped that the new department would facilitate the recruitment of the highly trained PSWs and MSWs by increasing movement between the community and institutions, and, implicitly, by improving social work's status, its salaries and its conditions of service.

The nub of the White Paper's proposals was the 'single door', but it was emphasised that there would also be a need to cooperate with other public and voluntary services. This was particularly the case with those services which would have fallen into a 'social education department'. It was suggested that education welfare officers should join child care in the new department, but attendance officers remain with the education authority. The assessment of children's needs would still be divided, with child guidance continuing as a responsibility of the education department: 'perhaps the heaviest price that has had to be paid for the proposal to create a Social Work Department not concerned solely with children.'[17]

Of all the proposals in the White Paper those concerning Probation were perhaps the most discussed. As we have seen, Probation had a number of unique features, and some probation officers reacted sharply to the tentative conclusions that 'on balance it would be better if all the functions of the Probation Service in Scotland were undertaken by the local authority social work department'. This section concluded by offering reassurance to both probation officers and sheriffs, through proposing special machinery to associate the courts with the social work department.[18]

As discussed, the White Paper concluded that services for the physically and mentally ill, the handicapped and the elderly should go immediately to the new department. This caused controversy not only because these services were less clearly connected to the original focus, children, but also because these had often been the responsibility of the medical profession. One, at the time, relatively minor service, was that of the home helps. In view of subsequent developments, the White Paper was percipient in predicting that the potentialities of the service had not yet been fully explored, and that it could have a very positive role to play in a social work department.

Lastly, the White Paper considered social work with children and the role of the children's panel. As we have seen, this was the work of the civil servants, rather than the Advisory Group. It was short, and the definitive statement remained the Kilbrandon Report, from which it did not differ significantly. The detailed provisions proposed by the internal working group to implement the children's hearings awaited the Bill.

Reactions to the White Paper

The medical profession's response to the White Paper was critical, not only because of the loss of responsibilities it entailed, but also because of fears that it would result in a harmful distancing between local health and local welfare services. This was perhaps accentuated by the relative slowness with which the proposed reorganisation of the National Health Service had advanced. However, although the Society of MOHs (Scottish Branch) had already made their views known to SHHD, they were slow to mobilise against the proposed reorganisation. They also found few allies. Professional social workers were determined to resist the tutelage of the medical profession. ACCO's evidence commented: 'In some areas the medical aspect has been dominant, and it is clear that doctors may not recognise that social work has a particular contribution stemming from professional knowledge and skills which are learned.' Even the more sympathetic Scottish Branch of APSW, concerned about 'the separation of medico-social and social problems, and the threat to developments that have been growing in cooperation between these services', pointed out that 'social problems are not necessarily medical problems nor the sick necessarily a social problem, and we feel that in view of the expanding social service it is now inappropriate that health and welfare should be in the one department in the Local Authority'. As we have seen, the White Paper was produced by a division of civil servants, based initially in SHHD and later moving to SED. Now, in recognition of the size of the task, this unit was reorganised as the Social Work Services Group. It was the new SWSG which was responsible for summarising the views of interested bodies and submitting them to Ministers in April 1967. They concluded: 'Professional organisations representing doctors and other medical interests such as nurses and health visitors . . . accept the need for rationalisation of social work services, but express strong opposition to the White Paper's specific proposals for achieving this.' The arguments were:
(1) health and social needs were inseparable and the services should be within one department under medical direction, and
(2) the local authorities serving the largest sections of the population already had unified health and social work services under the MOH.

These medical bodies also opposed the incorporation of the probation service for adults into the health-based local authority arrangements which the doctors and nurses proposed. Official advice to Ministers was that the case for the amalgamation of local social work services outweighed any potential risk of their becoming distanced from local medical services. Judith Hart and her advisers were sure they were right.[19]

The most sustained assault on the White Paper came from Probation and its main supporters, the sheriffs. NAPO was one of the few associations to react at a British, rather than Scottish, level to 'Social Work and the Community', and this turned out to have its disadvantages as well as its advantages. As we have seen, Scottish plans for reorganisation were in advance of those in England, and NAPO was not alone in suspecting that they might serve as a pilot for a similar scheme south of the border. Thus NAPO's comments on the White Paper, emanating from London, represented the views of the Association as a whole, 'since it is recognised that the White Paper is of significance not only to the Scottish probation service.' While approving the principle of a comprehensive local authority social work department, they did not accept the inclusion of probation. They pointed out that the service had reached 'the enviable position' of a fully trained entry, while the other services had a low proportion of trained workers. In regard to children, they reiterated their Kilbrandon position that the need was for a better organised juvenile court system. They dismissed the idea that an adult service, particularly the specialist treatment of offenders in the community, could satisfactorily be carried out within a local authority framework, quoting the recent Morison Committee view that this was the main reason for the underdeveloped service in Scotland. As a last ditch stand they proposed a rump adult service made viable through a combination with its counterparts in England and Wales.

Despite admitting that a minority of the officers in Scotland would nevertheless favour the White Paper proposals, NAPO maintained a protracted rear guard action, although this was less solid and successful than that later mounted in the South.[20] The sheriffs now parted company with NAPO by acquiescing to the proposal that: 'juvenile courts are to be abolished for the reasons given by the Kilbrandon Committee . . .' and accepting that 'the duties among juveniles under 16 now performed by probation officers could be performed in future by the staff of the Social Work Department'. However, they continued to reject the view that the supervision of adult offenders could be appropriately or satisfactorily undertaken by local authority social workers. Their fundamental argument was that: 'The essential reason for the probation officer's intervention in the affairs of any individual is that he has been found guilty by a court of an offence against the criminal law, and not that he is the victim of some deprivation or handicap.'

Moreover, the sheriffs felt that the White Paper's assumption that services to the court would be performed just as effectively by social workers employed by the local authorities was mistaken. They argued for a staff of social workers with specialist training and outlook 'assigned exclusively to work with offenders for a substantial part of their careers'. They further argued that, on the one hand, the popular view of probation was a 'let-off' would be strengthened by passing the care of the offender to a local authority, and, on the other, that the adult delinquency taint might discourage some people from approaching the new departments. Like NAPO, the sheriffs were aware of developments in England, but they understood that the Government 'has no intention of abolishing the Probation and After Care Service for England and Wales'. They also noted that 'under the proposed reorganisation the school attendance and school health services would not be included in the Social Work Department', and commented that these were no more tied to the schools than probation to the courts.[21] With suspicion remaining that social work needed probation more than the *reverse*, the sheriffs feared the loss of their valued ancillary service, and consequent diminution of the powers of their courts. While recognising Scottish probation officers genuine concern for, and devotion to, their cherished service, it must be recognised that NAPO's overall strategy was affected somewhat by considerations of impending threats to their main empire, as well as of the immediate reforms of social work and court aspects in Scotland. Kilbrandon and the White Paper carried a precedent for possible absorption of the services in England and Wales just as in Scotland.

Thus NAPO was the only organisation to continue to protest the case for maintaining the direct judicial role in the arrangements for dealing with juvenile offenders. By this stage, however, the children's hearings had become a side-issue. Generally accepted, with a low profile in the White Paper, there were no matters relating to the hearings which officials thought necessary to bring before ministers. NAPO officials conceded that the loss of identity of the probation service was the main issue. Officials and Ministers remained convinced that the arguments in the White Paper for the total amalgamation of the probation services still stood. Judith Hart was aware that the new departments needed probation, and also that a sizeable percentage (perhaps 40%) of probation officers had been persuaded that their future lay with the new departments. In this situation, and with the sheriffs less influential than the magistrates in England, she felt confident to go ahead.[22]

The Large Burgh Question

The only criticisms of the White Paper to bear fruit at this stage were those of the local authorities, specifically the large burghs. Traditionally, most of the existing social work services, particularly child care and welfare, were administered by the large burghs. However, probation services were *de facto* organised on a 'whole county' basis in all but one county. Similarly, education was administered by the county councils, and a decision in favour of large burghs administration for social work would weaken the education/social work link.

The Joint Working Group had recognised this problem, which was further complicated by the impending Royal Commission on Local Government. The White Paper concluded that: 'on balance it would be best to place responsibility for the new department on counties (including counties of cities), and to empower and encourage the counties with the smallest populations to join with other authorities to form joint departments serving their combined populations.'[23]

The Association of County Councils and the Convention of Royal Burghs (CRB) responded that a change of such magnitude in local authority responsibility should not be made before the Royal Commission on Local Government reported. The Convention of Royal Burghs went on to protest that the 'establishment of social work departments in Cities and Counties will lead to an illogical separation between the new departments and the health departments in large burghs' and that: 'Social work services should remain a function of large burghs.' The Secretary of State met local authority representatives in March 1967, and thanked them for the assistance of their representatives on the Joint Working Group. To the CRB's assertion that 'the intimate nature of the services made it more suitable for large burghs to run them,' the Secretary of State conceded that 'there were areas where the large burghs were ahead of the county in the provision of the services, but there was something to be said for organising the services in such a way that the higher standard would be spread over a wider area'.[24] Similar meetings occurred regularly over the next few months, and in between them the CRB bombarded the Secretary of State with letters opposing the 'whole county' proposals.[25] Official advice continued to be that Ministers should proceed with the White Paper's proposal for the exclusion of large burghs, but the Secretary of State acknowledged the main fears of the burghs that: 'they would lose services which on the whole they had developed better than the counties' — a statement owing as much to political necessity as strict evaluation.[26]

It was argued that to leave the large burghs to develop the new department on the basis of their existing services until the post-reform authorities took over would cause the least dislocation. However, 'It would ... be very unlikely that populations of up to 50,000 could justify and support the much wider range of facilities which future developments will entail, or ... provide the specialist and administrative staff ...'[27]

Political considerations began to play a part, as Scottish Labour MPs, with their tiny majority at Westminster, turned their attentions to the support of probation officers, and, more seriously, to the burghs, where they had their political roots. Following the General Election of 1966, Labour had a majority of three. In September 1967 Mr R. D. M. Bell, Under Secretary at SWSG, met with county and town clerks, at the Secretary of State's suggestion, to find a compromise solution — with no success. Agreement by Ministers to the social work proposals had to be achieved if the Bill was to be included in the Queen's Speech at the end of October 1967. Otherwise it would have to be put aside until the next session to stand its chances against other claims on the Government's legislative time. The Secretary of State reached the decision that the White Paper's proposal would be reversed, and that the large burghs should be responsible for providing social work departments within the burghs. The commitment to legislation had been made, the large burghs and their supporters placated, and, it was argued, the whole structure would be in the melting pot again in the foreseeable future. Some felt the decision to be a disaster: 'ACCO's immediate reaction appears to be complete dismay, based on two points, the proliferation of directors of social work and the splitting up of the probation service.'[28]

Social Workers and the White Paper

To social workers in Scotland the White Paper represented a unique opportunity to influence social policy. Throughout Britain in the 1950s social workers came to recognise the structural constraints of the 1948 legislation. As Phoebe Hall comments: 'by the early 1960s these constraints were rapidly becoming unacceptable, and, although at first they were poorly articulated, the demands for change grew . . .'[29]

Early discussion of reform laid heavy emphasis on training, as it was generally considered that the shortage of professionally trained social workers in the social services was a major factor contributing to poor service to clients. As we have seen in Chapter 6, this was linked to the problems of coordination and the need for prevention. At field level a bewildering number of social workers and agencies might be involved with one 'problem family'.

Lack of coordination could lead to an appalling degree of confusion, overvisiting and overlap as described, for instance, by Donnison in 'The Neglected Child and the Social Services'. The importance of coordination became obvious when one looked at the numbers of families which Donnison found to be in contact with a large number of Social Services. He pointed out that this did not avert family break-up because, 'although the aim of all social service is to contribute to the health, happiness, and unity of family, it is not the *chief* aim of any . . .' Donnison argued that the smaller the number of social workers visiting any one family the better, and strongly attacked suggestions for yet another functional authority for children, pointing out that the problem was one of too many services.[30]

Attempts to improve, or establish, the social work profession were seen as complementary to service improvements, and eventually unification of professional associations appeared as a goal. The rise and influence of the social work profession in Scotland in this period has to be seen against the background of current debates on professionalism. Of course, social workers rarely admitted explicitly that the achievement of professional status was a major goal: some, indeed, argued against it. In an address to ASW in 1956 Donnison had discussed social work as a profession. He argues that no attempt should be made to define or limit the skills of social workers because while caseworkers might feel the need of the protection of a defined role it was more important that the profession remained critical and heretical.[31]

Eileen Younghusband was a major supporter of proposals, such as Donnison's, for 'all purpose social workers'. In 1955 she was appointed Chairman of the Working Party on Social Workers in the Local Authorities' Health and Welfare Services, which involved the question of a general purpose social worker. The appointment of this Working Party aroused considerable interest among social workers and stimulated several of them to contribute articles on the subject to 'Case Conference'. Most correspondents recognised a need to rationalise the system so that each family would deal with one social worker, not several, although the social worker could call in specialist help if required.

As a result of meetings in 1956, APSW proposed that generic courses containing psychiatric placements might be considered suitable qualifications for membership. This became APSW policy at the end of 1957. When the Younghusband Working Party reported in 1959 the recommendations proposed increased coordination between services, rather than any attempt to amalgamate the social services. APSW supported these recommendations in a press release issued in May 1959, although their main preoccupation continued to be with training.

Huws Jones, reviewed this history at the 1956 Stirling conference and then discussed current proposals for reorganisation. The 'Family Service' concept raised criticism from such as Titmuss, he said, because it did not appear to serve the isolates, the elderly and the mentally ill. A Department of Social Service, on the other hand, would provide services for people irrespective of age, family background and relationships. It was against this background that the individual social work associations reacted to the White Paper. At this stage there was no group coordinating their responses in Scotland, although the majority were members of the British Standing Conference of Organisations of Social Workers. However, there are strong similarities between all the comments received from these associations, except for NAPO.

When SCOSW itself came to debate closer unification in 1966, one of its principle arguments was:
'Social workers would acquire a sense of unity and professional identity by having a common forum for discussion and greater opportunities for organising inter-disciplinary conferences; this would be in keeping with the trend towards a common basis in training.'
The same discussion paper also argued that:
'It is essential that in the future development of the social services, the clients needs remain to the fore, and social workers must speak with a united and authoritative voice to ensure this.'[32]

In Scotland the sort of professional cooperation envisaged by the Discussion Paper occurred between all members of SCOSW with the exception of NAPO. At the end of 1966 ASW suggested regular meetings with other associations in Scotland, and in early 1967 proposed a Scottish branch of SCOSW. Other associations hung back, fearing that ASW was being reckless, that they would lose their representation at the London based SCOSW, and that they would be swamped by NAPO representatives if a Scottish Standing Conference was set up. However, a 'Political Action Group' was formed in May 1967, as a result of a meeting called by ACCO, to allow social workers to speak about the future of the social services with a 'united and authoritative voice', and to lobby for the type of reorganisation which the Standing Conference desired. This Group was also variously referred to as 'The Professional Working Party' and the 'Interdisciplinary ad hoc Group'.

Unification did not come easily. MSWs, like PSWs, were jealous of their own high standards and fearful of dilution. Moreover, they were reluctant to be overtly politicised, and were not generally at home in a local authority setting. Although NAPO, whose viewpoint did not coincide with those of the other organisations, was not represented on the Political Action Group, the views of those who supported integration were indirectly conveyed by a probation officer. The convener was Vera Hiddleston, of ACCO, who had a close relationship with members of the Study Group. The seven associations represented workers in: welfare, children's, education, probation and health departments, child guidance clinics, hospitals, voluntary organisations, residential care, universities and colleges, and other settings. When, in October 1967, the Scottish Standing Conference was set up, there was a certain amount of conflict between ACCO and NAPO, who viewed the organisation more as a trade union, and APSW and IMSW who saw it as a strictly professional organisation. Although NAPO was consistently 'odd man out', ACCO appears to have attempted to avoid any major split on this issue, and was, in fact, one of the most enthusiastic supporters of a totally unified professional organisation — opposing even specialist sections.

In their memorandum on the Kilbrandon Report ACCO had argued that the necessity of having a professional head of department was a major factor in the case against a 'social education department'. Similarly, IMSW, while welcoming the White Paper in principle considered 'it essential that the Director of any new Department of Social Work should be a trained Social Worker'. PSWS's experience in a wide variety of fields gave them confidence to comment generally positively on the proposals for an integrated social work department. However, like several other Associations, APSW, was less unanimous in the belief that the Director should be a caseworker, although this was generally agreed to be desirable.[33]

Similar support for the White Paper's proposals on integration came from many of the professional associations outwith SCOSW. The Scottish Approved Schools Staff Association, for instance, wrote: 'Despite the obvious criticism which will inevitably be levelled against the proposals from other quarters, we would wish to state that in principle we commend the Government for making a real attempt to put the business of social work in the community upon a sound footing.'[34]

By October 1967 work on the Social Work (Scotland) Bill had started at an official level, and it was on this that the Political Action Group now concentrated its attentions. NAPO, under the leadership of David Keir, and the sheriffs, led by Aikman Smith, continued to exert pressure to keep probation out of the new department. Sheriff Aikman Smith persuaded probation committees to write to their MPs arguing for a separate probation service. The decision to organise on the basis of large burghs made the proposals even less acceptable to NAPO, a position which separated them from many of their supporters in Parliament. NAPO and the Sheriffs met with SWSG, who relayed their views to Ministers, warning them that 'Both Associations are almost certain to pursue their opposition during the Bill's progress in Parliament'. The Political Action Group, on the other hand, argued that the major objections to the Probation Service joining Social Work stemmed from uncertainty as to the role of the Probation Officer — was he a social worker or was he a law enforcement officer? As training developed, the trend within the Probation Service had certainly been towards identification with social work. They made an eloquent case for probation's inclusion and rebutted the arguments of their opponents.[35]

Despite the concessions made over the large burgh issue, there remained a real danger that the Bill might be lost. Judith Hart had left the Department in 1966, for Social Security in London, to be replaced by Bruce Millan, a less personally involved minister, and NAPO had considerable support amongst MPs. The Parliamentary Group lobbied the political parties in the House of Commons, and orchestrated the lobbying of constituency MPs. They prepared briefs for Government and Opposition, and attended all sessions of Parliament when the Bill was discussed to make social workers views known and to advise MPs on detail. Responding to this, Hugh Brown, an ally, and increasingly influential spokesman on social services after Judith Hart's departure, said 'I have been very impressed by the quality and ability of the social workers who have been putting pressure on us about the Bill. I respect their sheer professionalism. . .'[36]

As we have seen, the social work organisations were united in their opposition to basing the service on large burghs. The issue was taken up by the chairman of SCOSW in a letter to the Secretary of State, and the Professional Working Party likewise contended 'only larger units have the resources to support the full range of specialist services and consultative staff'.[37]

By March 1968, when the Bill was introduced in the Lords, its passage into law in some form was ensured by the decision of the Conservative Party not to approach it on a party-political basis. In the House of Lords, which included the honorary president of NAPO, and also a former probation officer, many Conservatives opposed the services being based on large burghs, and an amendment was carried against the Government by 76 votes to 47. However, in the Scottish Standing Committee in the Commons, the Lords decision to exclude the large burghs was reversed on a division by 11 votes to 8.

At the Report Stage in the Lords those opposed to the absorption of the probation service had devised an amendment that officers carrying out probation functions should be specially qualified, which was defeated by 58 to 43. In the Commons Committee the Government won a division against making probation a function of social work departments by 15 votes to 10. Donald Dewar, a Labour MP, 'introduced a new and pragmatic point, suggesting that the Government was making the proposal for complete absorption because the new social work departments "needed" the probation service'.[38]

During the Commons Third Reading there was general praise for the legislation which was recognised as ambitious, forward-looking and relatively free from constraints. The Bill received Royal Assent on 26 July 1968, seven years after Kilbrandon was appointed. While this progress might seem rapid, it was no record in the field of social legislation. From Ingleby to the Children and Young Persons Act, 1963, was also seven years, from Seebohm to the Local Authority Social Services Act was four years, and from Curtis/Clyde to the Children Act, 1948, was only three. What was impressive was the magnitude of change.

The 1963 Act, through section one, legitimised preventive work, but merely tinkered with the main issue of children in courts. The Social Services Act, unencumbered by the issue of juvenile justice, and after a decade of surveys, with Ingleby's limited success and two White Papers, required four years to finalise the amalgamation of children's and welfare services. The Social Work Act delivered in one parcel the exact recommendations on juvenile justice of one single, and singular, committee, Kilbrandon, and incorporated in an expanded and improved form their prescription for a supporting family service. The main impetus for this grand design came from the coordinated efforts of the expert advisers, civil servants and the minister. This was supported by a well organised group of professional social workers. Moreover, court-based interests were considerably less successful than their counterparts in England in diluting the plans.

Once again, as in the run-up to the Curtis Committee in England, it was a handful of able graduate women who exerted the crucial influence on the speed and direction of developments. In the process a more unusual feature was the extent to which, in the words of one protagonist, 'Social workers achieved all that they could have wanted (except in relation to large burghs).[39] This one defeat, while appearing a retrograde step, was an essential timely tactical concession to secure the uninterrupted passage of the Bill. In the long run it gave five years practice of implementation on a lesser scale, which provided working foundations for regional social work departments.

The probation question was also a major threat to the development of a completely integrated family service. The strength of the probation lobby, particularly in the House of Lords, was little less than that brought to bear on parallel processes for England and Wales. However, the situations differed in as much as the more advanced and coherent Scottish proposals were ably defended by an undivided Scottish Office.

Before concluding we may reflect on the outcome if the Scottish Bill had not dealt with both juvenile justice and social work re-organisation in one packet. Attention was focused almost entirely on the latter aspect, and serious scrutiny and opposition was confined to the large burgh question and inclusion of probation. It is interesting to speculate whether, if Part III 'Children in Need of Compulsory Measures' had been debated more thoroughly, it would have passed in its pristine form and would still have contained some of the difficult and debatable provisions, which have become apparent after 20 years.

Its survival intact might have been even more in doubt if, as normal, it had followed instead of preceded the much fought over Bill on juvenile justice, which was to become the Children and Young Persons Act 1969 for England and Wales.

On this occasion however Scotland had assumed a strong independent line in social policy, with remarkably few divisions or rivalries to inhibit national progressive plans. These inherent strengths, encouraged by a generally favourable political climate, ensured a remarkable success over residual vested interests both in Parliament and in the country. Moreover, with the birth of the Social Work Act, the social work professions, increasingly unified and influential, had arrived in Scotland.

Notes

1. Journal of the Royal Society of Health, vol. 186, no. 1, Jan.-Feb. 1966, p. 19; Interview with C. M. (Kay) Carmichael, (1.12.77).

2. Interviews by G. McMillan with: Judith Hart (4.2.77); D. J. Cowperthwaite (1974); Assistant Secretary 1948-74, Criminal Justice Division, SHHD; and J.O. Johnston (1974), latterly director Social Work, Glasgow.

3. R. Lees, Social Work, 1925-50, British Journal of Social Work, 1972, 1.4, pp. 371-375; SACCC, 1963, staffing of local authority children's departments, SED, p. 9; The Child Care Service at Work, Scottish Advisory Council on Child Care Report, 1963, SED, p. 43; Association of Child Care Officers (ACCO) — A Souvenir Portrait. Child Care 1949-1970, pp. 92-93, The Scottish Region, (by J. L.).

4. Memorandum submitted to the Kilbrandon Committee by the Association of Child Care Officers (Scottish Region); CYP(WE) 10 ACCO (Scotland) Oct. 61; ACCO (Scottish Region), Memorandum on The Report of the Committee on Children and Young Persons (Scotland) (Aug./Sept. 64).

5. Interviews by G. McMillan with: J. C. Rogers (7.9.77) formerly Treasurer, NAPO, Scotland, later Depute Director SWD Dundee; A. T. F. Ogilvie (1974) Secretary to the Kilbrandon Committee.

6. Ministry of Health, The Report of the Working Party on Social Workers in the Local Authority Health and Welfare Services, 1959 ('The Younghusband Report'), HMSO, paras. 224-8, 654 and 806-7; Hansard, vol. 649, 24.11.61.

7. K. McDougall, Future Developments in Training, BJPSW, September 1950, No. 4 (vol. 1) p. 8f; Noel Timms, Communication to BJPSW, 14 June 1956, no. 4 (vol. III), p. 29.

8. The Institute of Medical Social Workers, Scottish REgional Newsletter, June 1965; Association of Psychiatric Social Workers (Scottish Branch) Annual Report: 1965; interview by G. McMillan with Miss N. Young, Edinburgh University, 1974.

9. SWSG Records, JWG 10 paras. 3 and 9; SWG/JWG 1st meeting, 19.11.65, para. 3; SWSG/JWG 8, Consultation and Planning.

10. SWSG/JWG 10, paras. 1-20.

11. SWSG/JWG 10, paras. 21-37.

12. SWSG/JWG 10, paras. 2 & 38; HH 61/58 1; Younghusband Report, para. 249.

13. SWSG/JWG 10, paras. 40-47.

14. SWSG Scottish Home and Health Department Files, 17 KSG2, 16 September 1965, Reorganisation of Social Work, Draft for Working Group on the Social Work services, para. 2.

15. SWSG/K/2/2 14, 30.9.65, letter from J.O. Johnston to R. E. C. Johnson; A. J. B. Rowe, The Future of Scottish Social Work, p. 5.

16. SED, SHHD, Social Work and the Community (Cmnd. 3065), paras. 8-10 and A. J. B. Rowe, op. cit., p.7.

17. Social Work and the Community, paras. 11-12 and 19-25; A. J. B. Rowe, op. cit. pp. 9 and 14-15.

18. D. J. Cowperthwaite, The Emergency of the Scottish Children's Hearings System, University of Southampton, pp. 34-35; Social Work and The Community, paras. 27-29; A. J. B. Rowe, op. cit. pp. 15-17.

19. Interview with Judith Hart; APSW, comments on Social Work and the Community; SWSG/JWG 4; SAC (67) 1 6.4.67.
20. A. J. B. Rowe, op. cit. pp. 15-17; D. J. Cowperthwaite, op. cit., p. 36; NAPO Evidence SWSG/RT/E/84 8.2.67; Interview with J. C. Rodgers.
21. Sheriffs Evidence SWSG/RT/E/14.
22. D. J. Cowperthwaite, op. cit. 36; interviews with J. C. Rodgers and Judith Hart.
23. D. J. Cowperthwaite, op. cit. p. 36; Social Work and the Community, para. 52.
24. SAC (67) 1 6.4.67. SWSG/K/19/4 9 Draft by J.O. Johnstone for meeting with convention of Royal Burghs 17.3.67, SWSG/K/19/4 12 Record of Meeting.
25. SWSG/K/19/4 21 16.6.67. Letter from Convention of Royal Burghs to Secretary of State.
26. SWSG/K/19/4/32 28.7.67 Secretary of State's meeting with convention of Royal Burghs.
27. SWSG/K/19/4 41 4.8.67. Social Work Services Group note.
28. SWSG/K/19/2A 18 7.12.67. P. A. Cox to J.O. Johnston.
29. Phoebe Hall, Reforming the Welfare, 1976, PXI; New Society, (No. 60) 21 Nov. 1963, p. 19, Social Work United Breakthrough.
30. D. V. Donnison, The Neglected Child and the Social Services, Manchester University Press, 1954, p. 23, pp. 73-74, p. 77 and p. 118.
31. D. V. Donnison, the Social Work Profession, Case Conference, vol. 3, no. 3.
32. Kay McDougall, A Chairman's Eye View, Social Work Today, vol. 1, april 1970; Standing Conference of Organisation of Social Workers, Discussion Paper, No. 2.
33. Summary of activities of the interdisciplinary ad hoc group (Action Group); Memorandum of the views of a professional working party on the Social Work (Scotland) Bill; Association of Child Care Officers (Scottish Region), Memorandum on 'the report of the Committee on Children and Young Persons (Scotland)'; comments on 'Social Work and the Community' by the Association of Psychiatric Social Workers (Scottish Branch).
34. Appendix No. 3 to Mrs Carmichael's papers on the White Paper; The Scottish Approved Schools Staff Association, A Comment on 'Social Work and the Community'.
35. Memorandum of the views of a professional working party on the Social Work (Scotland) Bill; SWSG/K/19/2A 39 23.1.68. R. D. M. Bell to Mr Millan, Under-Secretary of State for Scotland; Vera Hiddleston, op. cit. p. 205.
36. The ACCO Story, Alan A. Jacka, p. 62; Vera Hiddleston, The Promotion of Social Welfare. CASW 1989 pp. 2-5.
37. SWSG/K/19/2A 21 SCOSW (Scotland) 19.12.67. Mary Coverdale to Secretary of State; Vera Hiddleston, op. cit. p. 5.
38. D. J. Cowperthwaite, op. cit. pp. 46-49; Vera Hiddleston, op. cit. pp. 3 and 9.
39. D. J. Cowperthwaite, op. cit. p. 49; Vera Hiddleston, op. cit. p. 9.

CHAPTER 9

The Making of Social Work Departments

'Unfortunately, however, the mere decision to bring about large-scale organisation changes with their far-reaching effects is no guarantee that the proposed changes will be formulated in a manner comprehensible either to those responsible for producing a change or to those affected by it — Changes are introduced without those responsible knowing what they are doing.'

This is not a quote from a cynic scarred by the Scottish reorganisation of social work, but an observation by workers of the Brunel Social Services Research Unit,[1] the validity of which may be assessed from the events now related and discussed. In contrast to the previous chapter's lively history of change and progress in the philosophies and practice of social services, this account of the practical implementation of realised ideals may seem a prosaic passage. Yet it was a period of maximum significance and complete re-orientation for Scottish personal social services. For those involved it was an exciting and challenging, if at times threatening, experience. It was also the crucible from which emerged the major operational methods and forms which have provided parameters for those employed in the service ever since.

The Act

The Social Work (Scotland) Act, 1968, received royal assent on 26 July 1968 and was implemented by stages through 1969 to 1971. With the Children Act of 1908, the National Insurance and National Health Acts of 1946 and 1947, it is one of the great landmarks of 20th Century social services.

Previous Acts provided services for limited categories of persons with specific needs. By contrast the White Paper heralded the new Act as giving 'power to provide all citizens, of whatever age or circumstances, with advice and guidance in the solving of personal and social difficulties and problems'. Local authority social services were to be open to all, in the same sense as health services were open to all. This was to be done through 'a single door on which anyone might knock' to ask for help with confidence of getting it'. The single door was certainly provided, but in early years of necessity, such confidence was not always justified.

The Act brought together into a comprehensive service existing provisions for children, elderly, physically and mentally handicapped persons and offenders, which had been exercised through the Children, Welfare, Health and Probation Committees. Circular No. SW1/1968, which was issued with the Act, stated 'the Act replaces them by provisions in general terms more appropriate to a sphere of local authority work, where the many developments which are likely to take place in the next few years, should not be hampered by narrowly drawn legislation'. This was done at a time when central government still believed in the importance of local authority independence, and democratic freedom.

Exceptional to the 'general terms' were children's services. Part III of the Act, almost one third of the whole, dealt with Children in Need of Compulsory Measures, the original springboard for the reforms. Part II, the next most substantial part, consisted largely of a detailed transcription of the local authority's responsibilities under the Children Act of 1948. Responsibility for services to the elderly was covered by the general duty of section 12 'to promote social welfare by making available advice, guidance and assistance'. This applied also to physically handicapped persons, whose support incidentally had previously relied on a similar section in the National Assistance Act of 1948. Probation services merited one specific separate section (27), which required local authorities to provide court reports and supervision for persons on probation or after-care. This section was considerably amplified by the duty to prepare a detailed probation scheme for the approval of the Secretary of State. The needs of mentally handicapped and mentally ill persons were met more specifically under section one of the Act, which transferred to the new social work committees appropriate existing local authority health powers, apart from medical and nursing, under the Mental Health (Scotland) Act of 1960 and the National Health Services (Scotland) Act of 1947. By the same section, powers under the Nurseries and Child Minders Regulation Act of 1948 were similarly transferred.

The Act thus placed on local authorities very wide responsibilities for child care, child life protection, the support of families in difficulties, the welfare of the elderly and physically handicapped, services to mentally ill and mentally handicapped persons, services for offenders, the organisation of home help, and the provision of residential or day establishments serving these various categories. Associated with the last was the encouraging and monitoring of provisions by appropriate voluntary organisations. Certain services to the education and housing departments of local authorities were also implicit. In due course, when Part III of the Act would be implemented, the major duty of serving children's hearings would also be required.

Above and beyond all this was the general requirement under Section 12 'to promote social welfare by making available advice, guidance and assistance on such a scale as may be appropriate for their area'. The advice and guidance aspect was an unlimited provision, but the assistance, to be given in kind or cash, which derived from section one of the Children and Young Persons Act of 1963, was restricted by categories and circumstances. Firstly, to children where its granting would diminish the need to take into or keep in care, and secondly to persons in need requiring assistance in kind, or, in exceptional circumstances constituting an emergency, in cash, 'to avoid the local authority being caused greater expense on a later occasion'. Persons in need were limited by the interpretation section (94) to those with needs arising from infirmity, youth or age, mental illness or handicap, physical handicap and homelessness.

The envisaged extended horizon of promoting social welfare is best described by the wording of circular No. SW6 of December 1968, which gave detailed guidance to local authorities as follows: 'The new duty is not, however, related only to the needs for advice or social support which may be felt by individual people. The duty to promote social welfare must include concern for groups of people, whether families or other small or larger groups forming, for example, the population of a particular part of the local authority's area. Moreover the duty is not merely that of reacting to known needs. It implies that the local authority should seek out existing needs, which have not been brought to the authority's attention, identify incipient needs and try to influence social and environmental developments in such ways as will not only prevent the creation of social difficulties, but will positively lead to the creation of good social conditions'. This was an unlimited charter for rectifying past omissions, and planning new panaceas for the social and environmental services, which, as will be shown later, had often to be, initially at least, more honoured in the breach than in observance.

Section 12 is unique to Scotland, and, as the Seebohm Report, an exact contemporary of our Social Work Act, was being translated into the Local Authority Social Services Act of 1970, there were interested looks north by professional groups, but scarcely at all by Seebohm. The former resulted in statements by the 'Seebohm Implementation Action Group' such as 'Major Omissions — General Duty to Promote Social Welfare. It is a matter of concern that the Government has not seen fit to include in the Bill a general provision making it a duty of Local Authorities to promote social welfare in their area — vide Section 12 Social Work (Scotland) Act 1968'.[2]

The passing of the Act was the climax of considerable campaigning and sustained effort. Its implementation in the years 1969 to 1971 was an even more herculean labour for all concerned. The initial stages required much planning and preparation of directions by the Scottish Office. Between the White Paper and the Act, by a combination of the relevant divisions of SHHD and SED, a special unit was established in March 1967 and christened Social Work Services Group — referred to as SWSG. Although SHHD, responsible for welfare services, probation and juvenile justice, had initiated Kilbrandon and consequently reorganisation, SWSG was fostered with SED for overall financial, administrative and political control. Whether this was due to the preponderance of child care in the new service, or the critical roles played by the senior civil servants concerned, has been much debated. An equally potent factor may have been the civil service's traditional approach of balance of departmental work load and influence.

The Group was responsible for the continuing oversight of the separate services, children, welfare and probation, the preparation of the Social Work Bill, advice during its passage, preparation of commencement orders and regulations for the Act, and a series of circulars of advice and guidance on its implementation. It was headed by an Under Secretary supported by three Assistant Secretaries, and an advisory service was established by the amalgamation of the former welfare advisers, child care and probation inspectorate, and HM Inspector responsible for Approved Schools. A Chief Adviser was appointed, Miss Beti Jones who had wide experience as a Children's Officer of a Welsh county from 1949 to 1968.

The Mackenzie and Seebohm Reports

The form and functioning of Children's Hearings had been fairly clearly pre-determined by Kilbrandon's recommendations, and defined by the codification of these in the Act. The design and formation of the 'matching field organisation', the social work departments, was quite another matter. The White Paper of 1966 had gone little beyond a declaration of principles and intent for 'a single organisation — a new social work department' and 'a single door'.

By contrast the Committee on Local Authority and Allied personal Social Services (for England and Wales), which led to the Local Authority Social Services Act 1970, were quite specific. In their report of July 1968, referred to as the Seebohm Report, they devoted a major chapter to the organisation of proposed social services departments, including specifications for area offices and the classic formula 10-12 social workers for populations of 50,000-100,000 (para. 590).

To fill this gap on the Scottish scene a working party was set up in May 1968 and reported in July 1969.[3] This was done on the initiative of the Department of Social Administration of Edinburgh University, with the support of SWSG and the financial backing of the Joseph Rowntree Trust. It had 12 members, representative of local authority administration, child care, welfare, probation and medical social work, voluntary organisations and the health services. Amongst the 12, notable figures were John Spencer, Professor of Social Administration, and Lewis and Lewis Waddilove, Director of the Rowntree Trust. It was chaired by W. J. M. MacKenzie, Professor of Government at Glasgow University, who was noted for his experience of local authority and constitutional questions in the UK and abroad. The secretary was a young local government officer, Gavin McNaughton. Although their document is often referred to as the Rowntree Report, the style adopted here, to match titles of the other major reports discussed, is the *MacKenzie Report*. The Committee defined its own remit as 'to survey the purposes of the Act and the organisation and the staff needed to give effect to them, having regard to the resources available and to the great difference that exist between different parts of Scotland'.

The first half of the MacKenzie Report reviews the role of the social work department, its local authority setting, and its interfaces with other statutory services, local and national. In the second half there are chapters on social work roles and methods, the organisation of departments, the panel system, staffing and training, all of which, even twenty-five years on, give a useful basic text for the student of the development of Scottish social work. On the interface aspect, MacKenzie left no stone unturned in identifying possible bonds and inputs for the new social work departments. With health alone, dialogue would be expected between the new directors and staff and the hospital specialisms of geriatrics, paediatrics and psychiatry, and also with such providers in the community as medical officers of health, directors of nursing services and general practitioners. Education, provided at only county level, was more straightforward, and there the expectations were confined to helping the schools to design programmes for the older pupils on community matters and assisting the Youth Service where developments were slow. For 'town and country planning' it was hoped that the new departments would become involved in collecting relevant social and demographic data as well as advising on social planning and public participation. Relations with police and courts were to make no great new demands. Housing, as could be expected, presented a major facet, not least because, before reorganisation of local government, it was provided by four cities, 31 counties, 21 large and 174 small burghs.

As regards the local authority setting, the report now sounds somewhat optimistic, if not naive, in its statement (para. 160) that 'Local authorities have accepted in general the implication of the Act that the social work committee should be one of the main committees of the council, and that the director should rank in salary and status with other chief officers'. Until local government reorganisation in 1975, education and health were the pre-eminent committees, and social work was an also ran. As regards status and salary the director was usually in a different league from the clerk, treasurer, director of education and medical officer. Content with the old order and old loyalties to welfare and children, not all authorities welcomed the change, and some were sceptical if not hostile. Their natural resistances were not mollified by the dawning awareness that the White Paper's bland assurance of little extra expenditure were misleading, and that implementation of the new service must perforce be costly. This face, apparent to those in the local authority cockpit, was not generally discerned through more sanguine eyes in the colleges or St Andrew's House.

Whereas for children's officers the Curtis Committee had prescribed a paragon young woman, at least a graduate, with relevant experience, MacKenzie was content that a director could not simply be a 'back-room boy' but must combine a flair for public relations with a gift for influencing elected members and be at the same time 'a careful administrator and a professional leader respected by professional staff'. For a director of social services the qualities Seebohm prescribed were administrative skill, capacity to lead and train staff from different backgrounds, ability to influence elected members for resources and acceptability to other departmental heads.

MacKenzie is probably most remembered for its proposals on organisation — the field unit, the work team, headquarters and intake procedures. Before reorganisation of social work, the separate departments, except in the cities where some decentralisation had just begun, provided service mainly from a central office in the large burgh or county town. MacKenzie proposed field units to be provided in centres of communication, shopping and recreation, serving a population of about 50,000 through ten social workers operating in two teams. The reason given for producing this formula was that it derived from the existing level of field staff in Scotland.

The Seebohm Report of July 1968 (para. 590) had produced the formula of 10-12 social workers serving a population of 50,000-100,000 in towns. This too was based on existing staff levels, the main difference being that it did not include probation, and made an allowance for directors and headquarters staff.

The formula was first promulgated in Scotland by Circular SW6 of December 1968, para. 72 of which reads, 'The number of social workers likely to be in post in the child care, welfare, mental health and probation services, when social work departments are set up, may approach 1,000. As the population of Scotland is approximately five million, this gives a ratio of about ten social workers to every 50,000 population, and experience shows that *a compact population of this size* may be a good base for a local team of social workers.'

The immediate basis for this statement can be traced back in SWSG Records (Files SW 2/5 and R/2 to the transactions of the Working Party

SWD (M) in June/July 1967. David Colvin, later to become Chief Adviser, produced a memo dated 4.7.67 on the structure and application of units so designed. However there are earlier minuted references (20th and 19th June) by administrators to the formula, in the context of arguing against smaller authorities (the large burghs) and the need for compact populations to be served.

Other pieces in the jig-saw come from SWSG Records dealing with Seebohm (SW9/2/1C), where it is evident firstly that the senior civil servants directly concerned — J.O. Johnston in St Andrew's House and P. I. Wolf, Secretary to the Seebohm Committee in Whitehall — were in contact by correspondence and meetings in London, and secondly that copies of the report of the Working Party SWD (M) were sent to Mr Wolf under a letter dated 19 January 1968. By that time, however, the Seebohm Committee was within a few months of reporting.

It seems highly doubtful whether this almost identical formula could have originated independently in Edinburgh and London at roughly the same time, and the question must remain pending further searches at the Seebohm end, as to how much Seebohm thinking influenced Scotland on this issue or vice versa. Exchange of views on the subject there undoubtedly were.

All that can be said definitely here by the author after discussions with survivors principally concerned and from knowledge of J.O. Johnston at the time, is that a Scottish version of the formula had been produced in St Andrew's House by mid 1967, which neatly fitted political needs, existing resources and professional considerations.

On the role of the central department in developing the new social service, MacKenzie ventured little beyond noting the civil service pattern which 'involves collaboration on a footing of equal status between administrators and professional social workers'. It was left to an interested Edinburgh academic to register the point 'that social workers have every right to expect an increasing flow of ideas and ever improving leadership from St Andrew's House'.[4]

By contrast, Seebohm was in no doubt (para. 647C) that 'In order to carry out its functions effectively, the central government department concerned must have a strong, accessible and well-respected inspectorate to advise local authorities, to promote the achievement of aims and the maintenance of standards, and to act as two way channels for information and consultation'. This may give some clue to the differences in development of advisory services north and south of the border, which have been evident since 1970. Seebohm reinforced the Whitehall belief in the kind of firm inspectorial guidance that the Home Office had provided for Child Care. MacKenzie merely reflected the Scottish Office acquiescence to a weaker tradition in monitoring of personal social services, bolstered by a comparatively high profile at senior administrative level. Twenty-two years later an inspectorial system similar to that in England and Wales has been established. It remains to be seen whether this will give Scottish social work a more positive lead.

The various references to Seebohm above should not be taken as implying a direct comparability, or as belittling MacKenzie. Seebohm was a major commission on social services, operating for three years and backed by the resources of four major ministries. MacKenzie was the creation of concerned academics and civil servants, which with minimal research and support had to do a rush job in just over a year. Its main achievements were its portrayal of the widest possible role pattern for the departments and its definition of their responsibilities in the local authority setting. It reviewed social work values and roles and sketched possible outlines of departmental organisation. Given its limitations the MacKenzie Committee produced a relevant analysis and a useful rough chart for the unknown territory and possible developments immediately ahead.

The Implementation of the Act

SWSG, established early in 1967, having serviced the processes that led to the approval of the Act in July 1968, thereafter through 1968 and 1969 issued a series of circulars which gave timely, detailed and encouraging advice to local authorities on the implementation of the Act. Contrary to fading folk memory, the glorious revolution of social work re-organisation was not achieved entirely on the one momentous day 17 November 1969. There were four main stages, beginning with 1 April for recognition of the appropriate authorities, the counties and large burghs, and their empowering to set up social work committees. Second came 1 July for the formal appointment of directors, and thirdly, 17 November was the day for the amalgamation of the separate agencies, and the launching of composite social work departments. It was originally hoped that the children's hearings would follow in about a year, but in the event the commencement order for Part III of the Act 'Children in Need of Compulsory Measures' was delayed till 15 April 1971.

At the end of 1968 SWSG produced a major circular SW6/1968 'Reorganisation of Services' giving detailed implementation guidance for provisions on child care, probation, home help, residential accommodation, and not least staffing, with the classic formula discussed above. Apart from its intrinsic merit this circular reflects different social mores, in that its issue and receipt in late December indicates that in these days work of major importance was not arrested by the festive paralysis which now strikes central and local government in that month.

The document is also interesting for its frank admission of the major difficulties facing implementation — financial restrictions and staff shortages. After noting that any substantial extension of the local authority service would take time, it produced the fine rationalisation 'The immediate extension which is essential to the purposes of the Act is not an extension of resources, although it is greatly needed, but an extension of thinking and planning. The major change needed at this first stage is not an increase in the amount of social work done, but a redeployment to secure that the volume of known need is tackled in the new context set up by the Act'. This late apparent reversal of the engines was no small shock to those to whom the clamant need for increased social work activity was foremost among the great expectations of the decade. In this the Scottish Office was now not only outstripping Whitehall in social work reorganisation, but even outclassing the Egyptians for subtlety of method in requiring more bricks without straw.

Be that as it may, on 1 April 52 authorities were designated for the purposes of the Act, only three combinations having been effected,[5] although this had been strongly urged by the Scottish Office, again with little more effect that for the Children Act in 1948. About half the designated authorities had total populations of fewer than 50,000, a handful had even less than half that figure, and their scanty resources would provide poor foundations for ambitious social service planning. These 52 authorities then duly established social work committees to take over all the functions of the Act, including services formerly provided by the children's, welfare and probation departments. From the local health authority were transferred functions concerning nurseries and child minders, and the mental health provisions other than those involving medical or nursing services. From education committees they were to acquire the running of any local authority approved schools and financial responsibility for children from their area in all such schools.[6]

These were the responsibilities for which the new committees were to organise their resources. Before this, however, they would need to prepare an overall plan for the merging of existing agencies and the development of the new department. To facilitate this the advice of a chief officer was necessary, and they were required to appoint as soon as may be directors-designate, who would become directors after 1 July. At an earlier stage, the Scottish Office had envisaged the possibility of a central advertisement and central approving machinery to establish a pool of suitably qualified or experienced candidates, from which authorities in turn might select their own individual. When this was rejected, the authorities were advised to advertise for a person of good professional calibre with the rider 'until such times as qualifications are prescribed by the S. of S., persons should be regarded as eligible for the post if they hold a recognised qualification in any branch of social work or social administration, or in a closely related discipline. In addition they should have experience at senior administrative level of the provision of social work services' (Circ. SW6/1968, para. 60).

The circular added that some serving officers without qualifications would merit consideration, and that the Secretary of State would consider their fitness on the basis of experience and proven capacity. For six months or so preceding 17 November the local authorities followed the appointments process of advertising, submitting applications to SWSG for assessment, and then appointing from amongst approved candidates. SWSG exercised a system of rating the submissions in terms of basic qualification, professional qualification and administrative and local government experience.

Of the 52 appointed, four were women, four came from SWSG,[7] and a dozen were from England, Wales or Ireland. The largest single source was former welfare officers, at least 20, appointed mainly internally, and illustrating in some cases the inherent temptation in local authorities to appoint their own men as a reward for long service or other loyalty. Some ten were from probation, but only a handful from child care, the discipline which had fought hardest for a family service. One appointment, for Edinburgh city, was a doctor who had been responsible for the joint health and welfare department there.

The proportion of women may now seem small, but was then advanced, when there were no women in education directorates and relatively few holding chairs even in social sciences. The directors from outwith Scotland, particularly those appointed to larger authorities, and this included a few 'carpet baggers', often brought with them the standards of more progressive places, and the capacity to influence committees to provide greater resources. They were a timely and influential transfusion to the more torpid Scottish social work body of the period. The four from central government, and even some probation officers, had to adjust to the very different dimension of local government, whose jungle quality they had probably underestimated from their previous more sheltered roles. For the welfare officers appointed in situ the transition was the least disturbing, and by the same token their appointing authorities experienced the least disturbance — in every sense. Of the 52 appointed fewer than half had a recognised qualification in any branch of social work. On the whole this great exercise was achieved as fairly as possible in the circumstances, and the results were generally accepted, apart from some desultory press correspondence from interested professional bodies. On the initiative of SWSG the new directors assembled twice before November, firstly in July at an Edinburgh hotel, where they received an address of welcome and muted inspiration from the Secretary of State, Bruce Millan, Secondly, in October they met at Peebles for a more extended briefing, which included discussion of the MacKenzie Report led by Professor MacKenzie himself. The opportunity was taken here to found an Association of Directors which has continued, apart from a short break in 1975, as an active force in the development of social work in Scotland.

Committees constituted and directors appointed, the tasks for the months leading up to 17 November were the overall plans for the new departments, and the preparation of probation schemes. The latter were necessary for various reasons. After the major debate whether the probation should be included or remain a separate court service as in England and Wales, the sheriffs and many senior probation officers still viewed the apparent dilution of their specialist service with considerable misgivings, which later were often justified. The Act's provisions for probation, unlike those for child care, were contained in the one single section, 27. A scheme was necessary therefore which would deal with the provision of reports to courts, and co-operation between the authorities and courts, including the appointment of sheriffs to social work committees. The schemes were required to be prepared in consultation with the sheriffs and submitted for the approval of the Secretary of State, in order to be operative from 17 November. It should also be noted that, unlike the officers of the other departments, probation officers were not employed directly by the local authorities concerned, and therefore required official transfer to the new authorities so as to be effective on the great day.[8]

The main detailed planning for the change took place in the months immediately before 17 November, during which the majority of directors took up post. Planning apart, these were hectic days for directors, meeting future staff and visiting establishments. Consultations were also involved with other service heads, local authority such as medical officers and directors of education, and voluntary, from WRVS to the societies for the various handicaps, physical and mental. The days extended into evening missionary meetings, addressing community or professional organisations such as the burgeoning pre-school play groups, old peoples welfare associations, headmasters groups, hospital doctors and social workers. Sometimes the greatest missionary effort was required internally among the new committees, many still sceptical of change.

The official guidelines for re-organisation lay mainly in the 19 pages of the already quoted circular SW/6 of 19 December 1968 with its central theme of services to local populations of 50,000, provided by ten social workers. Translating the evangelical enthusiasm of the White Paper period and the visionary provisions of the Act into practical reality in a Scotland with exiguous resources during a period of financial restraint was obviously a Herculean task calling for almost oracular advice from the shrines of St Andrew's House. The able and committed civil servants of the time, with their circulars and other devices, strove nobly to match the occasion.

17 November and Immediate Sequels

The great day came and the previously separate child care, probation and welfare officers, moved as social workers to their new posts, new roles and often new locations. There was considerable enthusiasm, much uncertainty, and not a little regret and anxiety.

The formula for local teams was adhered to, more or less, by the different types of local authorities, moderated by the parameters of population scatter, communications and existing resources. The cities like Glasgow and Edinburgh developed outposted area offices from previously largely centralised district teams.

At this stage only the few largest of the 21 large burghs needed to have recourse to decentralised outposts for teams. The agricultural counties tended to base their teams in the many small burghs in their orbit, which were the natural shopping and school centres. The industrial counties also used small burghs and other townships, but could not escape having teams for their landward areas operating from large burghs, which already provided their own service. This incongruous situation was the result of the change in the Bill discussed in the last chapter, and was to persist until local government re-organisation in 1975. The Highlands and Islands because of problems of communication, and existing patterns of community self help involving less specialist staffing, experienced much less upheaval and changes. Exceptionally, Argyll was able to follow the agricultural counties pattern having the small burghs of Oban, Dunoon and Campbeltown as population centres.

An example of the mix of area team fielded for 60,000 population in a moderately provided county was area officer, senior, three child care officers, three probation officers, two welfare officers and a mental health officer.[9] This was by no means typical either in mix or numbers, and some urban areas, particularly Glasgow, had great difficulty in mustering teams adequate to population or the incidence of problems. Less than 1,000 existing social workers were spread across Scotland in a very thin and uneven red line.

Finding adequate accommodation for these teams presented another major problem. At 17 November 1969 it was often necessary to use offices which were sub-standard or even dilapidated, where sanitary arrangements were unsuitable for mixed teams, and furnishing and equipment were seriously deficient. These discomforts and inconveniences, which incidentally militated against client comfort and service image, were sustained with or without major protest, partly because of enthusiasm for the cause, and partly because in many places low standards had been the norm for the separate departments which enjoyed little local authority status.

Further Commitments and Raised Expectations

For the remainder of 1969 and the year 1970 there was a lull in developments, which gave the new departments time to contemplate the extent of their commitments. By contrast, 1971 was a vintage year of SWSG circulars, 29 in all, of which at least a third brought extra new blocks of work for the already overstretched departments. Circular SW/ 2 announced the Chief Advisers Report on the Assessment of Children, with a recommendation that multi-disciplinary assessment teams be set up. Circular SW/6 foreshadowed the establishment of Childrens' Hearings on 15 April and some of the minor implications. Circular SW/ 17 gave 1 April as commencement date for section 14 of the Act, under which the local authority acquired the duty as opposed to a power, to provide the Home Help Service. It was made clear, however, that this need not be carried out by the social work department, and in some cases the service was left, until local government re-organisation, with the health departments, which had pioneered and provided it. Circular 22, drawing attention to the report of the Office of Population Censuses and Survey on the Handicapped and Impaired in Great Britain, 1971, requested authorities as a matter of urgency to up-date their information on severely handicapped persons living alone, to organise future notifications from the health services, and to ensure that an adequate service was available for people in this category including provision of telephones where essential. This may be seen as an official hand-washing measure to meet criticism that sections one and two of the eagerly awaited Chronically Sick and Disabled Persons Act of 1970, which required gathering of information on needs, and provision of service to meet them, had not been made applicable to Scotland. This was done ostensibly because of Scottish Office's proud belief in the omnivalence of section 12 of the main Act, a position that was soon to be modified by the introduction of the Chronically Sick and Disabled Persons (Scotland) Act, 1972, which extended to Scotland the application of the missing sections.

Circular SW/25 in November 1971, Future Development of Social Work Services, required detailed development plans for 1972 to 1975, and in more general terms for 1975 to 1978, to be submitted by May 1972. The circular makers did not then hibernate, but produced a further four right up till the last days of the year. The very last, SW/29, introduced sanguine prospects for the perennial problem of truancy under the new regime of childrens' hearings. It neatly divided truancy into three facets. Firstly, truancy simple might be dealt with by existing educational machinery. Secondly, if causes seemed school-based, it might be a matter for child guidance, or if due to family and external circumstances, it might be a matter for social work. When compulsory measures seemed unavoidable, it should be referred to the reporter. To frustrated headmasters and teachers, for whom the traditional measures of attendance officers, and persuasion or prosecution of the parents, had failed to solve this chronic baffling problem, the circular seemed to herald a new dawn. Such optimism was not widely shared by social work departments, who suspected deeper structural bases for the phenomenon.

The spate of circulars in 1971 included six on Approved School matters, transferring financial responsibility from education to social work committees; initiative for finding places from SWSG to local authorities; and for the recovery of absconders from the schools themselves to social work staff. Of generally mundane documents the least inspiring was that (SW/11), headed Future Description of Approved Schools. On the basis that various categories of schools were classified alphabetically by the Scottish Education Department, 'List D' was adopted as the new title, and so, highly individual establishments, with traditions of over 100 years as industrial schools, reformatories or approved schools, were relegated under the neutral nomenclature of clerical convenience.

The only further major responsibility added to social work departments in the first four years was for the prison welfare service taken over at 16 November 1973. The adoption of social work in hospitals and the health service generally dates from 15 May 1975 and was scarcely noticed amidst the major turmoil of local government re-organisation on that day.

Of the blizzard in 1971 the most overwhelming aspect for the new departments was clearly the introduction of childrens' hearings, about 17 months after the establishment of the former. For social workers, all of whom were adjusting to various new dimensions, and not all of whom were child care oriented, this meant assessing families and producing new-style reports to a highly motivated lay panel, whose induction processes had given them high expectations and not a little sense of importance. All this was to be done moreover in front of the family and under the critical eye of the reporter, who usually had apposite experience at a senior level in probation or a related discipline. Furthermore, various factors in the first years produced an inflated volume of activity of a quite different dimension to the previous demands in child delinquency or protection operations. At the earlier stages many reporters tended to pass on an unnecessarily high percentage of referrals, and panel members with crusading zeal explored every facet. By comparison, the former sheriff court procedure had been a simple and undemanding machinery.

The biggest factor, however, was that whereas the Sheriff Court had been a once and for all procedure, the hearings were to require reviews at regular intervals. As introduction to the new system there was, under the Transitional Cases Order of 1971, a great preliminary bombardment, in the year from April 1971 to 1972, of reviews of all existing court orders whether approved school, fit person or supervision order. This meant for the social worker, sometimes meeting the case for the first time, the task of identifying past responsibility for the case, consultation with the previous worker and/or the approved school or childrens' home, often at a distance, assessing family and school circumstances and preparing a string of reports. The volume of activity, the unfamiliarity of procedures, and the pressure of datelines all imposed severe strains in this period on social workers and their departments.

An observer, Andrew Rowe, writing between the White Paper and the Act, commented 'failure to provide a satisfactory service to support the new system for dealing with children in trouble would be more damaging to the system even than unsatisfactory panels themselves'.[10] In the event the main danger was different. The viability of departments was often as much threatened by the disproportionate demands of the hearings as that of the hearings by the deficiencies to the departments.

Shortcomings and Criticisms

And so in 1971 there was the serious situation of excessive expectations, unlimited demands and inadequate resources. The main requirements of the Act, leaving aside section 12's promotional powers, were mountainous commitments per se. The second waves of additional responsibilities battered the new launches still struggling for equilibrium. Management had to resort to rationing, and priorities became the order of the day. The removal of senior probation and child care officers to promoted posts weakened already inadequate operational staffing. In a situation of competition between authorities there was the further disturbance of a high degree of staff mobility. Cities like Glasgow, where the tides of rising demands and receding resources clashed, showed particularly obvious defects, and in lieu of planned casework it was often necessary to resort to crisis solutions of cash payments under section 12.

In the circumstances it is not surprising that in the early years few departments were equal to their new role, and many were improvising and struggling. Criticism, widespread and sharp, was in any case inevitable, but was exacerbated in the case of sheriffs and medical officers by the loss of the enjoyment or the control of valued specialist services, and not a little jealousy of this new over-promoted enfant terrible. Not least had this been fuelled by unrealistic expectations created by the White Paper, the MacKenzie Report, and such sanguine statements inspired by the directors themselves as 'Scotland will have a structure of social work which could be the basis of the most effective and humane service in Europe once the peripheral shortcomings have been ironed out'.[11] At the time, that optimism for the future did little for the stark reality of the present.

The medical officers, who had opposed the form of change, and some of whom regarded themselves as the natural inheritors of the new kingdom, saw responsibility for the valuable home help, nursery and day centre services pass into amateur hands, and did little to suppress their disapproval, which spread to their nursing services, to general practitioners and local authority members. The nurses, many of whom saw themselves as the experts with problem families, single mothers and handicapped people, looked with unconcealed scorn at the fumbling efforts of some young and inexperienced social workers dropped into these strange fields.

The courts were openly and forthrightly critical, seeing the new departments with some justification, as the death knell of the highly valued probation services. One sheriff described the Act as 'a most bungled piece of legislation', another speaking of the disastrous decline in service, described the new social workers as miniskirted 'Rosemarys and Gwendolines'. The chairman of the Parole Board, a very reverend gentleman, also troubled by miniskirted supervision of men sentenced for rape, complained that reports were now based on hearsay and 'worse than useless'.[12] Reasonable claims as often, were devalued by unreasonable rhetoric, and shortage of dress unnecessarily diverted attention from shortages of service. The directors of education viewed with suspicion the new 'semi-educated' upstarts, who seemed to question their primacy of knowledge with deviant children and difficult parents. The police were generally critical of social workers, not least for their poor performance with absconders, and tended to see the perceived soft line of childrens' hearings as largely social work inspired. Perceptions changed according to the angle and distance of viewpoint. Directors outwardly maintained their faith, and generally held that the admitted defects arose from paucity of staffing, and the skeletal base of residential and day facilities which they had inherited. Given time and money these could be easily rectified.[13] Richard Bryant in an article *Social Work: New Departments and Old Problems*, depicted departments in some areas struggling to avoid the breakdown of basic services, and identified the immediate causes as the administrative scale of the departments, the previous parsimonious traditions which had persisted through into social work committees, and the reinforcement of these by Scottish Office denial of the availability of extra resources. He thought it naive, however, to believe that resources were the complete answer without taking account of the 'structural nature of poverty in Scotland'.[14]

Even as late as 1 August 1974 the *Scotsman* carried an article *Social Workers under Siege*, inspired by two of the surprisingly few Scottish cases of major child abuse that came to public notice in the period. It claimed growing public disquiet about the effectiveness of the new departments, where demand far outpaced resources and case loads were often double 'the recommended level'. Identifying 'lack of human resources' as the greatest single factor, it pointed to the state of Edinburgh with vacancies for 70 in an establishment of 150. It also quoted a prominent Glasgow child psychologist on the difficulties of getting any supportive services. 'The Act was a good idea in theory, but was never thought out in practice and as the implications become clearer, heads are pushed further into the sand'. Fortunately few social workers had the time to read all these adverse reports, directors were well aware of being the focus of anxieties and the objects of aggression, and morale was maintained somehow. Work was a callus which insulated against grief.

If such reports give a gloomy picture of the infant departments in the first five years, it should be remembered that they represent selected snap-shots taken from interested angles at crisis times. The heavy criticisms came mainly from frustrated official users with undue expectations and often opposing interests. The defences, mainly from directors, were again partial and sometimes unduly optimistic, no doubt reflecting with Proverbs, 'where there is no vision', or hope, 'the people perish'. The overall picture was as always mixed. There certainly were major deficiencies, particularly in urban areas, at times approximating to near breakdown of basic services. In other places there was progress, pioneering and raising of standards. In most there was a heroic struggle by over-burdened and under-supported social workers, whose efforts and devotion were insufficiently appreciated by critics, councillors and collateral services.

The Generic Approach; Promotion of Social Welfare

It is convenient to examine here two ideas which pre-occupied the new departments, the generic approach and the promotion of social welfare. The great protagonist of the generic idea, Eileen Younghusband had made it clear that it was a mistake to expect newly qualified workers to engage in generic practice, but rather they should have early supervised experience, followed by concentration on a field of interest and further training.[15] The White Paper in its turn was explicit that social workers would continue to use their specialist skills.

In the early days of November 1969, there was little place for reservations, delays or training. On the Friday night there were 305 child-care officers, 281 probation officers, 276 welfare officers and 97 mental health officers. On the Monday morning there were 959 social workers with shuffled caseloads, and naive assumptions that they had been transmuted into generic workers. Those who doubted the transubstantiation were not infrequently suspect of heresy, and the workers concerned were often hesitant to pretend other than omnicompetence. Older and wiser heads recognised a generic department without necessarily declaring for instant generic workers. The subsequent re-organisation in England prompted the comment 'Departments tended to go enthusiastically for the new generic approach with caseloads being vigorously mixed, as specialists were obliged to tackle wholly unfamiliar tasks. Confusion was rampant.'[16] This was a repetition of much of the Scottish experience. It took bad experiences, calmer days, and time, almost two decades, before the inevitable importance of specialisation was fully recognised.

The Social Work Act has been much admired beyond Scotland, and even envied for its children's panels, its comprehensive family service, and not least for the central wide duty to promote social welfare. The various aspects of this last provision have been widely studied and described elsewhere and discussion here is limited to comment on its early usage.[17] The apparently simple duty of section 12 to promote social welfare splits readily into two parts — the wider promotion by advice and guidance to individuals, groups, and communities on the one hand, and on the other by practical assistance, including cash in exceptional circumstances, to narrowly defined cases. Referring to the neglect of the social implications in environmental and other planning, the White Paper had prophesied enthusiastically that 'The creation of a new social work department in touch with all the social problems and needs of the area will change this situation.' The Mackenzie Report went as far as 'The job of the new social work department is to give back reality to the very old idea of community self help in a world in which specialisation and mobility have become the basis of industrial organisation.' The Report also emphasised the importance of the community worker 'in planning the development of an integrated community'. Along with the Beatles and womens' liberation, social engineering and planning were a major phenomenon of the 1960s, and section 12 was hailed by enthusiasts as a missing key if not a magic lamp for much of this.

For the first four years, under an avalanche of demands on poorly staffed departments, the reality was again different from the dream. Much of the service given was of a short term reactive first-aid nature rather than planned promotion. There was talk of fences for the top of cliffs, but most energies were required for getting ambulances to the casualties at the bottom. Particularly in urban areas, even planned casework was often impossible, and crisis situations were resolved by cash assistance under section 12 to avoid evictions or loss of heating and lighting. For 1970, £212,000 was given or loaned to clients compared to £60,264 in the previous year under the 1963 Act, and such comparatively high figures continued until 1974.[18] To some extent housing authorities and fuel boards welcomed and exploited this new compassionate safety net for the casualties of their harshness. There was little time on the part of management or other non-operational staff to participate in social planning even if invited, but in a few areas community workers were recruited and given their head. The results at the time were generally seen as disappointing, whether because of the inadequate training and inexperience of the workers, or deficiencies of management and deployment, general factors which were identified in a later survey of the question.[19]

Nevertheless, in some areas important inter-agency work was achieved, and at national level, particularly through the Association of Directors with SWSG acquiescent support, considerable influence was exerted on DHSS, fuel boards and housing authorities to moderate punitive practices and produce agreed protocols. In this period the groundwork was laid for considerable social work successes, though the victories were not fully realised till after 1975.

Conclusion

In 1968 Scotland achieved through Parliament one of the most radical and forward-looking Acts of the 20th Century. The Act was one thing, its realisation another. The contra-indicators for success were manifold. Many of the administrative units were unduly small and even parochial. Some were only beginning after 20 years to provide basic services under the 1948 Acts. Some had failed conspicuously to do so. Many councillors were content with their moderate provisions for children and elderly, reflecting the complacency which obtained before the upheavals of Curtis and Clyde. Probation and services for offenders held little interest. Such attitudes had resulted in a limited infrastructure of establishments and supporting services. Whereas in 1989 there were about 5,000 qualified field staff deployed,[20] in 1969 there were less than 1,000, of whom only 300 had a professional qualification.

The change coincided with a period of financial restraint, and the Scottish office emphasis on the lack of resources only served to reinforce the general caution of the local authorities, many of whose members regarded social work departments as a sharp and unnecessary imposition. Moreover, the new departments, in the light of impending reorganisation of local government and health services, could only be viewed as provisional and temporary. It was not an encouraging setting for the rebirth of the personal social services.

Nevertheless the incarnation of the main features of the Act was realised on time in November 1969, largely through the idealism, optimism and labour of directors and staff, with, in some cases, more encouragement from central government than from their own local employers. The infant departments were scarcely up and walking in 1971 before they had to take on large, new responsibilities, not least the servicing of childrens' hearings. If anything seriously threatened the survival of the new young departments, it was the panel system with its disproportionate demands. And yet without the ideal of the latter, conceived by Kilbrandon, the former would not have been created by that time. Moreover, the demands of the new system, and the voices of local panel members proved strong supports for strengthened staffing.

And so, in the first five years in the struggle for growth and survival, in many areas little more than a basic service was patchily provided. In others, miracles were performed. The Act's great central theme was insufficiently realised, and section 12 acquired a cash value, which social work practice had little alternative but to adopt, and research activities further confirmed. Viewed against the background of the Scottish scene of the time the production of the Act has the appearance of a miracle. The implementation of the Act, within the time and the resources available if not a second miracle, was a triumph of hope over reality.

Local government re-organisation was the dawn of a new and richer era for social work. Since 1975, based on these foundations laboriously but successfully laid, and responding to a more favourable soil and climate, social work has established itself as a significant force in the land, and has made, by most *comparisons*, exceptional progress. That assertion, however, and the 1969 proud prophecy that 'Scotland will have a structure of social work which could be the basis of the most effective and humane service in Europe,' are the matter for another book rather than another chapter.

NOTES

1.   Rowbottom, Hey and Bills; Brunel Institute of Organisation and Social Studies, 'Social Services Departments', Heinemann, London 1974. Preface.

2. Phoebe Hall, Reforming the Welfare, Heinemann 1976, p. 149.
3. Social Work in Scotland: Report of a Working Party on the Social Work (Scotland) Act 1968, Department of Social Study, Edinburgh University, 1969.
4. A. J. B. Rowe, The Future of Social Work, Barnardos School of Printing 1968, p. 25. Prior to becoming a University Lecturer in 1967, Andrew Rowe was a principal in the Scottish Office, involved in work on the White paper etc.
5. Midlothian, East Lothian and Peebles; Aberdeen and Kincardine Counties; Greenock and Port Glasgow large burghs.
6. The Title 'Approved Schools' obtained until succeeded by 'List D' in April 1971. The 28 establishments were run by voluntary committees, with the exception of two provided by Glasgow Corporation, Balrossie and Kerelaw.
7. J.O. Johnston appointed to Glasgow, W. D. H. Grant to Aberdeen City, J. S. Murphy to Stirling County and J. G. Gardner to Midlothian etc.
8. SWSG Circular SW 6/69.
9. Stirling County, formula for teams based on Falkirk and Stirling, both places being large burghs.
10. A. J. B. Rowe, The Future of Social Work, Barnardos School of Printing, p. 12.
11. Scotsman, November 1969 'New Deal in Social Work in Scotland', article by Brian Barr based on discussions with Beti Jones and Directors.
12. Scotsman 30.1.73 'Where Probation is Failing', Article by Diana Geddes.
13. Association of Directors Conference, Presidential Address, Aberdeen May 1970. Text may be available from the Secretary of the Association. Association of Directors Conference, Presidential Address, St Andrews, April 1971, as reported in The Guardian of 7.4.71.
14. Richard Bryant, New Departments and Old Problems, the Red Paper on Scotland EUSPB, 1975, pp. 345-347.
15. Community Care 8.9.76, p. 19.
16. Terry Bamford, Managing Social Work, Tavistock Publications, 1982, p. 99.
17. For a useful outline see Michael P. Jackson, The Rediscovery of Restrictions, Policy and Politics, vol. 16, no. 4, 1988, pp. 277-283.
18. Ibid. pp. 279, 280.
19. Alan Barr, Community Development Journal, vol. 22, no. 1, p. 11.
20. SWSG Statistical Bulletin, October 1989, table 1.

INDEX